FILM/CULTURE

Explorations of cinema
in its social context

Edited by
SARI THOMAS

The Scarecrow Press, Inc.
Metuchen, N.J., & London • 1982

Library of Congress Cataloging in Publication Data
Main entry under title:

Film/culture.

    Includes bibliographies and index.
    1. Moving-pictures--Social aspects--Addresses, essays,
lectures. I. Thomas, Sari, 1949-
PN1995.9.S6F48   302.2'3   81-23254
ISBN 0-8108-1519-2   AACR2
ISBN 0-8108-1520-6 (pbk.)

Copyright © 1982 by Sari Thomas
Manufactured in the United States of America

To Esther and Abe Tannenbaum

CONTENTS

Introduction, by Sari Thomas, 1

Part I: The Industry

Writing Film History: The Struggle for Synthesis, Daniel Manny Lund, 13

Film Financing and Banking, by Janet Wasko, 27

Film and Not-for-Profit Media Institutions, J. Ronald Green, 37

Film and Labor: What the Credits Mean, Robert Gustafson, 60

The Economics of Film: What Is the Method?, Douglas Gomery, 81

Part II: Form and Content

Pictures Can't Say Ain't, Sol Worth, 97

Conventions and Meaning in Film, John Carey, 110

Home Movies as Cultural Documents, Richard Chalfen, 126

Filmic Objectivity and Visual Style, Warren Bass, 139

Genre Film: Myth, Ritual, and Sociodrama, Vivian Sobchack, 147

Part III: The Audience

To What Extent Does One Have to Learn to Interpret Movies?, Paul Messaris, 168

The Nature of the Viewing Experience: The Missing Variable in the Effects Equation, James M. Linton, 184

Film Effects and Ethnicity, Gorham Kindem and Charles Teddlie, 195

They Taught It at the Movies: Films as Models for Learned Sexual Behavior, Garth S. Jowett, 209

People's Attitudes Toward Motion Pictures, Bruce A. Austin, 222

Talking About Film, George F. Custen, 237

The Social Experience of Movies, Ian Jarvie, 247

Index, 269

ABOUT THE CONTRIBUTORS

Bruce A. Austin, College of General Studies, Rochester Institute of Technology

Warren Bass, Department of Radio-Television-Film, Temple University

John Carey, Department of Interactive Telecommunications, New York University

Richard Chalfen, Department of Anthropology, Temple University

George F. Custen, Institute of Communications, Muhlenberg College

Douglas Gomery, Department of Communication Arts and Theater, University of Maryland

J. Ronald Green, Department of Photography and Cinema, The Ohio State University

Ian C. Jarvie, Department of Philosophy, York University

Garth Jowett, School of Communication, University of Houston

Gorham Kindem, Department of Radio, Television and Motion Pictures, University of North Carolina

James M. Linton, Department of Communication Studies, University of Windsor

Daniel Manny Lund, Department of History, University of California, Los Angeles

Paul Messaris, Annenberg School of Communications, University of Pennsylvania

Vivian Sobchack, Theater Arts Board of Studies, University of California, Santa Cruz

Charles Teddlie, Bureau of Research, Louisiana State Department of Education

Sari Thomas, Department of Radio-Television-Film, Temple University

Janet Wasko, Department of Radio-Television-Film, Temple University

Sol Worth, Annenberg School of Communications, University of Pennsylvania (deceased)

INTRODUCTION

Sari Thomas

Sometime during the fourteenth and fifteenth centuries, after the advent of woodcuts--images cut on wood blocks that when covered by ink could be repeatedly transferred to paper--painting and sculpture began to be understood as "Art" in Western culture. Before this time canvases, murals, statues, and so forth were functional in their societies, but they were not accorded the "separateness" that we associate with products labeled Art. But in the late Middle Ages the social function earlier served by these media--the transmission of religious and other lessons in an attractive and readily understood form--could now be performed better by woodcuts and other techniques for the mass production of pictures.[1] These newer means could reach many more people with much greater efficiency. Thus painting, sculpture, and related fine arts were released from one kind of social responsibility and they became--came to be understood as--Art. In fact, the history of Western civilization shows us that other modes of human creation usually have become Art in this same fashion.[2]

Film is an example. Critics may exclude this or that movie, or even a whole cinema genre, from the category Art, but most people would probably agree that the film medium is an artistic one.

This film-as-art idea was not really popularized until as late as the 1950s.[3] It was at that point, following the advent of mass television, that film was released from having to perform some of the social functions that TV, with its greater efficiency, now assumed.[4] From that point onward countless articles and books were written to analyze, criticize, and generally consider film as a form of art.

These works, many of them masterpieces themselves, deal largely with aesthetics or cinematic structure and form, describing to us the essence of film art (e.g., Arnheim, 1966; Kracauer, 1960), the characteristics of movie genres, the styles of great directors. The shelves are also stocked with books that chronicle the history of cinema. In many such histories the authors work to integrate aesthetic and critical discussion into their temporal structuring of the material.

This philosophical/critical/historical material is unquestionably useful to the student who wishes to appreciate the stylistic creativity, personal expression, and evolutionary patterns involved in filmmaking. Indeed, film scholarship would be incomplete without careful examination of such works. Yet to a great extent the recognition of film as art has tended to blind the literature to other aspects of the medium, in particular the sociological, a perspective from which scholars typically examine mass communication.[5] Few writers treat motion pictures from descriptive, empirical, or sociohistorical viewpoints, in which art is approached as a social construct and not as an object for critical evaluation. There has been some excellent work detailing film-industry/institutional practices, but we must dig somewhat deeper to locate material on the form and function of film as a social phenomenon.

To talk about film as a social event is to assume a somewhat controversial stance--controversial considering the more popular "art orientation." This stance postulates that movies are but a process and product of the social world and cannot be fully understood apart from it. Students of the rules of film must likewise be students of the rules of society, regardless of whether they are interested in the movie industry, the form and content of cinema, or the behavior of people in relation to film viewing.

Such sociological, or "culturalist," arguments characteristically meet two related objections: 1/ that the "magic" of film fades in proportion to the extent that it is made subject to such "cold" analysis; and 2/ that science seeks ultimate answers, a practice incompatible with film study, which may provide numerous (and sometimes conflicting) theories but should not presume to reach conclusions. This book will argue that social analysis enhances rather than inhibits film appreciation. As articles here and elsewhere demonstrate, film, like any art form, does not belong to a realm untouched by everyday experience. Subjectivist criticism of film may attach a mysterious aura to ideas about film's construction and psychological force, but this does not mean that film production and consumption are inherently mysterious processes-- only that they are usually treated as such. Since cinema is inextricably entwined with social institutions (regulating production and policy), social codes (conventions of form and content), and social roles for behavior (producer, exhibitor, viewer), the elimination of this cultural context in the name of "Art" serves only to block a richer appreciation of film. Information, in other words, should not be equated with sterility.

Similarly, all analyses of film need not be limited to prescription--that is, advice on how film should be constructed or evaluated. There is also a need for descriptive analyses that are concerned less with criticism than with exploration of how film does function. Descriptive scholarship works toward conclusions that are not dependent upon variations in judgment, although these conclusions, and the methods and means for arriving at them, are made public and thus are tentative until more convincing data to the contrary are delivered.

o • o

The chapters in this volume are geared toward descriptive, socially oriented analysis of film. With one exception, the articles appear here for the first time, and while most of them have been written as "theory" (that is, as general propositions that are not always accompanied by empirical evidence in the text), the authors for the most part have based their analyses on data accumulated from earlier or ongoing research projects. We have chosen a theoretical rather than research-report format for most of the chapters so as to allow readers unfamiliar with research techniques to become better acquainted with the kind of issues being raised by social scientists interested in film. It is an unfortunate situation that scholarly journals devoted to film study usually do not present much "sociological" research and analysis and that, conversely, social-science journals do not devote much space to film study. We hope that this volume will contribute to the growth of and interest in this subject matter among both sectors.

The book is divided into three parts: "The Industry" involves the organization and economics of film production; "Form and Content," the conventions and categories of film; and "The Audience," the public's relationship with the medium. This three-part organization mirrors the classic communication model of "sender → message → receiver," thus indicating the breadth of possibilities in the application of socially oriented methods to film study. Readers should keep in mind, however, that this arrangement does not create either linearly related or mutually exclusive areas of analysis. The role of film in society should not be seen as a simple succession of financing, production, viewing, and subsequent effect--for example, production values may be affected by audience response, which may influence economic considerations, and so on. Similarly, it is often impossible to discuss viewing behavior without recourse to industry practices or film form. As chapters in this book demonstrate, when we talk about film, or any other "force" in society, we must see countless intricate and meshing variables involving countless phases of social interaction. (See Jarvie's chapter for a most explicit example of the complexity of social factors.) The use of any organizing principle for the division of material is a matter of convenience.

As noted, the first part of this book, "The Industry," concerns the organization of film production in the United States, viewed from a socioeconomic, and sometimes historical, perspective. The articles comprising this section were chosen on the basis of two criteria. One was breadth of coverage. Because much of the institutionally oriented literature on film is scattered among a wide variety of publications or is available in forms too cumbersome and detailed for the nonspecialist, it was thought that a useful service could be provided here by including relatively concise overviews of some aspects of the field. At the same time, however, an effort has been made to ensure that at least some of the selections would deal with aspects of this general area that have received relatively less extensive coverage in the existing literature. Originality, in this sense, was the second criterion of selection.

Daniel Lund opens this section with a concise history

of the movie industry, stressing the interplay between economic factors and film content and form. Lund's article begins to suggest how film production can be understood as a business. Janet Wasko's chapter, which follows, goes farther in demonstrating how film production can be viewed as just one facet of modern society's overriding industrial complex. Her discussion of the sources and manipulations of capital for film production, particularly as they involve banking interests, provides a clear basis for the examination of movies as a <u>business</u>, independent of whatever other "psychological" or <u>aesthetic</u> functions they may serve.

These first two chapters are oriented toward the commercial, mainstream movie industry. J. Ronald Green surveys the history and structure of another important institutional consideration: the use of film in nonprofit contexts. Although many film scholars and students often have (sometimes unrecognized) regular involvement with these "not-for-profit" channels, the literature rarely describes their institutional workings with such clarity. Also infrequently discussed is the vast labor force involved in major movie production. For the most part our interests are limited to producers, directors, writers, and actors, even though the responsibility for a film's production falls on hundreds of shoulders. Robert Gustafson's unique glossary is a reference guide to most of those individuals to whom credit belongs. Concluding this section is Douglas Gomery's overview of the methods of film-institution study. As with the study of any phenomenon, Gomery systematically points out that the means of approach have everything to do with the results.

Part II, dealing with the codes and conventions of film form and content, presents articles on matters frequently touched upon in more traditional film theory--but here the authors take an <u>acritical</u> stance. These chapters rely largely on earlier, systematic data analysis whose emphasis lies in how film works, or "means," as a communicational system.

The first chapter in this section comprises relevant excerpts from the late Sol Worth's "Pictures Can't Say Ain't." Although his discussion relates to visual communication as a whole rather than to film exclusively, Worth argues that "pictures" (including filmed images) communicate in ways different from language and that parallels between film and language are problematic. Worth's expertise in linguistics, anthropology, art history, and filmmaking, and his extensive social-science research on film interpretation, contributed to this most interesting piece on the nonlinguistic, yet convention-based, system of pictorial representation.

John Carey, writing on film conventions, in many ways takes up where Worth leaves off. He attempts to demonstrate how viewers learn to make sense from movies. Drawing upon his research into sixty years of fiction film, Carey describes how movies are structured so as to teach and standardize cues for the interpretation of filmed narratives.

Richard Chalfen deals with a specific class of film conventions, that belonging to "home movies." Not only does Chalfen give us some insight into the character and structuring of "home-mode" communication, but in his discussion of its special social functions he points to the anthropological significance of film in general.

Warren Bass, too, examines film conventions, but here as they relate to the notion of "objectivity." Bass, an established filmmaker, analyzes how film form and meaning are affected by the position assumed or level of involvement demonstrated by the filmmaker.

Finally, Vivian Sobchack's analysis treats the conventions of film not in terms of form, but in terms of content. There is, of course, an abundance of scholarship examining in strict detail the characteristics of the individual genres (the screwball comedy, the western, the science-fiction thriller, the horror movie, and so on), and some of this literature involves comparative discussion of those factors differentiating one genre from another. But Sobchack's chapter is a departure. Through the use of anthropological theory, specifically as it relates to myth and ritual, she describes how the conventions of genre films are socially functional. In other words, by treating them as an anthropological genre of story telling she shows how these films, taken together, are important for the maintenance and cohesion of society.

The final section of this book examines an issue that is the least represented in the literature--that of the social effects of film. Prior to the advent of mass television, substantial work was undertaken on audience response to cinema. Some scholars argue that the shift of social-science interest from film to television was caused by television's obviously greater command of the masses. However, one must recognize that the second half of this century has been marked not only by the popularity of television but also by the growth of the social sciences, as manifested in the expansion of social psychology, the official establishment of more specific areas of social investigation ("Communication," "American Studies"), and the general movement of older disciplines, such as anthropology, sociology, and political science, away from their more traditional areas of inquiry into other, contemporary concerns--for example, the application of anthropology to urban issues. Given that television's entrance into Western culture more or less coincided with this boom in the social sciences, and given my earlier point that TV's emergence began to enshrine film as Art, it is not surprising that the social sciences directed their attention to television rather than to film. Of course, none of these considerations detract from the ability of film (as Art or not) to act as an important element in the socialization process. It is important to note, however, that film should not automatically be equated with television in this regard. It is not safe to assume that whatever "goes" for television with respect to socialization also "goes" for film. (See Linton's chapter for more on this argument.)

Part III begins by examining certain issues raised in earlier chapters as they now apply to the film audience. Paul Messaris confronts the behavioral implications of film conventions, particularly as they have been explicated by Worth and by Carey. He explains that the business of "learning" to interpret movie narrative is not simply the matter of a viewer's prior acquisition of cinematic-symbolic competence. Drawing on his own research and that of others, Messaris constructs an important socioperceptual argument pertaining to those situations in which cinematic-code learning may or may not be requisite for "proper" film interpretation.

The next three chapters move away from the consideration of behavior in terms of narrative interpretation to look at its more "active" effects. James Linton explores the many variables involved in the film-viewing experience. By considering several issues more typically discussed with respect to other forms of mass communication, Linton describes how physical, social, and psychological forces can interact to cause different behavioral ramifications. Gorham Kindem and Charles Teddlie also direct our attention to the "effects" of filmgoing, but in this case by focusing upon a particular issue: attitudes toward ethnic groups. They discuss not only how films can cultivate certain beliefs about ethnic minorities but also how film effects in general may be a function of variations in both film style and certain characteristics of moviegoers. The next chapter, by Garth S. Jowett, is a historical account of film effects--specifically as they relate to the acculturation of sexual behavior. By employing several pieces of earlier research Jowett gives us an example of how movies teach values and provide performance guidelines, particularly with respect to those subjects that tend to be neglected in the explicit curriculum of the real (physical) world.

The next two chapters deal with film as a part of everyday experience. Bruce Austin explores the history of people's attitudes toward moviegoing, describing shifts in popular sentiment and arguing systematically for the importance of attitudinal research as it relates to film. George Custen's chapter explores an often-ignored social function of movies-- how they are used in conversation. Contrary to the impression that many students receive from lectures or texts, Custen's research indicates that people's use of a film in verbal interaction has little to do with its intended or even inferred "meaning."

The final chapter brings us full circle. Ian Jarvie focuses on the industry, technology, and content of films to provide an overview of their many and changing social functions. By applying the noted sociologist Edward Shils's model of social centrality, Jarvie takes us through the history of life with film, while at the same time demonstrating the value of applying sociological insight to film study.

Clearly, the chapters assembled in this volume cannot be presumed in any way to cover the entire range or depth of possibilities inherent in the study of film in its social context. The authors hope only that this book contributes to and possibly advances the course of such study.

Notes

1. Certainly, the slightly later introduction of movable type further diminished European need to rely upon painting, sculpture, and so forth for "instructional" purposes.

2. A much fuller exploration of this "becoming Art" issue can be found in Thomas (1981).

3. This is not to say that aesthetic orientations to film never appeared in print until this time. Eisenstein, for example, produced an enormous amount of written work in the 1920s, 30s, and 40s. However, what is important to note here is the relative dearth of such work before the 1950s and the ever-continuing rise in such approaches in the second half of this century. One need only to address the publication dates of "classics" in this area--e.g., Arnheim (1966), Bazin (1971), and Kracauer (1960)--and, in fact, to examine the reprint years of the earlier work--e.g., Eisenstein (1970)--to support the claim being made here.

4. For an excellent discussion of the social functions of television see Wright (1975).

5. In light of my earlier remarks concerning the post-television treatment of "film as art," it is interesting to note that the dearth of sociological analyses of film is most apparent in that same period when film becomes art, so to speak. Some seminal sociological analyses of film were completed prior to the popular advent of television--e.g., Thurstone (1931); the Payne Fund Studies, synopsized by Charters (1935); Hovland, Lumsdaine, and Sheffield (1949); and Wolfenstein and Leites (1950). Such evidence suggests either that the classification of an event under the rubric "Art" tends to preclude its sociological consideration or, conversely, that it is primarily when an event appears to serve no "higher" purpose than amusing the masses that sociological concern is aroused.

References

Arnheim, Rudolf. *Film as Art*. Berkeley and Los Angeles: University of California Press, 1966.

Bazin, André. *What Is Cinema?* 2 vols. Berkeley and Los Angeles: University of California Press, 1967.

Charters, Werrett Wallace. *Motion Pictures and Youth: A Summary*. New York: Macmillan, 1935.

Eisenstein, Sergei. *Film Essays and a Lecture*, edited by Jay Leyda. New York: Praeger, 1970.

Hovland, C. I., A. A. Lumsdaine, and F. D. Sheffield. Experiments on Mass Communication. Princeton: Princeton University Press, 1949.

Kracauer, Siegfried. Theory of Film: The Redemption of Physical Reality. London, Oxford, and New York: Oxford University Press, 1960.

Thomas, Sari. "Why Television Is Not Art: Toward a Functional Analysis of Art in Western Culture." Forthcoming.

Thurstone, L. L. "The Influence of Motion Pictures on Children's Attitudes." Journal of Social Psychology 2 (1931): 291-304.

Wolfenstein, Martha, and Nathan Leites. Movies: A Psychological Study. Glencoe, Ill.: Free Press, 1950.

Wright, Charles R. Mass Communication: A Sociological Perspective. New York: Random House, 1975.

Part I

THE INDUSTRY

WRITING FILM HISTORY: THE STRUGGLE FOR SYNTHESIS

Daniel Manny Lund

We have studied the movies by looking at them and writing about what we thought as we watched, or by researching the movie-making industry and writing about what we found. The first we call film criticism, a form of aesthetic activity; the second we call industry study, a form of economic history. These two approaches have reflected distinct intellectual pursuits, usually taken up by different people with seemingly different ends. This separation, however, is artificial. It conforms to arbitrary divisions associated with the modern university curriculum.

There are critical connections between the production, distribution, exhibition, and consumption of movies as commodity and as art, connections that have been visible from the inception of the industry. Our task in film history is therefore synthetic--to weave together in a meaningful pattern the separate strands associated with cinema. Clarifying the historical relation between film technique and studio budgets diminishes neither the director's skill nor the actor's art; it merely sets out some of the conditions in which they produced their work. Similarly, exploring the interplay of film content and the markets of exhibition trivializes neither the writer's skill nor the producer's vision; it merely helps us understand the film in relation to its intended distribution in a consumer's market.

14 FILM/CULTURE

An integrated historical approach to film requires a framework in which to fit the varieties of film study. This chapter will suggest a scheme based on the broad sweep of historical forces that have been crystalized in the character of film markets. This is not an argument to reduce everything in cinema history to its commercial aspects, but rather a call for understanding movies in the context of material historical processes.

From the origins of cinema to the present there are arguably four broad periods: 1895-1914: the worldwide diffusion of movies; 1915-1929: the worldwide dominance of U.S. films; 1930-1946: the rise of national-language cinemas and regional markets; and 1947-present: film in the modern media complex. Cinematic development is cumulative. The periods are not self-contained or exclusive. Once film had become established as a worldwide phenomenon, the movies of each period have contained some of the essential features of their predecessors. The silent-film era of broad United States domination was qualitatively changed with the introduction of sound, yet U.S. films continued to be generally the strongest single "national" cinematic force. The great era of national-language cinemas exploiting regional markets has passed, but it nonetheless shaped the character of the modern media complex. No single film is wholly intelligible apart from the history of film, just as the sweep of film history fades into abstraction without a lively sense of what appears on the screen.

1895-1914: worldwide diffusion

Once forms for the public exhibition of films were developed, the "movies" spread rapidly and widely. By the turn of the century film showings had occurred in most of the major cities of Europe and the United States, and many of the more modest population centers as well. There was a theater with a regular schedule in Mexico City, another in Buenos Aires. Residents of Shanghai could attend more or less regular film functions, and so could people in Tokyo.

If we focused only on the cities as sites for film diffusion we would miss an important dimension of this remarkable period. Edwin S. Porter, the director of The Great Train Robbery (1903), spent the late 1890s as a touring projectionist, along with scores of other young adventurous entrepreneurs. Porter traveled with his projector and a bag of film, visiting the hinterland of the United States, Canada, the Caribbean, and South America. Others brought mobile theaters to Australia, China, southeast Asia, India and rural Europe. Thus by the early twentieth century the number of people who had seen a movie was remarkably large.

The cinema arose at a point in time when the mechanisms for its immediate and universal diffusion were already in place. An elaborate worldwide trading and communications network was functioning with its key centers in Europe. Movies rode out of Europe, and to a much lesser extent at the beginning from the United States, on the waves of international commerce.

The early centers of film production for international distribution were France and Italy. Movies with ever-more-elaborate plot lines emerged, and multireel films quickly followed. Camera techniques were not necessarily more sophisticated than in the American one-reelers, but there was more to the movies. French filmmakers pioneered in the comedy and staged costume drama, and Italians were soon making operatic-style historical and biblical spectaculars. French films tended to dominate the British and Latin American markets, and Italian films quickly established a hold on the Far East, especially in Japan. Both French and Italian movies had an enormous impact on the American market and American filmmaking. Up to World War I the French Pathé Frères was the largest motion-picture producer in the world.

The rapid but ragged growth of the United States film industry was characterized by extensive development of the home market, with modest distribution abroad. The urban-immigrant audience for early American films was brought in principally by the nickelodeon storefront theater. Pre-World War I construction of "movie palaces," self-consciously appealing to the middle class and a "better" working-class element, expanded the movie audience but did not displace the nickelodeon and vaudeville networks in their market significance.

Once the large market for movies became evident, there emerged a tendency toward monopoly control of filmmaking. In the spirit of the late Gilded Age, Thomas Alva Edison proved to be as much an innovator in patent litigation as in merchandising technical advances in filmmaking. Edison's attempted control of the movies came through the licensing of his cameras for film production and the sale or rental of films only to those exchanges or exhibitors who agreed to the exclusive use of Edison licensed products, including projectors. There was even an agreement with Eastman Kodak (the only U.S. film manufacturer) to sell raw film stock only to Edison-licensed producers.

By 1908 nearly a hundred percent of film revenues were gathered in by the Motion Picture Patents Company, which comprised all of the American producers (including the last holdout, Biograph), along with the French Méliès and Pathé Frères. This level of monopoly control exercised by the Trust of Edison tended to limit innovation of filmmaking severely.

Nevertheless, the home market was simply expanding too fast to be serviced effectively by Edison's operation. Particularly as the Trust moved toward a conscious cultivation of the middle classes, the several thousand urban storefront nickelodeons demanded more product than Edison could provide. By 1912, when Justice Department lawyers filed an antitrust suit against the Motion Picture Patents Company, the Trust had already lost nearly half of the home-market revenues.

"Independents" emerged from every part of the filmmaking business to take advantage of the growing demand. These filmmakers were quick to pick up and expand on European innovations in cinema content and style. Carl Laemmle came out of the distribution sector to found his own production company. Adolph Zukor, who worked in the exhibition sector, hired Edwin S. Porter to make movies of well-known plays starring the famous actors who had done the stage versions. D. W. Griffith moved out of the Trust's shadow to make bigger and bigger films. Cecil B. DeMille was hired by the Jesse L. Lasky Feature Play Company to make The Squaw Man in California. By the time the courts ruled, in 1915, that the Motion Picture Patents Company of Edison was an illegal conspiracy in restraint of trade, the motion-picture industry had already moved to a new level, with multiple competing units.

Although no single dominant center emerged after the Trust, the pattern toward oligopoly was set by William Fox. Based initially in film exchange, Fox was an innovator in vertical integration for the industry--that is, he built up a network of production, distribution, and exhibition under a single ownership.

Thus by the outbreak of World War I the modern cinema in embryo was in place in the United States. There were feature movies with recognized stars, and comedies, mysteries, westerns, and costume dramas. Something like a studio system had emerged, increasingly centered in southern California and tied to elaborate film exchanges and chains of exhibition. Often controversial, movies were nonetheless the most popular aspect of what we can recognize as modern mass culture.

1915-1929: worldwide dominance by U.S. films

The First World War interrupted and altered much of European life, including film production. In 1915 the United States exported about 36 million feet of film. A worldwide market for cinema had been growing since the first footage had been glimpsed in 1895. European production could not meet the demands, and in 1916 U.S. film exports increased almost five times from the previous year. By the end of the decade an estimated eighty-five percent of screen time worldwide was taken up with U.S. products. Even the home market had been nearly totally mastered, with only two percent of U.S. screen time given over to foreign products.

Film history is thus tied to the sweep of political events and economic forces far beyond even the biggest mogul's control or the most innovative filmmaker's imagination. Filmmakers, in the broadest sense of that term, are in large part the makers of film history, but only under given conditions.

In this period the U.S. film industry came to rely on a revenue formula that has endured to the present day--a good year is one in which more than half of receipts come from foreign sales. But the recital of such a statistic can hardly capture even a portion of what the first truly international film celebrities meant in that era. Charlie Chaplin's tramp became one of the most widely recognized figures in the world. The social realism of his films combined with the sympathetic romanticism of his persona gave his appeal a depth of intensity that astounded observers of the day. Mary Pickford and Douglas Fairbanks wooed and wed to the din of unprecedented publicity, and their belated honeymoon trip to Europe became a continental processional beyond the legend of past royalty and the capacity of any contemporary monarchs.

The international dominance of American films was closely related to the expansion of U.S. trade and commerce. Without many statistics to back up the notion, filmmakers and commercial interests eagerly repeated a popular formulation: "trade follows the film." With or without data, no one seriously questioned a general link between American movies and the expanding markets for American commodities, especially fashions, cosmetics, appliances, and automobiles. The film was, in a sense, more important than the flag of traditional empire.

The volume of U.S. feature-film production reached seven hundred productions per year at the apex of the period in the mid-1920s. Although American production was awesome, other national cinemas began to arise. Germany was capable of producing more than two hundred movies annually; Great Britain and France reemerged as film production centers of some weight. India, Japan, and the Soviet Union all became important national centers as well. Movies were made in China and a nascent national industry was observable in Mexico. In fact, there were few areas untouched by moviemaking efforts. The very scope of American dominance encouraged a diffusion of the art and business of cinema.

The tremendous expansion of U.S. film production was carried out by an industry rapidly coalescing around production studios, most of which were part of vertically structured operations, bigger and more elaborate than William Fox's company. From time to time independent producers and exhibitors emerged, but in the main this was the era of industrial integration. Adolph Zukor's Paramount became the model for the studio system.

The American silent film developed an extensive vocabulary of cinematic motion. Most apparent in the comedies, yet visible in all other genres as well, there was motion. People in motion, machines in motion, even nature in motion were contrived on set, captured by camera, and manipulated in editing. American films were not the only aesthetic models of the time. German cinema was taken very seriously, and by the middle of the 1920s Soviet filmmaking was acknowledged as a rival center for the silent-film aesthetic.

Once again, however, the very scale of the operations of filmmaking in the United States seemed to become a fetter on innovation. The vertically integrated giants were bottom-heavy. Massive investments were made in real estate for the prestigious but not always very profitable movie palaces of the day. The technological breakthrough of sound film was available some time before the first talking film was released to great success in 1927 by the Warner Brothers' independent productions. There was some lag as motion-picture theaters were converted to sound, but the process was relatively rapid both in the United States and abroad. In general, by 1930 films talked. But at first, as they talked they moved less. Early sound technology required a more fixed camera, and exploitation of the novelty of sound tended to reduce action.

The universal appeal of American films lessened as the multilingual world market set the conditions for the development of national-language cinema. Historically, markets have emerged in association with language. For the first two periods of our survey film appeared to transcend linguistic limitations, and in a way it continues to do so. Sound, however, reintroduced some of the limitations of language in the medium and profoundly altered the shape and character of the next two periods.

1930-1946: national cinemas/regional markets

Once the novelty of sound had run its course, the U.S. share of the international market began to decline. American films, with their ever-more-extensive soundtracks, were less and less interesting. The general coincidence of this phenomenon with the Great Depression sharpened the processes involved but did not fundamentally alter the situation. Filmmakers in many nations stepped forward to produce for a market that wanted to hear a movie in its own tongue.

The American film industry tried a number of tactics to hold on to the international market. Subtitling was not satisfactory at the time, perhaps especially when general literacy was not as high as it has become. Dubbing was a technologically imperfect process, and did not really become even marginally satisfactory until later in the decade. The initial answer for the American industry was a kind of polyglot production program, involving feature films made in the language of the intended market of exhibition. Studios in Hollywood and New York produced Spanish- and Portuguese-language versions of standard American comedies, mysteries, and even musicals. Studio facilities were built in France to serve as a center for multilingual European production. A generation of Latin American (mostly Mexican, but including

Brazilian, Chilean, and even Spanish) film workers, technicians, and actors came to Hollywood to make Spanish-language productions. A few of the efforts, done from well-made scripts and crafted with care, were good films and were modestly well received in Spanish-speaking markets. In the main, however, they were mechanical imitations of current U.S. productions set in obviously American contexts, with a casting that tended to mix and mingle Spanish accent and dialect variations with a cavalier disregard for any sort of coherent cultural pattern. The resulting films were critically panned in the Spanish-speaking markets; audience ridicule or simple lack of interest convinced American producers to cut back and eventually abandon the polyglot experiment. Later in the decade the United States would find another formula to win back a share of the lost international market.

The very inability of the once-dominant American film industry to maintain its position in the sound era was an invitation to insurgent and reinsurgent national cinemas. Under difficult circumstances, cinema production began or continued in a remarkable variety of locales. Mexico and Argentina began to compete in Latin America, but Cuba, Chile, and Spain also made efforts to pick up a share of continental distribution. Similar situations emerged in parts of Asia, the Far East, and the Indian subcontinent. European national-language cinema probably expanded the most, somewhat unevenly aided by a protectionist system of tariffs, import quotas, and national screen-time regulations. This is not to say that U.S. films disappeared from view on any of the foreign screens; but once their overwhelmingly dominant position was challenged there was some space in the market for others.

The 1930s are remembered less as a time of national-language cinema than as a time of severe economic conditions. At least in the United States some aspects of the entertainment industry thrived during the Great Depression. People seemed to need a release from the hard times. In general, movies remained popular, and some particular movies, such as Gone with the Wind and Snow White in 1937, became box-office smashes beyond any prior films. But overall attendance was down, revenues were down, and those companies with bottom-heavy investments in real estate for the exhibition sector sank deeper into debt.

The Fox Company went into receivership in 1929 and was reorganized two years later with William Fox essentially removed from effective control. Paramount, the very model of the expansionist Hollywood of the prior period, also went into receivership. By 1933 RKO and Universal were both in serious trouble and joined their fellow companies in equity receivership. MGM remained solvent, and United Artists, unburdened by heavy investment in nonliquid assets like real estate, survived and even expanded its distribution network.

Since World War I, Hollywood had more and more required the services of the bankers; now, in the period of reorganization under equity receivership, the new corporate structures emerged with important financial groupings from New York and San Francisco well represented on boards and in top management.

In the United States home-market movie attendance had peaked in 1929-30, and by 1932 had fallen off a staggering thirty percent. Not until the war years of the 1940s would attendance fully recover and then only for the duration of the war.

The full scope of effective vertical integration of the Hollywood industry had been revealed in the various receivership actions. In 1938 the Justice Department once again took up the antitrust fight with a full-scale legal challenge to the major studios. The so-called "Paramount Case" (Paramount being the first listed company in the bill of particulars) dragged on for more than ten years before at last a formal divestment resolved the legal question.

Varieties of antitrust challenges hit the "majors" in their foreign markets as well. Legal restraint on monopoly-type control was mounted in Mexico and Argentina in this same period. The resolution of these latter challenges were accomplished by formal adjustment of the ownership patterns of subsidiaries.

Yet another aspect of economic challenge kept things lively for the studios--labor organizing and occasional strikes. Some studio craftworkers and projectionists had already been organized when the industrial-union movement of the 1930s swept Hollywood. In a relatively short time, directors, actors, extras, cartoonists, and studio workers of every craft were organized by one union or another. Such organizing was difficult, with studio resistance and jurisdictional disputes. The reality of gangsterism versus honest trade unionism was more dramatic and complex than most films of the period. The general completion of studio unionization in 1946-47 coincided with the last truly good year of Hollywood production and revenue before a pronounced decline in the movies as the dominant entertainment medium began.

One more brief discussion will suffice to draw the connections between national-film production, film genres, and the particularities of a given historical period. During the years 1941 to 1946 the Mexican film industry grew into one of the half-dozen largest in the world. In the late 1930s the U.S. film industry had established an elaborate distribution network throughout Latin America, based in part on the increasing distribution of Mexican-made films. With the loss of the critical European market in the late 1930s Latin America became key to maintaining U.S. film-industry receipts. During World War II nearly a third of U.S. film production was specifically war-related, in terms of training and educational films; of the feature films produced, nearly a third contained elaborately drawn patriotic themes. Such films did not travel well outside of the United States; there was simply very little foreign box office for "win the war" movies. In order to feed the hungry film-distribution network, other feature films acceptable to the Latin American market had to be secured. The Mexican motion-picture industry expanded with both private and government assistance from the United States to meet the particular market demands.

Thus the U.S. film industry was best able to deal with the phenomena of national-language cinema and the consequent language-based regional markets in the first period of sound production by expanding its interests in foreign production itself.

1947-present: film in the media complex

As in life, so in the cinema. The Second World War was followed by the Cold War; preliminary investigations, particularly into strike activities, culminated in early 1947 with the House Committee on Un-American Activities calling the first of what would be many rounds of Hollywood talent to account for premature antifascism, overdrawn Russian wartime sympathies, and the alleged spread of communism itself in America's most important mass medium. After a brief initial stiffening of the studios' collective spine there appeared to be a total collapse.

Politically defined blacklisting became the central feature of employment from the craft level to acting, writing, and direction. Some blacklisted workers went abroad and participated in the fragile postwar flowering of production and distribution in Europe and Mexico. Others worked as best they could, on the fringes of the industry or under assumed identities. Still others never really worked again in the medium.

In the complicated context of other postwar movie problems, ranging from difficulties in foreign markets to the television challenge, it is difficult to gauge the impact of the Hollywood red scare--except to note that it was only the beginning, and continued as an aspect of the postwar complex that hurt and held back American cinematic development.

Perhaps more significant in the long run was the Cold War division of foreign markets. Diplomatic indignation at the iron curtain around Eastern Europe and the Soviet Union appears in retrospect to have had less to do with the lack of free elections than with the loss of the "free flow of information and products." From Walt Disney to the major studios, wartime planning for the postwar period was built on entry into vast foreign markets. China's fabled (though never really exploited) market was effectively closed by the revolution of 1949. Even the European market was extremely hedged in by new formulas for tariffs, screen-time restrictions, and frozen revenue accounts. The latter, in Great Britain for example, could be thawed if the money was spent on film production in Great Britain; Walt Disney's Treasure Island was his way of using the hostaged funds.

Another effect of the trade barriers, whether commercial or ideological, was the apparent reinvigoration of the national cinemas. And, at least in the early postwar era, a review of films from anywhere in the world would reveal a general intensification and elaboration of identifiably national cinema styles and modes, from the Italian work of de Sica to the Mexican work of Fernández.

The antitrust challenge of the Paramount Case came to a formal end with a series of consent decrees in 1948. The five major studios agreed to divest production and distribution from exhibition. RKO and Paramount were quick to sign and implement the consent decrees; Twentieth Century-Fox delayed a while; and Warner Brothers did not really complete divorcement until 1951 and Loews-MGM not until 1959.

Key to this process was retaining the legal capacity to wed production and distribution functions. After nearly five decades of filmmaking it had become clear that exhibition was the most problematic sector, given the heavy capitalization required and the volatility of the market itself. Distribution was generally acknowledged as the fulcrum point, both for generating capital for production and for maximizing the return on investment in production. The next three decades would underscore that point.

The most crucial new development was exactly what the common wisdom of today argues in hindsight--television. TV changed the nature of the market for cinema. Broadly speaking, the film industry met the challenge in two ways.

The first was to utilize long-established technological breakthroughs on a commercial scale in an effort to make the movies "better than ever." Cinerama, a filming and projection advance that had been made in the 1930s, was introduced in late 1952. Also in that year audiences were treated to Natural Vision--3D. Soon Polaroid was manufacturing more than 6 million pairs of special 3D viewing glasses a week; but by 1955 another movie fad had run its course. In 1953 Cinemascope, a process developed in the 1920s, was employed to achieve a wide-screen effect at a small fraction of Cinerama's cost. The distortions of the Cinemascope effect were corrected with the film clarity and fidelity of Vistavision in 1954, refined from a 1919 technological achievement. The 1955 Todd-AO process represented further refinements on the wide-screen and big-sound process. The quest for novelty reached an apex of sorts with the Aromarama and Smell-o-Vision experiments of 1959. Besides illustrating that the application of technical breakthroughs must await propitious market and industry conditions, the period should be remembered for wildly promoted short-run novelty, a few long-term technological gains especially with regard to the wide screen and big sound, and the general failure to win back the ever-increasing television audience.

The second, and more successful, Hollywood response was to produce for and sell to television. Monogram and Republic, two minor studios, were the first to do so. RKO, in 1955, was the first major to sell or lease significant parts of its vast warehouse to television, and the other majors soon followed. These deals represented a kind of going-out-of-business sale. It was Columbia (ironically the leader of the noncooperation/all-competition line on radio in the 1930s) that caught the wave of the future. Its wholly owned subsidiary, Screen Gems, began to make film for television--first commercials, then half-hour shows. Disney and Warner Brothers quickly worked out ways by the mid-1950s to be a full part of television-related film production. Universal, however, was the studio most successfully given over to a made-for-television format.

As the media became more complex in their interrelations, so did the patterns of ownership and control. United Artists, with Transamerica backing, was part of a worldwide conglomerate. Paramount as a part of Gulf + Western was quintessential transnational media, and through its Desilu subsidiary was big-time television production.

In the 1960s it became more and more confusing to speak of national cinemas. Even a significant portion of U.S. screen time was occupied by "foreign" films. But what is the nationality of a film in the present period? Does a film acquire its nationality from the language of its soundtrack, the country of origin of its stars or director? Or does a film have a nationality based on who financed or who owns it?

Films from countries producing for particular home markets, as is much of India's production, would appear to be clearly national. Films made in socialist countries, such as Cuba, appear to be nationally distinct. Films out of a renewed or newly developing film center, such as recent German and Australian work, are identifiably national. However, films for particular regional markets, such as much of Hong Kong production, become less clearly identifiable in terms of nationality. Generally, the cinema commodity in the capitalist world, like the production and distribution apparatus behind it, is transnational. This is especially true of the American product, now diffused through television as a complementary medium on a scale and at a density unprecedented in the prior periods. The point here is that U.S. production in itself is less the crucial function than the transnational capacity of U.S. film capital to coordinate and utilize production in many lands.

The fulcrum point for development and expansion in cinema production is control over the distribution process. As the location or character of markets and market outlets shift, producers who, like Disney, have mastered their own distribution networks appear to thrive. In effect, television became less a competative medium than a part of the complex media market for film.

Old giants, like United Artists, were first and foremost distributing operations that became better able than others to finance production. Newcomers, such as Joseph E. Levine with Avco-Embassy, arose out of the distribution sector, as the Carl Laemmles of old. The newest mogul generation, epitomized in Francis Ford Coppola, appear to be generally more successful at filmmaking and distribution-dealing than in studio building. All this motion begins to assume some coherent pattern when we recognize that a key element enabling us to struggle for a synthetic, integrated view of film is a historical understanding of the shape and nature of the markets.

There are signs of the end of this last period, and the beginning of a new one. In the early 1970s film attendance began to rise, not just in the United States but around the world. By 1974 the pattern of generally increasing film-theater attendance was established, and it appears to continue. Yet more significant for the dividing of periods are the striking technological advances in home-video facilities and pay-cable viewing. Once again, the nature of the market appears to be shifting, with unforeseen consequences for the production, distribution, and exhibition of film--consequences in film content and film aesthetics as well.

FILM FINANCING AND BANKING

Janet Wasko

Motion pictures are produced, distributed, and exhibited in most capitalist societies under market conditions that affect the kinds of films that are made, who makes them, and how they are viewed by the public. Film is a business. And like any other commercial enterprise, the film business requires capital. Large sums of money are needed to cover production and distribution expenses before a film can be exhibited. How this money is supplied is an important consideration in understanding film in its social context.

Initially capital came from the personal savings of entrepreneurs out to make a fortune from the nickelodeon craze that was sweeping the country in the early 1900s. But capital requirements increased as films became more technically advanced, more diverse, and longer. It was natural for film people to call upon a variety of financiers and banking institutions for backing.

It took some time, however, for the industry to prove itself worthy of such financial support. Yet as movies became more widely accepted as a form of entertainment, the profit-making potential became more apparent to both moviemaker and financier. During the 1920s development and expansion in all phases of the film industry--production, distribution, and exhibition--increased the need for capital and legitimized the industry in the eyes of the financial elite. Valuable real estate acquired for centralized studios and large movie theaters attracted even further attention from financiers. Although the industry found numerous sources of financial backing, it was the bank that established the strongest and most profitable relationships (see Wasko, 1980).

Growth of the majors

As the industry made the expensive shift from the slients to the talkies in the late 1920s, the banking connection became even more intense. Financial support, as well as control of vital sound patents, came from the two largest banking groups in the country--the Morgans and the Rockefellers--while many other banks, most notably the Bank of America, continued their lending activities and involvement in the filmmaking business (Klingender and Legg, 1937). During this period and into the 1930s the industry became increasingly concentrated, or dominated by a few large corporations known as the "majors": Loews, RKO, Paramount, Warners, and Fox. There was also continued integration, as the majors owned or dominated all branches of the industry (Huettig, 1944).

The antitrust actions, which resulted in the Paramount decrees in the late 1940s, finally separated exhibition activities from the major film corporations, as well as required certain changes in monopolistic trade practices (Conant, 1960). The major film corporations were also threatened by competitive challenges from other leisure-time and media activities after World War II, especially television (Guback and Dombkowski, 1976). The majors were thus forced to develop new strategies in order to maintain their domination of the industry.

The growth of independent films (produced outside the majors' studio facilities but often distributed by the majors) contributed to this adjustment process during the 1940s and 1950s. The majors had formerly produced large numbers of films at their own studios using contract actors, directors, and producers. For various reasons they began during this period to provide financing or distribution for fewer films produced by their satellite production companies and producers or by nominally independent producers.

Conglomeration, diversification, internationalization

Although most of the major production-distribution companies experienced a critical period in the late 1960s and early 1970s, they adjusted successfully by the mid-seventies, again becoming strong and profitable. Today the majors are involved in activities other than the production and distribution of feature films. Following a trend in other industries, all of the major production-distribution corporations went through a process of conglomeration. Business activities completely unrelated to the production and distribution of film were gathered under one corporate umbrella. This process was accomplished in a number of ways. Several companies, such as Columbia Pictures, Walt Disney Productions, and Twentieth Century-Fox, went through a process of self-conglomeration, adding subsidiaries to their existing corporate structures. Other companies, such as Universal Pictures and Warner Brothers, merged in various ways with other closely related companies. Paramount Pictures and United Artists became subsidiaries of already-existing conglomerates (Gulf + Western and Transamerica, respectively).

Although antitrust action stripped them of their ownership of domestic theaters, the majors have found new and profitable distribution outlets. At first a threat, video distribution--network and syndicated television distribution, cable, pay-cable, videocassettes, and videodiscs--has become an important source of revenue. In addition to these new outlets for feature films, the majors have become involved in the ownership of some of these channels, such as television stations, cable systems, and videocassette systems, as well as in the production of new products for these markets--television programs, made-for-television movies, commercials, and so on. A few of the major distributors also maintain ownership of foreign-theater circuits.

Other media and leisure activities have been gathered under these corporate umbrellas, among them publishing companies, amusement parks, ski resorts and other tourist attractions, mechanized games, sports centers, and sports teams. Although such activities as record and music publishing and distribution had previously been part of film companies' activities, this diversification process was intensified during the 1960s and 1970s. The production and distribution of feature films for theatrical release is, more than ever, only one part of the business of the major corporations in the American film industry.

Geographical expansion of markets also occurred during the sixties and seventies. The international market for American-produced films has traditionally been an important source of profits (Guback, 1969). In the early sixties, however, it became more common to use international locations for the production of American-financed feature films, which consequently became eligible for subsidies provided by foreign governments. In addition there was an increasing number of coproductions abroad and joint efforts by the American majors in international distribution. Both production and distribution have become increasingly concentrated at an international as well as at a domestic level.

So, while the changes of the late 1940s and early 1950s increased the risk of producing and distributing feature films, the major corporations have successfully spread this risk by intensifying the industrial processes of conglomeration, diversification, and internationalization. Concentration continues as the majors are able to dominate the marketing of feature films in the United States, even without theater ownership, through the production of feature films at their own studios as in previous eras.

Financing films

This adjustment process involved some changes in the methods by which films and film corporations are financed and consequently affects relationships with financing and banking institutions. To repeat, financial sources have varied over the years, as entrepreneurs and wealthy individuals have invested in film production through various schemes. But because banking institutions have provided continuous support for the entire industry, as well as established long-term, ongoing relationships with film companies and filmmakers, it is important to look at this relationship and its possible consequences.

Generally there are two types of financing applicable to the film industry: debt and equity financing. Debt financing, which covers bank loans, involves commercial banks extending credit, or a specific sum of money lent for a specific period of time for a specific amount of interest. For the film industry these loans have taken two forms: production and corporate loans. Production loans have been basically short-term, or interim, with money provided for production expenses, to be repaid most often from receipts generated from a picture's release. Corporate financing, on the other hand, includes not only loans from commercial banks (short-term, long-term, and various types of credit lines), but also the issuing of notes, bonds, and debentures by investment banking firms for general corporate use, which may include activities other than filmmaking. Debt financing does not involve ownership rights, but merely a creditorship relationship: the bank merely collects the money lent plus interest after a certain time period. The film company's ability to repay this sum is therefore of particular concern to the lender, which sets restrictions and conditions for the operation and management of the company.

Equity financing, another important part of a corporation's capital structure, is the issuing of corporate stock, or shareholdings, and involves investment-banking firms. Equity financing requires conditions and restrictions similar to those of debt financing; very often board members are appointed to represent a bank's interest in the company, or the bank holds large blocks of the company's stock.

Both debt and equity financing, as well as other services offered by commercial and investment banks, have been important to the film industry (Perry, 1966). In fact banks have at times come to directly control and even own film companies. Although direct ownership or overt control by banking institutions has not always been apparent, there has over the years been a continuous involvement by banks in the film industry through a combination of relationships: through the supply of capital (both debt and equity) for large corporations and independent filmmakers; through varying, and often unknown, amounts of corporate stock held by individual bankers, by investment--and, at one time, commercial--banks, or in commercial bank trust accounts; and through other services offered by banking institutions, especially financial advising. Additional relationships have involved bank approval, or placement, of management and key personnel in film companies; the presence of interlocking directors (directors who sit on both the bank's and the corporation's board); and the activities of industry representatives in financial and political spheres. In other words, it is through the totality of these complex and ongoing relationships, built over the years between a small number of banks and film corporations, that the potential for the exercise of power has been made possible.

Power has been obvious in ownership relationships

when banks have directly controlled the majority of stock in
a corporation (for example, Chase National Bank's control of
the Fox companies during the 1930s). But banks have also
decided which companies, and very often which filmmakers,
receive capital. The extension of credit has allowed banks
to influence decisions and policies made by corporate managers, and it has even given them the legal right to influence
who these managers will be. Further, these relationships
have provided a small group of banks and bankers with extensive knowledge of the film industry and its participants,
and thus another source of power.

"The movie business is a business"

Bankers and financiers have generally been attracted to the
motion-picture industry for reasons other than an interest in
film or filmmaking per se. Film as a creative art form or
communication medium has been much less important to bankers than film as a commodity. Yet their interests have been
not only in film as a product in itself but also in those valuable properties associated with film companies (e.g., real
estate and other assets); in the film industry as a market
for other products (sound equipment); or in the film business
as one component in the diversified activities of large multinational conglomerates. Bankers' attitudes toward film have
been molded primarily by economic considerations. As Peter
Geiger, of the Bank of America, has simply stated, "The
movie business is a business" (Geiger, 1974).

Among the primary banks active in the corporate financing of the American film industry are the largest and
most powerful banks in the country and in the world. Out
of the top sixteen bank-holding corporations, ranked by assets
in early 1980, fifteen were active in lending to the film industry during the 1970s. Most of these institutions were involved with the industry, although in varying degrees, at least
since the 1930s, and some even earlier. Nearly all of them
have years of expertise and experience with the film business.

Historically New York banks have been important for
the film industry because of their key location in the financial capital of the country, which naturally developed as the
film industry's financial headquarters. However, California
banks, such as the Bank of America, also have been important, primarily because of their location near Hollywood, the
film-production capital. Other banks became involved with

the industry due to the interest of individual bankers in expanding into areas where their large banks could profitably lend excess funds. The First National Bank of Boston is the best example of an institution now extremely active in the film industry due to the interest of one executive (McGilligan, 1976; Mayer, 1974).

It must be recognized that these banks hold powerful positions in the general economy, maintaining crucial political ties and affiliations. The film industry has relatively little political and economic clout compared with these multinational institutions with their extensive political, military, and industrial ties, as well as their control over vast sums of international capital.

In this context the position of the film industry relative to other sectors of the economy must also be considered. For example, a large oil corporation, such as Exxon, can draw income during any one three-month period equal to the total box-office gross for the entire film industry for one year. In fact, the total output of only fifteen countries in the world exceeded the total sales of Exxon in 1979. Obviously, these multinational giants and their multinational banks command far more political/economic attention than even the most prosperous film company.

The exercise of power

Despite this dominant position, though, it has generally been unnecessary for bankers to exercise their power over film corporations directly. Especially since the mid-1930s, bank-approved managers or other surrogates have represented banks' interests in the industry. But as these interests have very often been similar to those of film corporations, it has been unnecessary to use this potential power, or even to specify expectations. Managers or corporate directors, if not directly representing banks, often have similar financial backgrounds. The same class interests are represented, whether banker, large stockholder, or corporate executive is involved, and overall goals and policies are usually accepted by all participants.

As long as business runs smoothly and according to prescribed financial expectations, there is no need for the overt exercise of bank power. After all, bankers do not want actually to run corporations, and especially, they insist, not _film_ corporations (McGilligan, 1976). They do not generally read scripts or select stars or directors. Nevertheless, potential power over these corporations still exists, and during periods of crisis or challenges for control, it can be unleashed, revealing the details of complex and often hidden power structures.

These relationships have had consequences for the operations, policies, and organization of the film business during various periods of its history. In general, a concentrated, oligopolistic structure has been encouraged and intensified by bank support of the diverse activities of the major production-distribution corporations that currently dominate the industry.

More specifically, though, banks have aligned with major corporations and have become a part of the community of interests operating in the film business. Certain customers are favored over others--a challenge to the notion of a free marketplace for film distribution and exhibition. This community of interests, or favored-customer policy, is especially applicable to independent production financing. Banks have generally supported those producers aligned with, or approved by, the major distribution companies, without regard for the quality of a proposed production or the talent of the filmmakers. Independent producers and distributors have been placed either at the mercy of the majors or out in the cold; either they become closely aligned with them or they have to be content with box-office leftovers.

The effect of the banks/film industry relationship on film content, style, and form is important, but this relationship must first be established in order to identify and fully understand any possible effects on the production process. Active participation by bankers or their studio representatives was prevalent in the late 1920s and 1930s, and cases of direct banker influence on film content can be cited. This direct involvement, however, has not been the only way that financiers have influenced filmmaking. The amount of capital and the terms under which it is provided (budget limitations and other restrictions, for example) have also inevitably influenced _how_ films have been made.

To a great extent, direct involvement by bankers and other financial interests in film content and form has been unnecessary. The parameters have been set by the system in which filmmaking operates: films are products that are made, distributed, and exhibited by profit-making organizations. Bankers do not have to enforce these boundaries. They were long ago accepted by the film industry itself.

References

Conant, Michael. Antitrust in the Motion Picture Industry. Berkeley: University of California Press, 1960.
Geiger, Peter W. "The View from the 48th Floor." Hollywood Reporter, November 29, 1974, p. 70.
Guback, Thomas H. The International Film Industry: Western Europe and America Since 1945. Bloomington: Indiana University Press, 1969.
_____. "Theatrical Film." In Who Owns the Media?, edited by Benjamin Compaine. White Plains, N.Y.: Knowledge Industries, 1979, pp. 179-249.
_____, and Dennis J. Dombkowski. "Television and Hollywood: Economic Relations in the 1970s." Journal of Broadcasting 20 (Fall 1976): 511-527.
Howe, A. H. "Bankers and Movie-Makers." In The Movie Business: American Film Industry Practice, edited by A. William Bluem and Jason E. Squire. New York: Hastings House, 1972, pp. 57-67.
Huettig, Mae D. Economic Control of the Motion Picture Industry. Philadelphia: University of Pennsylvania Press, 1944.
Klingender, Francis D., and Stuart Legg. Money Behind the Screen. London: Lawrence & Wishart, 1937.
Kotz, David M. Bank Control of Large Corporations in the United States. Berkeley: University of California Press, 1978.
McGilligan, Patrick. "Bank Shots." Film Comment, September-October 1976, pp. 138-141+.
Mayer, Martin. The Bankers. New York: Weybright & Talley, 1974.
Murdock, Graham, and Peter Golding. "For a Political Economy of Mass Communications." In Socialist Register, edited by Ralph Miliband and John Saville. London: Merline, 1974, pp. 205-234.
Perry, Donald L. "An Analysis of the Financial Plans of the Motion Picture Industry for the Period 1929-1962." Ph.D. dissertation, University of Illinois, 1966.
U.S. Congress. Senate. Committee on Government Operations. Disclosure of Corporate Ownership. Report by

the Subcommittee on Intergovernmental Relations and the Subcommittee on Budgeting, Management and Expenditures of the Committee on Government Operations, 93rd Cong., 1st sess. Washington, D.C.: Government Printing Office, 1973.

Wasko, Janet M. "Relationships Between the American Motion Picture Industry and Banking Institutions." Ph.D. dissertation, University of Illinois, 1980.

Zeitlin, Maurice. "Corporate Ownership and Control: The Large Corporation and the Capitalist Class." American Journal of Sociology 79 (March): 1073-1119.

FILM AND
NOT-FOR-PROFIT
MEDIA INSTITUTIONS

J. Ronald Green

In a capitalist economy, like that of the United States, success is measured by profits. Such a system is very businesslike. Results are apparently easy to read, since institutions can be compared summarily by looking at the balance sheets, the bottom-line ratios of income and expenses. It is also brutally efficient, since the competitive marketplace determines survival, and the inefficient and ineffective institutions are supposedly eliminated by "natural selection." But there are disadvantages as well. Because profits are the measure of success, one cannot assume any motivation or social goal but that of financial gain. This is not to say that there are no other motives operating, but that they are incidental to the system of economic rewards. This system is too simple to account for the range of human goals and the historical complexities and social inequities that inform our present society.

The United States tax law provides for another type of business, one that is to some extent protected from the battlefront of profit-measured competition. The Internal Revenue Service does not tax certain organizations, and it does not tax profits, of businesses or individuals, that are donated to certain of these organizations. These untaxed, tax-deductible institutions are judged by the IRS to be operating for other reasons besides profit (which may or may not be the case--

the legal definitions are imperfect in that respect), and thus are called "not-for-profit." It is this type of media institution that will concern us here, a concern justified by its proliferation, by its importance to film, and by its neglect in the developing scholarship of film institutions, which has focused on the dominant, commercial industry.

Definitions

The definitions that follow should be read as a taxonomy to be fleshed out: as an indicator, on the one hand, of the ways film is embedded as an institution in society, and, on the other hand, of the basic categories of film as an ideal organizational model in society.

"Not-for-profit"--does not mean that institutions so designated cannot make a profit, but rather that any profits they make cannot accrue to any individual (or generally to the benefit of any individual). Of course, they may give money to individuals, such as pay reasonable salaries for services, like management and labor, or make grants to individuals according to the goals and purposes of the organization (though this is much more difficult now than it used to be, due to past abuses). Such payments are not considered profits; they are operating expenses. In a profit situation--such as General Motors or a private bank--profits over and above expenses are the personal property of the owners of the institution; in a not-for-profit organization profits may be made, subject to certain regulations, but they must remain in the coffers of that institution and cannot be claimed by its directors, owners, or managers.

"Media"--in this chapter comprises (in addition to film) video, television, audio, and radio, since they are all significantly related in our society and since many not-for-profit institutions deal with more than one medium.

"Institution"--a formally incorporated organization that provides services, which can be categorized as six media-culture functions: funding, production, preservation, distribution, exhibition, and study or education.

"Funding--includes activities meant to attract funds into the culture, or training and information programs directed toward that end. Examples are grant development, consultation with regional organizations and individuals concerning market analysis, public relations, and lobbying.

"Production"--comprises shooting, recording, editing, mixing, processing, printing, and (in electronic image and sound making) synthesizing, image manipulation, and certain aspects of hardware-system research and development of improved and less expensive technical and managerial means for handling the above functions.

"Preservation"--ensuring that works are not lost and are accessible for the future.

"Distribution"--transferring the work from the maker to the exhibitor or viewer. The most prominent means are nontheatrical film and video distribution through rentals and sales (commercial, cooperative, governmental and educational circuits, and public libraries); also television, radio and cable, and satellite. Distribution involves acquisition, print and tape production and care, transporting, rights and agreements protection, and promotion of product.

"Exhibition"--presenting the film or tape work to an audience. Involves program or series development; historical and aesthetic research; research into the location, price, and condition of prints and tapes; transport; maintenance of physical screening space and projection standards, print projection; and audience comfort. Also includes rights negotiation, publicity, audience development, and acquisition, storage, and handling of exhibition prints and tapes.

"Study"--increasing the understanding of the moving image and sound experience. Involves primary materials and methodological research; education from beginning to advanced levels in traditional or nontraditional institutions; curriculum development; interviewing; lectures, seminars, conferences, workshops, and summer institutes; publication; access to archival collections; development of and access to analytical viewing equipment, libraries, and (especially) professional and public information services.

The media-culture system: an institutional model

These definitions comprise an institutional model of the not-for-profit media culture. The model functions as a system, which simply means that all the activities we have talked about are interrelated and form a larger entity. If any one element were removed, the whole fabric would be endangered, as in an ecologic system.

The elements of the model are the media themselves: film, video, television, audio, and radio. Their interrelations and behavior are the services and functions: funding, production, preservation, distribution, exhibition, and study. One simple way to illustrate this behavior as a system is to draw these activities as a circle, or cycle, starting with "funding." Funding, or "financing" as it would be termed in profit organizations, is the life-blood, the circulatory aspect of the system; whatever is going to happen must generally be paid for first (whether "up-front" or not is irrelevant at this point--some idea of where the money is going to come from usually must precede any institutional activity). Once financing is in place, the first activity one thinks of is production, since without film, video, or audio product there is nothing to preserve, distribute, exhibit, or study. Once something is produced, it can be preserved, which is necessary if the system is to have a history or a future of distributing, exhibiting, or studying the productions. If a work is preserved, then it can go into distribution. Once distributed, it can be exhibited and seen or heard, and once it is seen, it can be studied. And here the circle closes and the cycle starts over--studying the production serves as feedback, a critique of the failures and successes of the production in its journey through the system. These critiques when fed back to the beginning of the functional cycle inform the decisions concerning the funding of the next production, and the subsequent preservation, distribution, exhibition, and study of it--and so on. [1]

The two terms that form the link in the cycle, "funding" and "study," can also be understood as applying directly to any of the other five functions, thus generating subcycles within the system. In other words, one can discuss as a subcycle the funding, study, and refunding of exhibition alone, or distribution, or for that matter, funding or study activities themselves.

A list of institutions

The discussion thus far has been theoretical; the table on page 41 presents a cast of characters taken from the real world, analyzed according to the theoretical model. The list is highly selective and makes no judgments as to quality.

TABLE OF INSTITUTIONS AND FUNCTIONS

Institution	FUNDING	PRODUCTION	PRESERVATION	DISTRIBUTION	EXHIBITION	STUDY
Academy of Motion Picture Arts and Sciences, Los Angeles			x	x		x
American Federation of Arts, NYC				x		x
American Film Institute, DC and Los Angeles	x	x	x	x	x	x
Anthology Film Archive, NYC			x		x	x
Appalshop, Whitesburg, Kentucky		x	x	x	x	x
Association of Independent Video and Filmmakers, NYC	x					x
Centro de Communicacion, San Antonio					x	x
Corporation for Public Broadcasting, DC	x					
Educational Film Library Association, NYC				x	x	x
Film Fund, NYC	x			x		x
Film in the Cities, St. Paul		x	x	x	x	x
Film Oasis, Los Angeles					x	
George Eastman House, Rochester			x		x	x
Media Study, Buffalo		x	x	x	x	x
Millennium, NYC		x			x	x
Museum of Modern Art, NYC		x	x	x	x	x
National Endowments for the Arts and Humanities, DC	x					x
Northwest Film Study Center, Portland, Oregon		x		x	x	x
Pacific Film Archive, Berkeley			x		x	x
Pittsburgh Film-Makers		x	x	x	x	x
Public Broadcasting Service, DC	x			x	x	
Public Interest Satellite Network		x	x			
Rocky Mountain Film Center, Boulder		x		x	x	x
Society for Cinema Studies						x
South Carolina Arts Commission, Columbia	x	x		x	x	x
Third World Cinema, NYC		x		x	x	x
UCLA Film Archive, Los Angeles			x			x
University Film Association						x
University of Wisconsin Center for Theatre Research, Madison			x			x
Walker Art Center, Minneapolis					x	x
Whitney Museum, NYC					x	x
Young Filmmakers, NYC		x	x	x		x

Goals of not-for-profit institutions

Why was the Museum of Modern Art motivated to set up an expensive program to preserve and distribute films that had been made by a powerful, fabulously wealthy industry? According to the market approach to economics, anything that was valued by society would find appropriate financing through the natural workings of the system; that is, if it is important, then someone must want it enough to be willing to pay for it --there must be a market for it. There are many problems with a straight market approach to economic and social systems, some of which are discussed below. At this point it is enough to realize that the profit organizations of the industry have allowed countless important films of their own making to disintegrate, to get lost, or to be tossed out, because they were no longer capable of generating a significant profit. Other films of great social value were never commercially viable, even when they were made, such as certain documentaries, avant-garde--socially and culturally iconoclastic-- works, and, in this country, foreign films of all kinds. Goals of not-for-profit institutions spring from the social failures of the for-profit industry.

The Museum of Modern Art Film Library

When the Museum of Modern Art established its Film Library in 1935, it was virtually impossible to see a film made in Hollywood that was not a recent release. There were no film societies, no museum repertory screening programs, no university film-history courses, no film in public libraries --because there was nothing for such institutions to show. Richard Griffith, Director of the Museum of Modern Art Film Library in 1956, wrote in the Report on the Film Library: 1941-1956:

> It was a miracle of judgment on the part of the founders which rejected the idea (then seriously proposed) that the Film Library should be merely an archive in which a few scholars could putter among "historic" films, and which instead embraced the concept of a central circulating system from which films would be made available to anyone in the country [1956: 4].

That policy decision opened the way for today's great variety of not-for-profit film activities. The availability of old, documentary, avant-garde, and foreign films allowed for the development of film societies, university film courses, and museum and library film exhibition programs. These phenomena in turn became a substantial market for "noncommercial" films, thus generating a profitable business in nontheatrical film distribution to serve that market. New profit distributors were in effect welcomed as unofficial partners by the Museum of Modern Art. The Museum simply kept track of the films that were picked up for distribution by its "competitors" and adjusted its own distribution catalog accordingly, dropping commercially distributed films and picking up neglected work.

Also, the preservation activities had a noticeable effect on the growth of noncommercial film activity all over the world. Obvious examples are the establishment of such professional organizations as the British Film Institute in London, the Cinémathèque Française in Paris, and the Fédération Internationale des Archives de Film, founded in 1939 at a meeting at the Museum of Modern Art.

The beneficiaries of the Museum's preservation and distribution policies were not just formal institutions. Less well known is the effect of this program on the rise of American avant-garde filmmaking, as pointed out by Lewis Jacobs:

> Behind this phenomenal post-war revival [in experimental film] were two forces which had been set in motion during the war years. The first was the circulation at nominal cost to non-profit groups of programs from the Film Library of the Museum of Modern Art. Their collection of pictures and program notes dealing with the history, art, and traditions of cinema went to hundreds of colleges, universities, museums, film appreciation groups, study groups. These widespread exhibitions as well as the Museum of Modern Art's own showings in their auditorium in New York City exerted a major influence in preparing the way for a broader appreciation and production of experimental films [1968: 563].

Not-for-profit film institutions proliferate

Within twenty-five years of the founding of the Film Library at the Museum of Modern Art, noncommercial film institutions had grown and diversified into a jungle of independent service agencies, on the one hand duplicating services and resources, and on the other leaving enormous resource gaps. Colin Young, in his proposal for an American Film Institute, published in the Summer 1961 Film Quarterly, discusses some of these organizations: the Hollywood Motion Picture and Television Museum (in planning at that time), the San Francisco Museum of Art, the Eastman House, the Library of Congress, the National Archive, the Academy of Motion Picture Arts and Sciences, Cinema 16, the American Federation of Film Societies, the Wisconsin Film Society, and the UCLA Extension Media Service. The list reflects his initial concern with preservation, distribution, and exhibition. Later, discussing education, he adds these: the University Film Producers Association, the Society for Cinema, various film councils (e.g., those in New York and Washington), the Motion Picture Association of America, the Writers' Guild, the Directors' Guild, the American Society of Cinematographers, the American Cinema Editors, as well as "many public libraries and high school or university extension adult education departments" (page 46). Elsewhere in the article he discusses the Educational Film Library Association, the American Library Association, the Flaherty Seminars, the UCLA Theatre Arts Department, the New Yorker Theater, the Center for Mass Communication at Columbia University, the Theater Owners Association, the International Film Importers and Distributors Association, and the San Francisco Film Festival.

Young goes on to list even more organizations. The point here is that twenty-five years after the founding of the Film Library, the proliferation of not-for-profit film organizations (many directly or indirectly spawned by the Film Library's policies, some thrown off directly from activities of the commercial industry) was being pointed out in public for its variety and overall disorganization. The not-for-profit film field had grown to the point that it needed a national coordinating institution.

The American Film Institute

The American Film Institute was founded in 1967 partly to answer the need for coordination and central planning for that proliferation. A report developed by the Stanford Research Institute, Organization and Location of the American Film Institute, commonly called the Stanford Report, was the blueprint for the formation of the AFI. This report recognized a broad constituency, much like that delineated by Colin Young, in the body of its analysis and recommendations, and in the wide range of its informants from the field of not-for-profit film. Nevertheless, because of certain conclusions of the report, particularly its judgment that commercial, theatrical film was to be considered primary, along with the decision to prefer autonomy over broad affiliation for the board of directors, the AFI developed as a service organization oriented primarily toward those not-for-profit interests most closely associated with the commercial industry as centered in California. However, certain recent changes in the AFI have produced a realignment of priorities that will allow the Institute to assume a greater role in the not-for-profit film world existing outside of the Los Angeles commercial industry.

Regional media centers

Just after the American Film Institute was formed, a new phenomenon began to emerge: The regional media center. Some centers, such as the Pacific Film Archive in Berkeley and the Rocky Mountain Film Center in Boulder, began by showing films to the public that otherwise could not be seen in their regions, very much like large nonmembership film societies. Others, like Pittsburgh Film-Makers and the South Carolina Arts Commission, were originally motivated by the need to provide centralized equipment resources or other services directly to filmmakers doing noncommercial work. A third group--the University Film Study Center in Cambridge, Massachusetts, and Anthology Film Archive in New York City are examples--set out to collect certain kinds of films for the research or study use of not-for-profit clientele.

Whatever the initial goals of these institutions, there developed a general tendency in all of them to expand their services toward a full offering of all the functions of film culture: funding, production, preservation, distribution, exhibition, and study. Since each organization emerged out of a specific region with its own problems and strengths, each had a different attitude toward the balance of these functions. This in fact was the strength of the phenomenon: the centers were able to serve their regions directly and efficiently.

Pittsburgh Film-Makers: case study of a regional media center

Pittsburgh Film-Makers was founded in the early seventies

to provide a centralized pool of equipment--particularly large and expensive pieces, such as flatbed editors and sound transfer and mixing studios--for the use of an open membership of independent, noncommercial film producers. (The practice of pooling resources, of forming partnerships and cooperatives for the purpose of joint proprietorship and time sharing of expensive capital equipment, is common in commercial and noncommercial enterprises: e.g., farmers' coops or oil-drilling partnerships.) The founders of Pittsburgh Film-Makers were interested solely in production. They were not concerned about a theoretical "full film culture."

However, after setting up and running their own cooperative work space for awhile (with grants from local foundations and later the National Endowment for the Arts and other agencies), they discovered that other people wanted to join, and that some of these wanted to learn filmmaking or photography and would be willing to pay for the instruction. Though the original filmmakers had not thought of this, they were not averse to teaching people who wanted to learn, and they could use the income to live and to make their films. Since most of the production expertise of the Pittsburgh area was associated with Pittsburgh Film-Makers, since they had already invested significant capital in equipment, and since they had teaching experience, the universities in the area who wanted to begin filmmaking curricula sought cooperative arrangements with Pittsburgh Film-Makers to handle their new courses in production. The original filmmakers, who had wanted only to make films, now needed to show films in order to teach, and discovered, as a consequence, that it helped their own work.

In connection with teaching activity Pittsburgh Film-Makers also developed a reference library of books and periodicals that became a study resource for the region, providing a base for a subgroup called the Research Project in American Film. The Project conducted interviews with important independent filmmakers, wrote articles, published a journal, pursued preservation of certain works, and made documentaries about American filmmakers. Pittsburgh Film-Makers became more directly involved in preservation activities, as members often lacked the money to take the proper preservation measures.

Distribution was recognized as the last priority, since the two national film-distribution cooperatives for independent producers, Film-makers Cooperative in New York and Canyon

Cinema Cooperative in Sausalito, were as freely accessible to filmmakers as any cooperative in Pittsburgh would have been. On the other hand, Pittsburgh Film-Makers, because of insights and problems arising from their regular screenings and their film programs and workshops, felt the need to establish a distribution system whereby new works from any independent filmmaker in the country would be collected in Pittsburgh and then cycled through ten regions around the country and shown to potential renters and purchasers only, in an effort to get new independent films seen by a maximum number of possible renters and purchasers. This was a marketing program, related directly to distribution and exhibition, and, more to the point, increased funding for filmmakers, in the form of returns.

Pittsburgh Film-Makers is a paradigm case history of growth from an original exclusive concern in 1971 for film production, through progressive relations with film study and exhibition, then preservation, distribution, and funding. The original singleness of purpose grew, through practice rather than theory, into a broad concern for all aspects of the system. The members found that as producers, they could not survive without some institutional relationship with the other functional aspects of the film culture. In fact, this case study demonstrates a dependence of independent filmmakers on multi-system institutions, and their interdependence among themselves, as realized, perhaps unwittingly and often unwillingly, through their own necessary cooperative practices. Thus the "independent" filmmakers were independent of commercial institutions, but not of their own not-for-profit (or profit) institutions, or of each other.

Regional and national organizations

There are many local and regional media centers like Pittsburgh Film-Makers, all of them different. They represent a significant sector of not-for-profit film activitiy in the United States, after a short ten years of growth. Their combined capital assets run in the tens of millions of dollars, as do their annual operating budgets. Recently they have begun to organize themselves in multistate regions and, most importantly, nationally. Some 120 media centers have formed the National Alliance of Media Arts Centers, a major step in the evolution of film culture. This Alliance creates a federalist institutional structure of, on the one hand, decentralized root institutions serving individuals and locales, representing

48 FILM/CULTURE

pluralistic interests and clientele, and on the other hand, national-level coordination. This federalist structure allows for local, indigenous development and services, directed to individuals, other institutions, and independent film producers; unity of identity and purpose in a pluralistic field; and the ability to accomplish common goals.

Summary

The last few pages have shown how a pioneering policy decision by a not-for-profit film organization, the Museum of Modern Art, in 1935 led to the proliferation of diverse commercial and, particularly, noncommercial film activities, ranging from university curricula to museum exhibition to independent film production. This proliferation helped bring the American Film Institute into existence. At the same time, filmmakers and other individuals formed media centers to deal with the complexities of the burgeoning film culture in their own locales. These centers eventually coalesced into a national coordinating body for a federalist institutional network, one that now takes its place beside several other large systems, also spawned more or less directly by the original Museum of Modern Art distribution policy. These include the Fédération Internationale des Archives de Film, the Educational Film Library Association, the University Film Association, the Society for Cinema Studies, the American Federation of Film Societies, and others, comprising a huge not-for-profit institutional film and media culture.

Public policy

The emergence of a strong and diversified not-for-profit film culture gives new importance to issues of public policy in this field. In the past few years discussion in the United States about film institutions has increased, but with overwhelming focus on the commercial industry (see Hampton, 1970; Jacobs, 1968; Jarvie, 1970; Sklar, 1975; Balio, 1976; Gomery, 1976, 1978, 1979; Allen, 1979; Staiger, 1979; Andrew, 1979).

It is important that we expand this discussion to include the noncommercial systems, and also public policy. Public policy is action, or plans of action, deliberated and set by governments at all levels, local or federal, or by their agencies; it need not be legislated, but can be unlegislated and tacit. In other words, public policy should be studied not only in its formal manifestations but as it is practiced in the world of action and social behavior. The agencies of government are not only the well-known ones that comprise the alphabet soup that has become a part of our quotidian language--NEA, NEH, NSF, DOD, HEW, OSHA, FCC--but also the numerous pseudogovernmental, officially private institutions that directly depend for their existence on government. Some examples: the Corporation for Public Broadcasting, a private organization created and funded almost entirely by government; the American Film Institute, a wholly private body with an autonomous board of directors, which was "authorized" for significant funding and singled out for special mention by President Lyndon Johnson on the occasion of the founding of a true federal government agency, the National Foundation for the Arts and Humanities; and the Children's Television Workshop, which produces Sesame Street and other programming through a heavy dependence on financing from various government agencies.

A comparison of these three institutions shows that they represent a spectrum in their relationships with government. The Corporation for Public Broadcasting is virtually a government agency, since its dependence on line-item government funds is almost a hundred percent. The only reason it was not set up as a true government agency was to buffer public television programming from direct government control. The American Film Institute is another step away from government, with its fully autonomous, self-perpetuating board of directors and its non-line-item relationship to the federal budget. The Institute must compete with other organizations for grant and contract funds distributed by agencies, with an implicit possibility that, under the conditions of normal review of these grants and contracts, funding could be cut off, reduced, or increased at any time without upsetting or changing any statutory government policy. The same relationship to government pertains to the Children's Television Workshop, with one difference: it was never singled out by the nation's President or any other official for special mention and "authorization" as an institutional priority. Thus it has no direct statutory argument for obtaining government funding. It must compete on equal terms with other organizations. It is into this category that most of the institutions and systems of institutions in the not-for-profit film culture fall.

Some policy issues: access

The broadest and most important policy issues center on access--who has access to what, and through what procedures? And the most important access issues have to do with the processes of policy formation--are policies formed from the bottom up or the top down; who is enfranchised and at what level; who is informed? The centrality of access issues springs from the very nature of the politico-economic system in the United States. The legal basis of American "free enterprise" capitalism is the right of citizens to own property and to dispose of it in their own way at their own discretion (Sutton et al., 1956: 57). Large companies are logical extensions of this right, having evolved in scale through the accumulation of capital via profits. The legal basis of capitalism is individual proprietorship, and, by implication, private limitation of access to resources and to their management. This fact is one of the major reasons for the emergence of not-for-profit institutions in this politico-economic system. Incorporation of a not-for-profit organization legally undercuts the individual proprietary basis of the economic reward system and gives economic advantages to organizations with extraproprietary goals, including access-oriented policies and programs.

Efficiency and effectiveness

Another issue is that of accountability. The profit system claims advantages in this area, arguing that the orientation of management around the balance sheet and its bottom line (profit or loss) ensures efficiency and effectiveness through absolute accountability for productivity. Both government and not-for-profit organizations are accused by business of being "naturally prone to waste, corruption and favoritism," and of "failing to call individuals to account for their use of funds and economic resources and for their decisions" (Sutton et al., 1956: 66). This distinction is not as clearcut as business interests have traditionally portrayed, since balance sheets are subject to crude guesswork, flexible or arbitrary accounting conventions, and countless details of interpretation in their construction that must be reinterpreted and can be misinterpreted (Sutton et al., 1956: 74). Nevertheless, there is no doubt that economic survival in a competitive marketplace, as figured in a proper balance sheet, is a stringent test of an institution's relative productivity. The profit system is an enviable evaluative mechanism.

The government evaluations, reporting procedures, auditing, and record keeping that are strangling business, grantees, and contractees, are a response to that common criticism. There is no easy solution to the problem. Numerous value systems must be brought to bear on decisions of public policy, representing numerous interests and constituencies. They are not always comparable, as are numbers on a balance sheet.

If the not-for-profit sector of the film culture grows, the problem of evaluation and standards will become more critical; the problems described above will be a large part of institutional life. Designing means of evaluation will be a major challenge in this field, and scholarly discussion of the related larger issues is essential. The National Endowments for the Arts and Humanities recognize this need and simply move it into a formal arena: judgments of quality, social and cultural need, and productivity are made not by bureaucrats but by peers working in the same or related fields as those of the grant and contract applicants, peers who are brought to Washington for meetings. This peer-review panel system assumes the need for judgments beyond (though including) the arithmetical. There are, however, many corollary issues surrounding that system. How is conflict of interest avoided if the best people are needed and expected both as grant applicants and grant arbitrators? How are panelists chosen so that the judgment process is not improperly skewed by bureaucrats or politicians?

In the larger sense, too, discussion is needed in order to inform and exercise the thinking of our peers, and to develop criteria, with respect to complex institutional policy issues, not only so that the evaluation systems will work progressively but so that institutions and systems of institutions will <u>be managed</u> progressively.

Managing not-for-profit film institutions

As this chapter has repeatedly suggested, there are fundamental differences in the social goals of profit and not-for-profit enterprises. The extract that follows suggests important areas of concern that do not commonly appear in the self-proclaimed social successes of American business:

> In both its discussion of what constitute the achievements of American capitalism, and its

> explanation of these achievements, the business ideology is highly selective, in comparison with a broader, more neutral social science discussion of these problems.
> The creed, as we have seen, concentrates on the material and the practical in its enumeration of achievements. Claims that the business system has yielded significant cultural or esthetic gains are almost completely absent. Spiritual and moral achievements are limited largely to Freedom.
> It is hardly surprising that the creed rarely makes any claim on the esthetic quality of modern life, the superiority of the moral standards of our present society over those of earlier societies or of other countries, or the piety of life under the System. To concentrate on such matters would be foreign to the fundamental American value system within which the values of business creed are framed. Nowhere in the creed is there any suggestion that conflict exists between religion and capitalism, humanitarianism and money seeking, although discussion of such conflicts is frequent in European writing.
> Little space is given to other noneconomic achievements of the society which are more compatible with our system and might well be credited to the System. The great improvement in health over the last century and the resultant increase in the average length of life are little discussed, although they are clearly achievements of industrial capitalism. True, they are listed among the achievements of the System in the NAM [National Association of Manufacturers, Economic Principles Commission] treatise, but they rarely appear in more popular conveyors of the creed--advertisements, pamphlets, and speeches. The same can be said of equal opportunity in education [Sutton et al., 1956: 49].

Some of those areas needing the attention of not-for-profit organizations are inherent in the omissions from the American profit enterprise success story. Not-for-profit goals are often formed around those omissions.

Also inherent in those omissions is the necessity for different management approaches and procedures. We have seen one demonstration of the difference between management procedures in not-for-profit enterprises in the film-distribution policy of the Museum of Modern Art Film Library in 1935. The Museum decided to act upon an assessed need even when there was thought to be no market formed around that need. This subsidized program (preservation and distribution of films that had social but no commercial value) evolved to the point where a market large enough to support small profit enterprises was created. The Museum adapted to the competition of profit enterprises by adopting a nonproprietary stance toward the films; they dropped any that were picked up by commercial distributors and added new ones that were not in distribution. As I have attempted to demonstrate, these management approaches, inherently complementary to profit-enterprise practices, gave rise to an exponential increase in not-for-profit film activities dealing with a range of important social and cultural issues.

Value, and economics of scale

An interesting issue faces not-for-profit managers as the size and complexity of their organizations increase. Douglas Gomery, in his 1979 article "The Movies Become Big Business: Publix Theatres and the Chain Store Strategy," explains aspects of the film industry's discovery and development of economics of scale for maximization of profits.

> The chief advantage for a chain operation lay in cost reduction through scale economies and monopsony power.[1] Chains could spread fixed costs over more operations and purchase inputs at lower prices. To maximize such savings, chains relied on what was labeled "scientific management." Here large circuits would secure trained managers, experts and other skilled labor to operate the firm at peak efficiency: no waste, rapid turnover, maximum profits and growth. To assure that a standardized product would be sold in a "clean and dependable atmosphere," the chain's managers, operating from a central office, divided up the firm's activities, and had each department perform its specialty at maximum efficiency and minimum cost. Gradually the managers would internalize more and more of the transactions, increase the speed and regularity of operations, and continue to lower costs. Simultaneously the chain would purchase more outlets, grow more powerful, and garner more monopsony power for necessary inputs. Costs would fall even

54   FILM/CULTURE

> further. Chains advertised widely and developed trade-marks for instant recognition. Large accounting departments provided managers with a continuous flow of information in order to circumvent unneeded expenses. Greater profits facilitated new financing, and chains quickly moved to capture new markets during the 1920's ...
> [1]Monopsony power results when a firm is one of a limited number of buyers of a certain input, and thus can bargain for a lower purchase price [pages 27, 38].

In his discussion of the arts in Economics and the Public Purpose (1973) John Kenneth Galbraith points out some characteristics of large- and small-scale organizations and their effect on the arts.

> Where manufacturing requires a measure of artistic effort and is judged in part by this, the artistic superiority of the small firm will often allow of its survival in competition with the large organization. Since the good artist cannot or will not be subordinate to organization, the large, relatively immobile enterprise commands not the best talent but the most accommodating. This, more or less by definition, is second-rate. Nor is this purely a matter of poor or perverse taste on the part of the organization. The large firm must have designs that will lend themselves to long and economical runs. Artistic sense must also yield to the will of those who, on the basis of instinct, experience or market research, are knowledgeable on what the public can be persuaded to buy. Artistic judgment is subject to a supervening view of acceptability, and this, in turn, is powerfully influenced by the common working assumption, sometimes articulated, that no one ever went into receivership underestimating the popular taste. In consequence the large firm gets long runs, technical efficiency, low costs and a considered marketing strategy at the expense of good design. The automobile industry, the mass producers of furniture, the household appliance industry, the container industry and numerous others amply illustrate the point [page 61].

The tendency of business organizations to get larger is well known, and as Gomery and Galbraith point out, there are efficiencies--such as long production runs, the spreading

Not-for-Profit Media Institutions 55

of fixed costs over large operations, and the ability to serve large markets--that encourage and justify such scale, if the only value is profitability. We have noted already that not-for-profit organizations tend to grow as well, due to the same pressures and attractions of serviceability and efficiency. As this occurs in the film culture, managers will need to balance economic values with the other values inherent in not-for-profit institutional goals.

Gomery points out that, within the large-scale economics of the film industry, certain <u>functions</u> are more susceptible to management for scale <u>economics</u> than others.

> Hollywood-owned circuits increasingly presented a more standardized product, on a national level, at decreasing cost--all directed by a central authority in New York. <u>Exhibition was the branch of the industry which could most easily adopt "big business" practices and thus accumulate the greatest excess profits</u> [page 26; emphasis added].

Galbraith makes the same observation about the relations of functions and scale for completely different reasons.

> A few industries--the motion picture firms, television networks, the large advertising agencies--must, by their nature, associate artists with rather complex organization. All have a well-reported record of dissonance and conflict between the artists and the rest of the organization.... Frequently the problem is solved by removing actors, actresses, scriptwriters, directors, composers, copywriters and creators of advertising commercials from the techno-structure of the film studio, television network or advertising agency and reconstituting them in small independent companies. The large firm then confines itself to providing the appropriate facilities for producing and--more importantly--marketing, exhibiting or airing the product. Similarly painters, sculptors, concert pianists and novelists function, in effect, as one-man firms or, as in the case of rock, dance and folk music groups, as small partnerships and turn to larger organizations to market themselves or their products [page 60]. [2]

We have seen examples of the coalition formation of organizational marketing and self-support functions in the case of Pittsburgh Film-Makers, and in discussing regional and national organization we saw the formation of a large, complex organization of organizations, the National Alliance of Media Arts Centers, designed to protect the regional and professional autonomy of the smaller institutions. Clearly the economics and the values inherent in organizational scale must be managed subtly and consciously.

Conclusion

All productive activity arises from a cultural context. Individualistic work, or the work of small groups of individuals, is potentially of great interest to society, provided it can be integrated into that society. The film culture is responsible for such integration. This chapter has attempted to widen the discussion on the film culture, which directly affects and manages film product, to include institutions whose stated purpose and legal configuration is not-for-profit. It has also attempted to increase understanding of the phenomenon, past and present, and to encourage study and more detailed discussion. The issues involved, particularly those of public policy, affect, more and more, our informing environment-- the films we make and films we see.

Notes

1. Some of the ideas of this paragraph have evolved in public, unpublished discussion of regional media centers and independent film in the past decade. It is difficult to credit sources for their formulation. One formulation appears in "The Spectrum of Cinema," by Gerald O'Grady (1977: 15).

2. I. C. Jarvie in Movies and Society approaches Galbraith's issues from a different angle. "To sum up, we have tried to answer sociologically the question of whether the filmmaker is at any special disadvantage because he must need work within a complex production organization. Our answer has been that the advantages outweigh the disadvantages, which anyway tend to be made up of artistic idealizing, and naive juxtapositions of art and commerce. It is not at all clear that responsiblity gets lost in organizational complexity; but it is true that organizational advantages have tended

to favour the middle ground as far as quality is concerned" (1970: 37). Jarvie's criticism of "naive juxtapositions of art and commerce" does not apply to Galbraith's analysis, even though Galbraith does not present anything comparable to the depth and breadth of Jarvie's description and sociological analysis of the film industry itself.

Jarvie's criticism is important to bear in mind when discussing not-for-profit institutions. It is not, for example, the purpose of this chapter to imply that there is anything inherently "good" in not-for-profit enterprises or "bad" in profit enterprises. There are interesting problems and advantages to both. The intention of this chapter to encourage discussion of the public sector of the film culture is, first of all, in recognition of a newly significant phenomenon. The growth of that phenomenon, not-for-profit media institutions, is an implicit criticism of certain inadequacies of the profit system, some of which this chapter attempts to identify.

References

Allen, R. C. "Motion Picture Exhibition in Manhattan: Beyond the Nickelodeon." Cinema Journal 18, 2 (1979): 2-15.

Andrew, D. "The Postwar Struggle for Color." Cinema Journal 18, 2 (1979): 41-52.

Galbraith, J. K. Economics and the Public Purpose. Boston: Houghton Mifflin, 1973.

Gomery, J. D. "Film Industry Studies: The Search for a Theory." Quarterly Review of Film Studies 1, 1 (1976): 95-100.

──────. "The Picture Palace: Economic Sense or Hollywood Nonsense?" Quarterly Review of Film Studies 3, 1 (1978): 23-26.

──────. "The Movies Become Big Business: Publix Theatres and the Chain Store Strategy." Cinema Journal 18, 2 (1979): 26-40.

Griffith, R. Report on the Film Library. New York: Museum of Modern Art, 1956.

Hampton, B. B. A History of the Movies. New York: Covici, Friede, 1931. (Reprinted, as History of the American Film Industry from Its Beginning to 1931, New York: Dover, 1970.)

Jacobs, L. The Rise of the American Film. New York: Harcourt, Brace, 1939. (Reprinted New York: Teachers College, 1968.)

———. "Experimental Cinema in America: 1921-1947." Hollywood Quarterly 3, 2 (Winter 1947-48): 111-124. (Reprinted in The Rise of the American Film.)

Jarvie, I. C. Movies and Society. New York: Basic Books, 1970.

O'Grady, G. "The Spectrum of Cinema." Film Library Quarterly 8, 1 (1975): 7-16.

Staiger, J. "Dividing Labor for Production Control: Thomas Ince and the Rise of the Studio System." Cinema Journal 18, 2 (1979): 16-25.

Sutton, F. X., S. E. Harris, C. Kaysen, and J. Tobin. The American Business Creed. Cambridge: Harvard University Press, 1956.

Young, C. "An American Film Institute: A Proposal." Film Quarterly, Summer 1961, pp. 37-50.

Additional Reading and Reference

Anthony, R. N., and R. Herzlinger. Management Control in Nonprofit Organizations. Homewood, Ill.: Irwin, 1975.

Elsas, D., ed. Fact File--Film and Television: A Research Guide. Washington, D.C.: American Film Institute, 1977.

Gottesman, R., and Harry Geduld. Guidebook to Film. New York: Holt, Rinehart and Winston, 1972.

Internal Revenue Service, Department of the Treasury. Exempt Organizations Handbook: IRM 7751. Washington, D.C.: U.S. Government Printing Office, 1976.

———. Private Foundations Handbook: IRM 7752. Washington, D.C.: U.S. Government Printing Office, 1976.

Melton, H. "A Guide to Independent Film and Video." Film Culture, No. 62, 1976.

Netzer, D. The Subsidized Muse: Public Support for the Arts in the United States. Cambridge: Cambridge University Press, 1978.

Perry, T. Performing Arts Resources. New York: Drama Book Specialists/Publishers, 1975.

Phillips, A. The Arts, Economics and Politics: Four National Perspectives. New York: Aspen Institute for Humanistic Studies, 1975.

Prieve, A. E., and Ira W. Allen. Administration in the Arts: An Annotated Bibliography of Selected References. Madison: University of Wisconsin, 1973.

Rose, E. D. World Film and TV Study Resources. Bonn: Friedrich-Ebert-Stiftung, 1978.

Zolberg, V. L. "Autonomy for the Arts: The Dilemma of Public Funding." In Studies in the Sociology of the Arts. Budapest: Budapest Institute for Culture, 1980.

FILM AND LABOR: WHAT THE CREDITS MEAN

Robert Gustafson

For many viewers the long list of titles and names following almost every feature film is neither a "real" part of the movie nor something requiring much attention. Yet that list of workers whose labor was required to bring the film to the screen is something quite real and important. Despite the auteurists' claim that the director is the ultimate author of the film, despite the fan-magazine clamor given almost exclusively to actors, and despite the occasional glimpses we are given of mogul-producers, there are hosts of others without whose participation we would not have movies. This chapter attempts to provide some insight into the myriad of professionals involved in the film business.

The following glossary lists screen credits alphabetically and gives a brief job description for each. Because the motion-picture industry is so highly unionized, the appropriate labor organization is noted. Occupations that normally do not receive screen credits are also cited.

Special attention should be given to the studio employment chart following the glossary, which shows the hierarchy of authority and responsibility.

ACTOR: see Star, Featured Player, Extra, Stunt Man, Stand-In.

ADAPTATION: responsible for transforming the film's literary or dramatic source into a screenplay or shooting script. Screen Writers' Guild.

ADDITIONAL PHOTOGRAPHY: films scenes used in the motion picture that are shot outside of camera-crew operations. International Photographers of the Motion Picture Industry.

ADDITIONAL RECORDING: records audio sections used in the film that are made outside of the sound-crew operations. International Sound Technicians of the Motion Picture Industry.

ADDITIONAL SCENES AND DIALOGUE: submits extra script material during the screenwriting process or during the filming itself. Screen Writers' Guild.

ADDITIONAL SONGS: submits a song or songs to the musical score of the film. American Federation of Musicians.

AGENTS: represent the occupational interests of clients to potential employers, particularly production companies. Not credited. No union affiliation.

ANIMAL TRAINER: responsible for the care, handling, and performance of animals used in the film. No union affiliation.

ANIMATION: responsible for creating the series of drawings that when photographed produce the illusion of movement. Used for credit sequences, diagrams, cartoons, etc. Cartoonists' Guild.

ART DIRECTOR: oversees the drawing, planning, and designing of the sets and costumes. Art Directors' Union.

ASSISTANT ART DIRECTOR: responsible for the coordination of the design of sets, furnishings, and costumes. Art Directors' Union.

ASSISTANT CAMERAMAN: loads camera, mounts lenses, and assists in all photographic tasks. International Photographers of the Motion Picture Industry.

ASSISTANT DIRECTOR: (also known as Assistant to the Director) responsible for administrative duties, such as budgets and schedules. Screen Directors' Guild.

ASSISTANT FILM EDITOR: physically cuts and joins the film and records the placement of the cuts. Motion Picture Film Editors.

ASSISTANT PROPS: responsible for the procurement and inventory of set properties. Affiliated Property Craftsmen.

ASSISTANT SOUND MAN: handles and sets up microphones and recording equipment for the Sound Engineer. International Sound Technicians of the Motion Picture Industry.

ASSISTANT TO THE DIRECTOR: see Assistant Director.

ASSOCIATE DIRECTOR: see Unit Production Manager.

ASSOCIATE PRODUCER: generally the actual producer of the film when the individual listed as Producer acts as the Executive Producer. See also Producer and Executive Producer. No union affiliation.

AUTHENTICATOR: see Technical Adviser.

BACK PROJECTION: operates film projector on a translucent screen placed behind live action. Affiliated Property Craftsmen.

BEST BOY: (also known as Best Boy Grip) arranges set pieces, such as furniture. Assistant to the Key Grip. Studio Grips' Union.

BEST BOY GRIP: see Best Boy.

BLACKSMITH: creates metal props and set pieces. Affiliated Property Craftsmen.

BODY MAKE-UP: applies cosmetics to the bodies, but not to the faces, of the cast. Make-Up Artists and Hair Stylists.

BOOM OPERATOR: (also known as Boom Swinger and Sound-Boom Man) positions and handles the microphones that are suspended by a metal pole above the cast. International Sound Technicians of the Motion Picture Industry.

BOOM SWINGER: see Boom Operator.

CAMERA CRANE OPERATOR: (also known as Crane Operator) raises and lowers the camera by means of a motorized platform. International Photographers of the Motion Picture Industry.

CAMERA OPERATOR: (also known as Operating Cameraman and First Assistant Camera) the only individual who actually sees the image through the camera's viewfinder. Responsible for camera movement and for properly framing the image. International Photographers of the Motion Picture Industry.

CAMERAMAN: see Director of Photography, Camera Operator, First Assistant Camera, and Second Assistant Camera.

CARPENTER: constructs wooden sets. Brotherhood of Carpenters.

CASTING: see Casting Director.

CASTING DIRECTOR: (also known as Talent Coordinator) interviews actors, develops cast list from script requirements, chooses cast, sets salaries within the budget. No union affiliation.

64 FILM/CULTURE

CHIEF ELECTRICIAN: see Head Gaffer.

CHIEF PHOTOGRAPHER: see Director of Photography.

CHOREOGRAPHER: creates and directs dance performances. No union affiliation.

CINEMATOGRAPHER: see Director of Photography.

CLAPPER-BOY: works the hinged clapboard, or slate, that is used to identify each take and to make the sync mark on the soundtrack. Screen Directors' Guild.

CLASS B GRIP: see Laborer.

COLOR CONSULTANT--COSTUMES: responsible to the Art Director for the appropriate color selections and color coordination of all costumes. Motion Picture Costumers.

COLOR CONSULTANT--SETTINGS: responsible to the Art Director for the appropriate color selections and color coordination of all sets and set pieces. Set Designers' Union.

CONSTRUCTION COORDINATOR: oversees the cooperation between the Set Erector's crew and the Set Decorator's crew. Affiliated Property Craftsmen.

CONSTRUCTION MANAGER: works under the instruction of the Art Director and is responsible for the physical execution of the sets. Affiliated Property Craftsmen.

CONTINUITY: see Script Clerk.

COSTUME DESIGNER: creates all garments worn by the cast and controls the manufacture or selection of the garments. Motion Picture Costumers.

COSTUMERS: see Wardrobe.

CRANE OPERATOR: see Camera Crane Operator.

Film and Labor   65

CRANE STEERER: guides or drives the motorized platform that controls the hydraulic camera-raising arm. International Photographers of the Motion Picture Industry.

CULINARY WORKERS: prepare and serve the food to the cast and crew. Not credited. Culinary Union.

CUTTER: see Editor.

DANCE DIRECTOR: see Choreographer.

DIALOGUE DIRECTOR: works with the cast to ensure that what they say in the film is consistent with the dialogue in the script. Script Supervisors' Union.

DIRECTOR: plans and selects the shots, guides the performance of the actors, and is responsible to the Producer for bringing the script to life. Screen Directors' Guild.

DIRECTOR OF MUSICAL NUMBERS: plans and executes those scenes primarily containing music and not dialogue. American Federation of Music or Musicians, Composers and Lyricists' Guild.

DIRECTOR OF PHOTOGRAPHY: (also known as Cinematographer) responsible for the camera and lighting set-ups that the Director has ordered for each shot. American Society of Cinematographers or International Photographers of the Motion Picture Industry.

DOLLY GRIP: pushes the wheeled device that carries the camera. Studio Grips' Union.

DOUBLE: see Stunt Man.

DRAFTSMAN: creates the blueprints from which the sets are constructed. International Brotherhood of Painters, Decorators and Paperhangers.

DUBBING EDITOR: see Sound Editor.

EDITOR: (also known as Cutter, Film Editor) reassembles the various pieces of filmed scenes and soundtracks into the final print. Motion Picture Film Editors.

EDITORIAL COORDINATOR: responsible for the consistency between the publicity, advertising, and exploitation of the film with the production of the motion picture itself. Screen Publicists' Guild.

ELECTRICIAN: there are two distinct types of Electricians: those who work with lighting equipment and are members of the Motion Picture Studio Set Electricians (see Gaffer), and those who work with permanent electrical installations and are members of the International Brotherhood of Electrical Workers.

EXECUTIVE PRODUCER: has the final managerial and corporate authority over the entire production. Is often head of all studio productions. No union affiliation.

EXTRA: actor having no lines to speak, but appears most often as an anonymous passerby. Not credited. Screen Extras' Guild.

FEATURED PLAYER: actor whose name is ranked second under those of the stars. Screen Actors' Guild.

FILM EDITOR: see Editor.

FILM LABORATORY WORKER: operates the film-processing machines, contact printer, optical printers, sound transfer equipment, etc. Film Technicians' Union.

FIRST-AID WORKERS: stand by during the production and assist in the event of a medical emergency or similar problem. Not credited. First Aid Union.

FIRST ASSISTANT CAMERA: (also known as Focus Puller) follows focus, sets exposures, maintains and repairs the camera. International Photographers of the Motion Picture Industry.

FIRST ASSISTANT DIRECTOR: see Unit Production Manager.

FIXTURES: arranges all large set pieces that are attached to the set, for example, windows, doors, bookcases. Affiliated Property Craftsmen.

FLORIST: selects and maintains the flowers used in the film. Affiliated Property Craftsmen.

FOCUS PULLER: see First Assistant Camera.

FOLLOW-UP MAN: coordinates the activities between the Construction Manager and the Set Designer. International Brotherhood of Painters, Decorators and Paperhangers.

FOUNDRYMAN: creates metal castings for the production of props and set pieces. Affiliated Property Craftsmen.

GAFFER: (also known as Electrician) works with the lighting instruments and equipment. Motion Picture Studio Set Electricians.

GREENERY MAN: (also known as Landscape, Greensman) maintains and arranges all trees, shrubs, and grass used in the film. Affiliated Property Craftsmen.

GREENSMAN: see Greenery Man.

GRIP: handles and moves the scenery and camera equipment. Studio Grips' Union.

GUARD: (also known as Policeman) maintains order and controls admittance to the studio property and sets. Not credited. Building Service Employees International Union.

HAIR STYLIST: see Hairdresser.

HAIRDRESSER: (also known as Hair Stylist) arranges, cuts, and prepares the hair of the cast. Make-Up Artists and Hair Stylists.

and prepares the hair of the cast. Make-Up Artists and Hair Stylists.

HEAD ELECTRICIAN: see Head Gaffer.

HEAD GAFFER: (also known as Chief Electrician, Head Electrician) foreman of the lighting crew, works directly with Cameramen to arrange the lighting setups. Motion Picture Studio Set Electricians.

HEAD GRIP: see Key Grip.

HEAD SPECIAL EFFECTS: supervises and organizes the creation and use of all sensational devices used in the production, such as wind machines and explosives. Affiliated Property Craftsmen.

HELICOPTER CAMERA: operates camera from within a helicopter in order to shoot very high angle shots. International Photographers of the Motion Picture Industry.

INKING: traces the outlines of drawings onto animation cells. Cartoonists' Guild.

JANITOR: caretaker of the studio's physical plant. Not credited. Building Service Employees International Union.

KEY GRIP: foreman of all Grips, responsible for the movement and arrangement of scenery, set pieces, and camera equipment. Studio Grips' Union.

LABORER: (also known as Class B Grip) transports and arranges all movable pieces of scenery and sets. Motion Picture Studio Laborers and Utility Workers.

LAMP OPERATOR: maintains and repairs all lighting instruments. Motion Picture Studio Set Electricians.

LANDSCAPE: see Greenery Man.

LAYOUT: designs animated scenes including background, character placement, color choice, and camera movement. Cartoonists' Guild.

LIGHTING CAMERAMAN: see Director of Photography.

LIGHTING DIRECTOR: creates and designs the placement, color, and intensity of lighting instruments. Motion Picture Studio Set Electricians.

LOADER: see Second Assistant Camera.

LOCATION: selects and oversees the use of a setting that is not within studio property. No union affiliation.

LOCATION EQUIPMENT: procures and oversees the use of material and properties that are part of a nonstudio setting. No union affiliation.

LOCKSMITH: maintains and repairs all small metal devices and hardware. Affiliated Property Craftsmen.

MACHINIST: (also known as Studio Machinist) builds, maintains, and repairs the large devices-- dollies, cranes, and mechanical set pieces, such as stationary automobiles. Affiliated Property Craftsmen.

MAKE-UP: (also known as Make-Up Artist) applies cosmetics to the faces of the cast. Make-Up Artists and Hair Stylists.

MAKE-UP ARTIST: see Make-Up.

MAKE-UP DESIGNER: creates and oversees the cosmetic changes in the appearance of the cast. Make-Up Artists and Hair Stylists.

METAL POLISHER: responsible for the appearance of all metallic set pieces shown in the film. Affiliated Property Craftsmen.

MINIATURES: (also known as Models) creates and builds small-scale models that are made to look actual size in the film. Ornamental Plasterers, Modelers and Sculptors' Union.

MIXER: see Sound Mixer.

MODELS: see Miniatures.

MOLDER: puts detailed wooden and plaster pieces onto sets, for example, decorative strips around doors and window sills. Affiliated Property Craftsmen.

MUSIC COMPOSER: writes the compositions for the film whether used as background sounds or as songs. American Federation of Musicians.

MUSIC CONDUCTOR: directs the musicians and musical performers. American Federation of Musicians.

MUSIC SUPERVISOR: oversees the coordination and cooperation between the Music Composer, Music Conductor, and Sound Recording crew and staff. American Federation of Musicians.

MUSICIANS: perform the selections chosen by the Music Supervisor or Music Conductor. American Federation of Musicians.

OFFICE WORKERS: perform the secretarial and clerical duties during the production. Not credited. Screen Office Employees Guild.

OPERATING CAMERAMAN: see Camera Operator.

OPERATOR: see Camera Operator.

OPTICAL EFFECTS: laboratory worker who is responsible for the creation and execution of the visual effects, such as fades and dissolves. Affiliated Property Craftsmen.

ORCHESTRATION: scores the music written by the composer

PAINTER: see Scenic Artist.

PLASTERER: covers sets with plaster to give the illusion

of stone, masonry, etc. Ornamental Plasterers, Modelers and Sculptors' Union.

PLUMBER: installs, maintains, and repairs the system of water and sewage pipes on the set. Plumbers' Union.

POLICEMAN: see Guard.

POST-PRODUCTION ASSISTANT: coordinates those tasks performed after shooting is completed, for example, the dismantling of sets and the return of rented properties. No union affiliation.

PRODUCER: (also known as Supervisor) oversees all personnel working on the production, delegates responsibility to each of these persons, controls the budget, is held responsible for the financial success of the film. No union affiliation.

PRODUCTION ASSISTANT: prints scripts, schedules, call sheets, and rehearsal dates. No union affiliation.

PRODUCTION COORDINATOR: (also known as Production Manager) responsible for the administrative details of the production, for instance, the scheduling of equipment and facilities, estimating and keeping the budget figures, and preparing the shooting schedule. Unit Production Managers' Guild.

PRODUCTION MANAGER: see Production Coordinator.

PROP MAKER: creates and builds those properties that cannot otherwise be purchased or acquired for the film. Affiliated Property Craftsmen.

PROP MAN: handles all furniture and properties that decorate the set and all nonclothing items used by the cast in the film. Affiliated Property Craftsmen.

PROPERTY MASTER: oversees the use, repair, and inventory of all movable properties used in the film. Affiliated Property Craftsmen.

72 FILM/CULTURE

PUBLICITY: creates and distributes the promotional material regarding the production. Screen Publicists' Guild.

RECORDING SUPERVISOR: responsible for the compilation of all soundtrack material. International Sound Technicians of the Motion Picture Industry.

RE-RECORDING MIXER: see Sound Mixer.

ROTASCOPE: transfers live-action footage into animated drawings by tracing live-action frames onto cells. Cartoonists' Guild.

SCENE PAINTER: covers backdrops only with paint. Moving Picture Painters and Scenic Artists.

SCENIC ARTIST: covers set surfaces with paint according to the directions of the Set Designer and Set Decorator. Moving Picture Painters and Scenic Artists.

SCREENWRITER: author of the screenplays or shooting scripts that form the blueprint for the production of the film. Screen Writers' Guild.

SCRIPT CLERK: (also known as Script Girl, Continuity Girl) keeps a highly detailed record of what is seen in each shot so that no inconsistencies will appear in the finished film. Script Supervisors' Guild.

SCRIPT GIRL: see Script Clerk.

SCRIPT SUPERVISOR: oversees the scriptwriting process by reading scripts and requesting changes in them. Script Supervisors' Guild.

SECOND ASSISTANT CAMERA: (also known as Loader) loads and unloads the camera magazines, fills out camera log sheets, sends exposed film to the labs, keeps track of the inventory of unexposed film. International Photographers of the Motion Picture Industry.

Film and Labor 73

SECOND ASSISTANT DIRECTOR: relays instructions from Unit Production Manager to the Camera Crew and to the Electricians. Screen Directors' Guild.

SECOND UNIT DIRECTOR: responsible for filming scenes that do not contain lead actors within primary sets, most often shoots exterior setups with Stunt Men performing action sequences. Screen Directors' Guild.

SET DECORATOR: responsible for the detailed interior appointments in a set, for example, the placement of draperies and carpets. International Brotherhood of Painters, Decorators and Paperhangers.

SET DESIGNER: works from the script to draw the sketches and blueprints for set construction, supervises all set decoration. International Brotherhood of Painters, Decorators and Paperhangers.

SET DRESSER: arranges all interior set pieces, such as furniture. Affiliated Property Craftsmen.

SET ERECTOR: raises large flats that represent walls, storefronts, etc. Affiliated Property Craftsmen.

SHEET-METAL WORKER: forms set pieces from broad, thin sheets of metal. Affiliated Property Craftsmen.

SOUND: see Sound Man.

SOUND-BOOM MAN: see Boom Operator.

SOUND-CABLE MAN: positions and handles the cables that connect the microphones with the recording equipment. International Sound Technicians of the Motion Picture Industry.

SOUND EDITOR: (also known as Dubbing Editor) records or otherwise obtains all music, sound effects, and dialogue and prepares them for the re-

74 FILM/CULTURE

cording session, where they will be mixed onto a master track. International Sound Technicians of the Motion Picture Industry.

SOUND EFFECTS: responsible for the collection and use of recordings that furnish authentic-sounding noises for stage activities, for example, the sounds of gunshots, thunder, dogs barking. International Sound Technicians of the Motion Picture Industry.

SOUND ENGINEER: see Sound Man.

SOUND MAN: (also known as Sound, Sound Engineer, Sound Recordist) handles the recording of all sounds used in the film. International Sound Technicians of the Motion Picture Industry.

SOUND MIXER: (also known as Re-recording Mixer) records synchronized sound, balances and combines the input levels of various microphones. International Sound Technicians of the Motion Picture Industry.

SOUND MIXER ASSISTANT: works with the Sound Mixer on a second set of recording and mixing equipment. International Sound Technicians of the Motion Picture Industry.

SOUND RECORDIST: see Sound Man.

SPECIAL EFFECTS: creates a wide variety of sensational scenes, for example, fires, storms, explosions, crashes. Affiliated Property Craftsmen.

STANDBY PAINTER: assists Scene Painter by carrying paintbrushes and buckets. Moving Picture Painters and Scenic Artists.

STAND-IN: takes the place of a lead actor during the long periods of preparation before the actual shooting begins. Not credited. Screen Extras' Guild.

STAR: actor whose name generally appears before

Film and Labor 75

the title of the film, has a considerable number of fans. Screen Actors' Guild.

STILL PHOTOGRAPHER: photographs scenes during the production that will be used for publicity purposes. International Photographers of the Motion Picture Industry.

STORY ANALYST: checks script material for potential problems and gives suggestions for its improvement. Screen Story Analysts' Guild.

STUDIO MACHINIST: see Machinist.

STUNT MAN: (also known as Double) takes the place of an actor in scenes too risky or dangerous for the actor. Stunt Men's Association.

SUPERVISING EDITOR: oversees the cutting, splicing, and assembly of the film into its final version. Motion Picture Film Editors.

SUPERVISOR: see Producer.

TALENT COORDINATOR: see Casting Director.

TECHNICAL ADVISER: (also known as Authenticator) responsible for researching and establishing the accuracy of all script details. Is an expert on that particular subject under research and is not affiliated with a studio or a union.

THIRD ASSISTANT DIRECTOR: acts as an apprentice or messenger for the Director and staff. Screen Directors' Guild.

TITLE DESIGN: (also known as Titles) graphic artist who presents through animation techniques the list of personnel involved in the film's production. Motion Picture Painters and Scenic Artists.

TITLES: see Title Design.

TRANSPORTATION CAPTAIN: organizes the transportation of the cast and crew to various locations. Teamsters' Union.

UNDERWATER PHOTOGRAPHY: swimmer who operates a specially modified camera in and under water. International Photographers of the Motion Picture Industry.

UNIT MANAGER: works closely with Unit Production Manager and assists in the management of the production by keeping track of the entire production's hours of work, overtime, union regulations, etc. Screen Directors' Guild.

UNIT PRODUCTION MANAGER: (also known as First Assistant Director, Associate Director) gives advance notice to Director of shot and lighting changes, relays Director's instructions to Camera Crew. Screen Directors' Guild.

UPHOLSTERER: covers furniture with fabric chosen by the Art Director and Set Designer. Affiliated Property Craftsmen.

WARDROBE: organizes costumes according to cast member and is responsible for the costumes' appearance and repair. Motion Picture Costumes.

WARDROBE SUPERVISOR: maintains the inventory and oversees the use of the garments worn by the cast in the production. Motion Picture Costumers.

EXECUTIVE PRODUCER

PRODUCER
- PUBLICITY
- EDITORIAL COORDINATOR
- STILL PHOTOGRAPHY

ASSOCIATE PRODUCER
- OFFICE WORKERS
  - SCRIPT SUPERVISOR
  - SCREENWRITER
    - STORY ANALYST
    - ADAPTATION
- GUARDS
- JANITORS

DIRECTOR

DIRECTOR OF PHOTOGRAPHY
- KEY GRIP
  - BEST BOY
  - GRIPS
    - CAMERA OPERATOR
    - DOLLY GRIP
      - HELICOPTER
- FIRST ASS'T CAMERA
  - SECOND ASS'T CAMERA
  - CLAPPER BOY
  - CRANE OPERATOR
    - CRANE STEERER
- ADD'L PHOTOGRAPHY
  - UNDERWATER PHOTOGRAPHY
  - BACK PROJECTION

SPECIAL EFFECTS
- MINIATURES

LAYOUT
- ANIMATION
- INKING
- COLORIST

SECOND UNIT DIRECTOR
- ROTOSCOPE

LIGHTING DIRECTOR
- HEAD GAFFER
- ASS'T GAFFERS
- ELECTRICIANS
- LAMP OPERATORS

Art Department Organization Chart

- **DIRECTOR**
  - ART DIRECTOR
    - SET DESIGNER
      - DRAFTSMEN
      - COLOR CONSULTANT-SETTINGS
      - COLOR CONSULTANT-COSTUMES
    - FOLLOW-UP MAN
    - CONSTRUCTION MANAGER
      - CONSTRUCTION COORDINATOR
        - SET ERECTOR
          - CARPENTERS
          - FOUNDRYMEN
          - PLUMBERS
          - SCENIC ARTISTS
            - SCENE PAINTERS
            - STAND-BY PAINTERS
          - PLASTERERS
          - SHEET-METAL
          - MOLDERS
          - MACHINISTS
          - LABORERS
        - SET DRESSER
        - GREENERY
        - UPHOLSTERER
        - FLORIST
        - FIXTURES
        - LOCKSMITH
        - METAL POLISHER
        - BLACKSMITH
        - PROPERTY MASTER
          - PROP MAN
            - PROPS ASS'T
            - PROP MAKER
      - SET DECORATOR
    - COSTUME DESIGNER
      - WARDROBE SUPERVISOR
        - WARDROBE
    - MAKE-UP DESIGNER
      - MAKE-UP
      - BODY MAKE-UP
      - HAIR-DRESSER

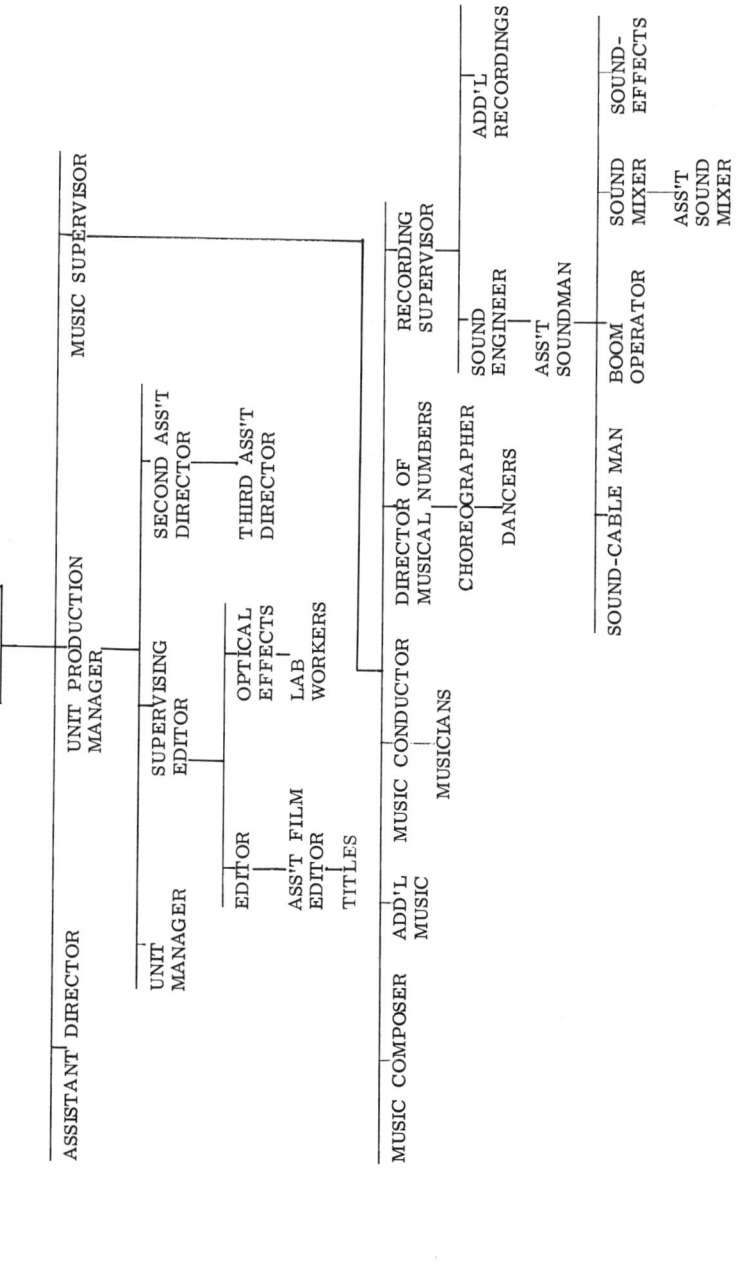

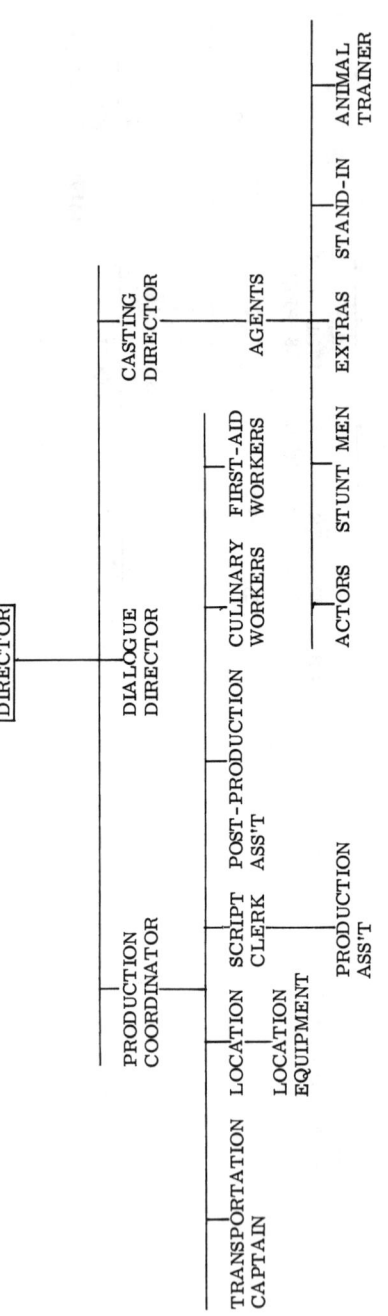

THE ECONOMICS OF FILM:
WHAT IS THE METHOD?

Douglas Gomery

Headlines from the trade press of the U.S. motion-picture industry proclaim constant change and turmoil. "Urban Cowboy No Longer Paramount's as Hollywood Tax Shelter Fever Builds" reads Boxoffice, June 30, 1980. Translation: Rich businessmen from all over the United States had purchased "limited partnerships" in a John Travolta film in order to avoid paying personal income taxes. Two months later the banner headline announced: "Airplane! Gross Over $23 Million After 19 Days" (Boxoffice, July 28, 1980). This disaster parody had generated unexpected revenues: $23 million in 1,000 situations, $7 million the first week, and $8 million the second. Paramount, the film's distributor, was elated to learn that Airplane! had overtaken the Star Wars sequel, The Empire Strikes Back, to become the box-office leader for the lucrative 1980 summer season. Yet euphoria did not reign in all quarters of the movie business in 1980. On May 21, 1980, weekly Variety heralded on page one: "Pix Face Bulging Budget Crisis." Samuel Z. Arkoff, former president of American International Pictures, warned all moguls that industrywide production-budget excesses would lead to a depression in Hollywood. Is Arkoff right? Why then the clamor to invest in Urban Cowboy, and the large revenues from Airplane!? More generally, how can interested observers, students,

82 FILM/CULTURE

and potential filmmakers make sense of the contradictory
claims found in these news reports? This chapter is a brief
introduction to the methods and theories scholars employ to
analyze the actions of the U.S. film industry. Using these
basic tools, anyone can begin to formulate systematic answers
to the complex issues of movie economics.

It is commonplace to assert that the production, distribution, and exhibition of motion pictures require vast sums
of money, and thus no research in cinema can be complete
unless one addresses questions of economic influence and effect. Studies of the movie business line the shelves of libraries, but none seems to pose and answer related questions.
Some recount efficient ways to acquire grants for independent
filmmaking; others describe and criticize the Hollywood corporate colossus. A minority attack the economics of movie
production in capitalist cultures (read the United States). Such
confusion materializes because motion-picture economics does
not constitute a single, unified field of study. At least three
competing theories exist. And since the method that a researcher uses determines the form and scope of the analysis,
I shall isolate and discuss all three, presenting a detailed
case study for each.

The movie business

Many students confuse the terms "business" and "economics."
U.S. business schools train people in management, finance,
accounting, and marketing. Students master the practical
skills necessary to steer a corporation, partnership, or
small enterprise toward larger and larger profits. Economists, on the other hand, investigate the processes that
households, firms, and government institutions employ to
produce and allocate goods and services. They construct
abstract models to analyze why and how economic systems
function the way they do, and rarely ever concern themselves
with the question of the day-to-day management of an individual enterprise. The difference between business and econom-
ics--practice and theory--is common in other areas of study.
For example, students learn pragmatic skills in art and engineering programs, but their theoretical counterparts are
housed in art history and physics departments.

Most business studies of film describe techniques for
resolving the problems of finance, production, and distribution. Independent filmmakers (those not directly affiliated

with major studios) seek help with the vexing questions of subsidies, copyrights, contracts, and taxes. The giant Hollywood corporations--Paramount, Warners, Twentieth Century-Fox, Metro-Goldwyn-Mayer, Columbia, United Artists, Universal, and Disney--hire, train, and maintain sizable staffs of experts to formulate business strategies and advise in areas of accounting, marketing, and taxation. But independent filmmakers, working alone or with only a handful of coworkers, must continually search for assistance, and consequently, it is to them that most books on the business of film are directed. (The Hollywood corporations do internally generate knowledge of business techniques, but for competitive reasons rarely divulge such information.) The typical book on the movie business takes the form of a manual and is authored by a former executive, arts administrator, entertainment lawyer, or some other "retired" specialist. Typical of such efforts is The Film Industries: Practical Business/Legal Problems in Production, Distribution, and Exhibition, Revised Edition (1978), by Michael F. Mayer, an entertainment lawyer.

Based on lectures given at New York University, Columbia University, and the New School of Social Research, The Film Industries is divided into three major parts. The first covers film production. In five chapters the author succinctly analyzes contracts used to "option" a story or screenplay, negotiation procedures with actors and actresses, policies for acquiring capital and subsidies, and sources to help one predict the popularity of a motion picture. Since the chapters never exceed ten pages in length, Mayer does not give the novice enough detail to deal with the complex worlds of security flotation, release forms, or other intricate business practices. Indeed, most handbooks on film business are caught up in this contradiction. As an example, Mayer outlines in three sentences the nature of the rights covered in an option agreement. The reader must assume that the author would direct any questions to a qualified motion-picture lawyer or business consultant like himself. Mayer could answer all such questions in his Columbia or NYU classroom. Such a technique, however, cannot work for the average reader/filmmaker. In addition, as indicated by the headlines that opened this chapter, the procedures and tactics in the film business are constantly in flux. Readers should be aware of the potential datedness of all handbooks of the movie business.

Part Two of Mayer's manual deals with film distribu-

84 FILM/CULTURE

tion and exhibition. Here he must be praised for tackling matters most writers avoid. In ten chapters Mayer discusses typical distribution and exhibition agreements, competition from foreign films, overseas distribution, antitrust laws, conglomerates, and publicity and advertising. The lack of specificity and examples remains a drawback. Moreover, when Mayer strays from areas of his expertise, inaccurate information and misleading counsel seem all too common. For example, Mayer covers American antitrust legislation and the U.S. film industry in nine pages. He summarizes the monopolistic practices, the effect of the Supreme Court decision of 1948, and recent developments. For further reading he cites the case itself. This is hardly cogent advice for the inexperienced. (But, of course, that is precisely where lawyer Mayer would turn.) U.S. v. Paramount Pictures et al. (1948) remains one of the most complicated antitrust litigations in history. Mayer would have better served the reader by citing Michael Conant's book <u>Antitrust in the Motion Picture Industry</u>. In sum, potential readers of film-business manuals beware! Rare is the expert who can know it all.

The final section of <u>The Film Industries</u> is excellent. Here Mayer handles concrete legal problems: censorship, copyright, defamation, privacy, and rights for music. These eight chapters are crammed with details, examples, and legal citations. Unlike previous sections, this one provides almost too much information, some of which may be of incidental interest to the novice filmmaker. Mayer does achieve, however, just the right balance of theory and practice for the serious student or scholar of motion pictures as an institution. <u>The Film Industries</u> furnishes sage advice for anyone seeking to navigate the complex legal waters that flow through the world of film production, distribution, and exhibition. Mayer has written a classic manual on the movie business.

<u>Industrial-organization economics</u>

If business texts prescribe, economists try to explain. Economists analyze the production and allocation of goods and services within a society. All economies must answer two questions: What types and quantities of goods and services should be produced? and How should the end-products be distributed to members of a culture? Noncommunist economies --the U.S. or Western Europe, for example--employ the market system to solve these two problems. Consumers and producers make their decisions in response to prices generated by the interplay of supply and demand. People seek the most satisfaction from their incomes; business enterprises attempt to maximize long-run profits (revenues minus costs). And as a result, in the United States, corporations and partnerships produce and distribute the bulk of goods and services. (Governments create the rest.)

Industrial-organization economics examines how profit-maximizing business concerns interact with the market forces of supply and demand. Often, however, the actions of corporations, the dominant form of business enterprise in the United States, fail to conform to the goals of the economy: efficient production and fair allocation of goods and services. For example, a few firms, an oligopoly, emerge to control an industry. In this country the prevalent ideology dictates that economic power should not be concentrated in the hands of a small number of companies. Consequently the federal government, in the form of the Justice Department, may institute an antitrust suit to "break up" the economic juggernaut and return the industry to a competitive, efficient, equitable status.

Industrial-organization economics overlaps many other specialities in the field of economics--labor economics, banking and finance, international trade, and public finance, among others. The industrial-organization economist seeks models by which to better understand the behavior of business firms. Knowledge of labor, finance, world trade, government expenditures, and taxation is important, but total understanding would constitute more than a single specialty of study. Such a stance does not argue that other fields in economics are not important. Certainly they are. But since the division of labor in modern economics treats them as unique entities, any student of the literature of the U.S. film industry should be aware of that separation. In particular, economics have written several important studies of labor relations in the motion-picture industry. But this chapter will focus only on the dominant method used for film-industry studies: industrial-organization economics.

Moving beyond questions of taxonomy, how does the industrial-organization economist go about analyzing a single industry? Chart I outlines the most influential model-- structure, conduct, and performance. Starting at the base, with performance, economists attempt to spell out the qualities a society desires from a particular industry. Criteria

Chart I

A MODEL FOR INDUSTRIAL ORGANIZATION ANALYSIS: STRUCTURE, CONDUCT, AND PERFORMANCE

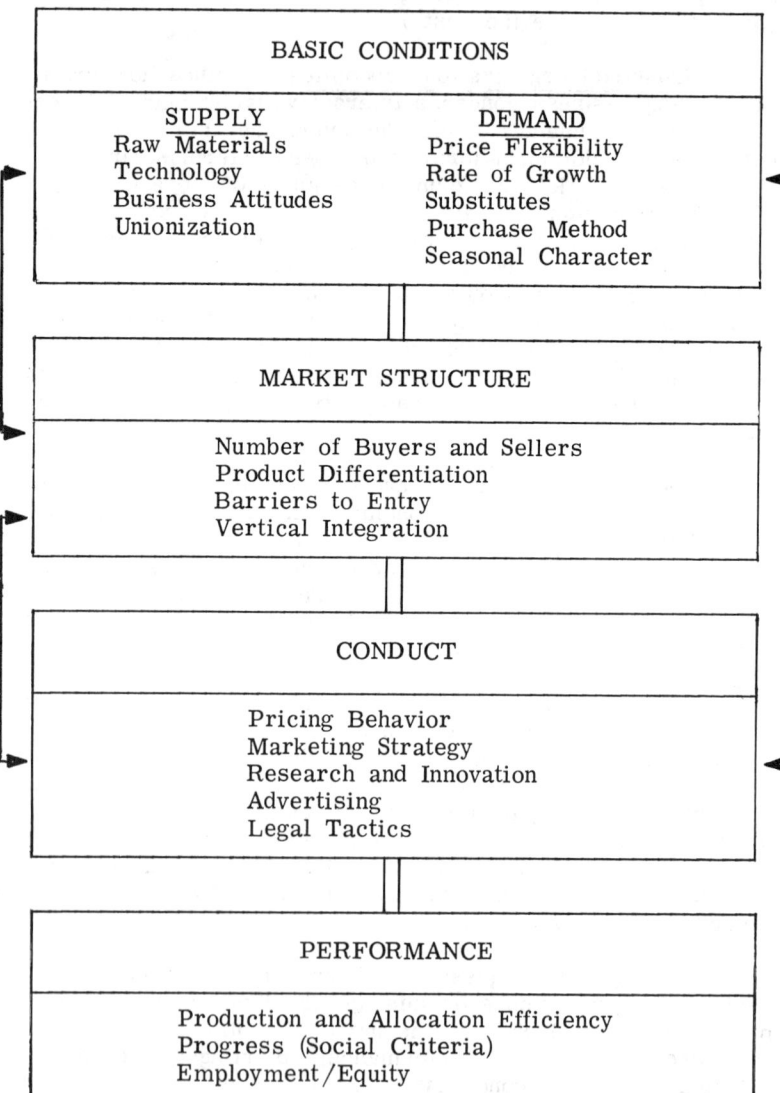

usually include some form of fair and efficient use of scarce inputs and an equitable distribution of the end-product. It can be difficult to determine what values a society embraces from speech and practice. For example, in regard to the U.S. film industry, are citizens interested in difficult production of movies, or are they more concerned with undiscriminated access to the channels of production, distribution, and exhibition? The latter criterion served as the basis for the famous antitrust case U.S. v. Paramount Pictures et al. (1948). In that suit the Justice Department successfully tried to open the film industry to more producers and exhibitors ("better performance") by diffusing the concentrated power of the eight major corporations.

But how an industry performs, asserts the model, depends directly upon the economic <u>conduct</u> of the firms involved. How do corporations price their products? Is there overt or tacit cooperation among companies? What strategies do companies adopt for marketing, advertising, research, and patent and copyright protection? For the U.S. film industry three examples illustrate the importance of these kind of questions in today's market. Pricing decisions dictate whether a consumer views a motion picture on a theater screen, on pay television, at a film society, or on "free," over-the-air television. The theater experience may cost the most, but we see a larger-than-life image with no commercial breaks. Several months later, for a smaller fee, the film is shown in some markets on pay TV. And so on. In all four situations consumers pay a different fee. The film companies establish the price and release schedules in order to maximize the profit for all productions that year. Second example: all Americans are familiar with recent innovations in marketing motion pictures. Before a feature film ever appears in a local theater, a seemingly endless stream of "previews" are presented on free television. Movie companies try to turn each new feature film into a media event, using talk shows, newspapers, and magazines, as well as shirts, mugs, and toys. Copyright protection provides yet a third example. Consumers can now buy a movie on a videocassette or disc. How should the film companies alter their sales practices to accommodate this new market? Such a question necessitates basic analysis of motion-picture-industry conduct.

Corporate behavior, however, does not occur in a vacuum. Conduct, industrial-organization economists argue, depends in turn upon the <u>structure</u> of the industry. How many buyers and sellers are there? Can other firms enter the industry if profits rise high enough? How are individual enterprises organized? All these important questions concern the market structure of any industry. In regard to the U.S. film industry, much has been written about the limited number of producer/distributors--the oligopoly. During the 1930s and 1940s Paramount, Twentieth Century-Fox, Warner Bros., Metro-Goldwyn-Mayer, Columbia, United Artists, Universal, and Disney generated the bulk of film-industry profits. Critics charged that such a structure produced inefficient and unfair conduct. For example, the members of the Hollywood oligopoly maintained barriers to potential competition. Economists argued that the source of this power lay in vertical integration (control of all phases of an industry by one firm). That is, prior to 1948 the giant movie corporations owned all the most profitable theaters in the best locations in the United States. They participated in the film business from production through distribution to exhibition (before television). The final decision of the Paramount case forced the vertically integrated Hollywood oligopolists to sell their theaters. The court argued that such a change in market structure would lead to more acceptable conduct and hence better performance. The concepts of oligopoly and vertical integration must be part of any analysis of market structure.

The final step in the model, as seen in Chart I, argues that market structure is in turn influenced by basic conditions of the supply of inputs to, and the nature of, the demand for the industry's product. On the supply side for the U.S. film industry, some basic conditions are the cost and availability of talented performers and technicians, the utilization of sets and studios, the innovation of new technology, and the actions of labor unions. Since this section of the model analyzes the process of production, it is at this point that the interests of the industrial-organization economist intersect with research on the business of film. But remember the crucial difference! The economist analyzes the production process and its effect on the structure, conduct, and performance of the industry. The business student of movies desires only the knowledge necessary to make more money, regardless of its ultimate implications. Moving to the demand side, the economist of the film industry tries to analyze how aware consumers are of changes in price, the rate of growth in movie attendance, the development of close substitutes for leisure-time activity, and seasonal variations in viewing habits.

As shown by the heavy arrows in Chart I, industrial-organization economists are concerned primarily with those relationships involving a causal flow from market structure and basic conditions to conduct to performance. Questions, theories, and methodologies are framed accordingly. To be sure, not all influences flow in one direction. There are feedback effects (arrowed lines in Chart I). For example, vigorous research and development efforts may alter a firm's technological base (conduct) and provide a greater barrier to entry (structure). Companies that do not have the technology cannot compete as effectively, and so, all else being equal, the number of firms in the industry should remain stable. Some smaller firms may even drop out because they cannot afford the investment necessary to acquire the new apparatus. Precisely this type of behavior took place when Hollywood converted to sound in the late 1920s. A second example can be found in the Paramount case. Unsuccessful legal tactics (conduct) affected vertical integration (market structure). Michael Conant's admirable study, cited above, provides an in-depth discussion of this very issue. His book, Antitrust in the Motion Picture Industry (1960), furnishes a classic example of how an industrial-organization economist can analyze and evaluate government attempts to affect the performance of a single industry.

Since the 1920s policy makers in the United States have been concerned with the breakdown of competition in the film industry, and the subsequent domination by eight giant corporations (an oligopolistic structure). This interest in improper performance led industrial-organization economists to study the conditions, structure, and conduct of the film industry. From 1938 on the federal government attempted to realign the oligopolistic structure, and produce "better" performance. Many scholars have researched U.S. v. Paramount et al., notably Michael Conant. In Antitrust in the Motion Picture Industry he eloquently lays out the specifics of improper performance. For example, less than five percent of the top-line feature films came from so-called "independent" (nonoligopolistic) studios. The oligopolists also held dominion in distribution. But, Conant argues, the ultimate source of their monopoly power stemmed from the exhibition sector. Since movie going was an urban-based phenomena, the bulk of any movie's revenues emerged from theaters in America's hundred largest cities. And it was in these urban environs that the vertically integrated Hollywood giants controlled the market. Consumers saw films from only eight companies. Moreover, the "Big Eight" had erected imposing barriers to entry with this exhibition-based system, and only a handful of independent producers, distributors, and exhibitors were able to remain in the market.

Conant locates the source of this oligopolistic structure and restrictive conduct in the special nature of the product.

> The demand for any motion picture is ephemeral; the great majority do not have a lasting public appeal, [and] perishability is thus the most important element to be considered in marketing pictures. The volume of production and program policies of exhibitors are geared to this [page 2].

Simply put, films function as fashionable or "fad" merchandise, similar to trends in other branches of retailing. Filmmakers try to charge the maximum possible price when the film is "in fashion," and less later on. This principle, plus savings available from worldwide distribution and monopoly power available from the exclusive contracts with stars, enabled the Big Eight to develop considerable economic muscle.

It was this set of conditions, structure, and conduct that the Justice Department assaulted in 1938. After ten years of legal struggle the Supreme Court ruled that the large Hollywood corporations had to sell their theaters (a structural remedy). The eight oligopolists also had to stop fixing prices, dictating terms of rental agreements, and manipulating deals totally in favor of themselves (a conduct remedy). In his best work Conant examines the ramifications of this radical judgment by the Supreme Court. He focuses on the implications for independent producers, the Hollywood oligopolists, the divorced theater circuits, independent theater owners, and the public at large. His overall evaluation of the Supreme Court decision is positive.

> The Paramount decrees have destroyed the nationwide combination that controlled the motion picture industry.... The bottleneck in the flow of films created by the majors' near monopoly of first-run theaters was broken. Large numbers of subsequent-run theaters received earlier access to films, and were relieved of the oppressive restrictions of block booking [pages 218-219].

And the public benefited from greater access to films from independent producers.

Michael Conant's is the most complete and sophisticated industrial-organization study of antitrust actions by the U.S. federal government against the American film industry. This brief analysis and summary glosses over the wealth of statistical detail contained in his book. Antitrust in the Motion Picture Industry offers a classic example of how powerful the structure-conduct-performance paradigm can be. Yet implicit in this type of economic analysis is the assumption that antitrust action really can "correct" flaws in an otherwise fine system. The market works, if only we can realign it into a proper competitive situation. Marxist economists disagree with this premise. For them the capitalist market system leads to fundamental problems, and no amount of "corrections" can help to overcome its structural inadequacies.

The Marxist critique

The industrial-organization model described above is a clear method of economic analysis, but it makes several assumptions that some economists find untenable. If the market system works so well, why do so few corporations hold so much power? Why do so few persons possess so much wealth? Why are there constant cycles of prosperity and recession? Marxist economists argue that such shortcomings emerge as a logical outcome of capitalist systems. Moreover, for the study of film economics the industrial-organization method cannot answer certain important questions. For example, while Marxist theory analyzes the relationship between film style and theme, and economic origin, industrial-organization economics asserts that such questions are beyond the scope of its model. In addition, it ignores historical change. Using the structure-conduct-performance paradigm, one can only analyze an industry at a single point in time, disregarding questions of transformation over time. On the other hand, a theory of history forms the base of Marxist analysis.

Classic Marxist economics offers a radical critique of capitalist economies, such as that of twentieth-century America. A pure-market economy is recognized as only one option, in fact a stage that the United States passed through many years ago. During the twentieth century the U.S. economy should be characterized as advanced monopoly capitalism. Giant corporation and financial institutions and a vast government bureaucracy jointly control the wealth and power. The majority of citizens (workers) only own their labor, and are continually exploited by the powerful ruling class (the capitalists). The driving force of this system is the desire to accumulate more and more wealth and power by the members of the capitalist class, while the workers continue to suffer. This process leads to greater economic power in the hands of smaller numbers, exploitation of third-world countries, and continual economic crises (recessions). Thus for the U.S. film industry it is expected that an oligopoly controls production and distribution. A few make a great deal of money, and most make very little. The films produced reaffirm, not challenge, the status quo. A complete, classic Marxist analysis would go far beyond the scope of this chapter. But before we move to a concrete example of such a study, it should be noted that, as a field, "radical" economics is currently undergoing a fundamental challenge and rethinking. Anthony Cutler, Barry Hindess, Paul Hirst, and Athar Hussain, for instance, in their Marx's Capital and Capitalism Today (1977) find the traditional Marxist model wanting. Still, as radical methods of economic analysis undergo transformations--possibly even a complete restructuring--Marxist economists studying film industries continue to employ the classic Marxist model.

An accessable example of Marxist economics applied to film can be found in Thomas H. Guback's The International Film Industry: Western Europe and America Since 1945 (1969). Guback studies the relationships between the American and European film industries. Exploitation of the European market ("economic imperialism") by Hollywood has had, Guback argues, major economic effects on the behavior of film industries on both sides of the Atlantic. We have here a classic case study of economic exploitation of the weak (the European film industries) by the strong (the U.S. film industry), twentieth-century style. Given this perspective, Guback wishes to study more than effects of economic structure-conduct-performance. Since film, he argues, functions as such an important vehicle of communication in our modern world, it possesses the possibility of expanding the boundaries of the human experience. Guback lays out his basic assumption: "Economic imperatives have in part determined what elements will be embodied in film" (page 5).

For his analysis Guback proceeds in three logical steps. In true Marxist fashion his book moves from a discussion of the economic base (European-American trade in motion pictures) to an analysis of the meanings thus generated by a particular film. In the first hundred pages of text the reader learns how Hollywood has exploited the expanded European market for movie going that has grown up since World War II. (Foreign films have come to America, but in nowhere the same numbers.) With the direct assistance and backing of the U.S. federal government, the Hollywood oligopolists formed a legal cartel to coordinate actions in Western Europe. This institution, the Motion Picture Export Association, pressed for "free" trade in motion pictures between the United States and Europe. Then the Hollywood oligopolists could extract maximum profits from the one-sided relationship. In his most fascinating chapter Guback details how the U.S. film industry and Defense Department cooperated to take over exhibition in West Germany after World War II, employing Hollywood feature films to "reeducate" the German population. European nations in time did proffer their own government schemes to "protect" their small, native industries. Heavy taxes, quotas, and exhibition restrictions on American products helped little. The United States has continued its hegemony in Western European markets.

The last quarter of Guback's book attempts to explain how this one-sided economic exchange has affected what is ultimately shown on the screen. Guback finds that Hollywood's successful exploitation has resulted in a homogenized products, blurring differences vital to the essence of national cultures. The International Film Industry argues that many of the 1960s' "international" films border on a dehumanization by brutalizing sensitivity, often deflecting attention away from reality (the implication being that realistic films should be highly valued). Such "international" productions develop audience response with synthetic, machine-mode images. Shallow, cardboard characters pollute the screen, camouflaged by vivid colors, panoramic vistas, and a "slick," bland style. Since capitalist filmmaking has created such poor results, it is not surprising that Guback pleads for more economic independence and cultural integrity. Only when national autonomy increases, Guback argues, will the chances for fostering the positive values of diversity of products and point of view (theme) rise. His closing remarks artfully summarize his position on film as an economic, social, and cultural institution:

> Because film is an art which portrays man's interpretation of life, it is imperative that contrasting perspectives be given the opportunity to exist and develop. The movement toward oligopoly and monopoly in American industry in general is now spreading elsewhere, paralleling American expansion. While this might spell efficiency in economic terms through the elimination of duplication, with fewer producers serving larger markets, it is to be avoided in the field of culture. It would be a pity to have but one control over all printing presses in a nation--or in the world. The same can be said for film production and distribution. Yet this is coming about in the world of the West [page 203].

The stern warning ends Guback's Marxist analysis of film-making relations between America and Europe. Note how the pessimism of his critique of industry/government interaction contrasts with Conant's view that government action can make the film industry perform better.

Conclusion

This chapter has attempted to demonstrate that there does not exist a single unified approach for studying movie economics. Since the answers a researcher obtains depend on the method employed, students of film economics should be careful to distinguish which approach they have in mind. Three dominant methods have been summarized: business studies, industrial-organization economics, and classic Marxist economics. Detailed discussions from three major examples provided insights of how others have used these approaches. In general, business provides the most narrow, industrial-organization economics a wider, and classic Marxist economics the broadest view. Reexamining the quotations found in the opening paragraph, one can see that the meaning of each depends on the approach one takes to understand it. For example, to a businessperson the Airplane! headline might signal success in marketing and publicity. The industrial-organization economist might seek to understand how such revenues reflected economic conduct. A Marxist might view Airplane! as yet another product of the exploiting Hollywood system. Not only can these three methods be used to examine the meaning and implications of the other headlines, but they can be employed in developing a fuller understanding of various issues pertaining to movie business and economics.

References

Conant, Michael. Antitrust in the Motion Picture Industry. Berkeley: University of California Press, 1960.
Cutler, Anthony, Barry Hindess, Paul Hirst, and Athar Hussain. Marx's Capital and Capitalism Today. London: Routledge, 1977.
Guback, Thomas. The International Film Industry: Western Europe and America Since 1945. Bloomington: University of Indiana Press, 1969.
Mayer, Michael F. The Film Industries: Practical Business/Legal Problems in Production, Distribution, and Exhibition. (Revised Edition.) New York: Hastings House, 1978.

Part II

FORM AND CONTENT

PICTURES CAN'T
SAY AIN'T[1]

Sol Worth

In this paper I should like to begin an exploration into how, and what kinds of things, pictures mean. I also want to explore how the way that pictures mean differs from the way such things as "words" or "languages" mean. In order to explore these things, I shall compare them along dimensions that I believe are central to the existence of both verbal and visual signs as communicative modes. I shall argue that pictures--paintings, movies, television, or sculpture--cannot be either true or false signs, and that therefore they cannot communicate the kind of statement the meanings of which can be interpreted as true or false. I shall then argue that picture interpretation is very different from word interpretation as regards its so-called pictorial code, convention, or "grammar," and also that syntactic, prescriptive, and veridical aspects of verbal grammar are very difficult to apply to pictorial events.

What is it, then, that pictures cannot do that words can do? Not only are words able to deal with negatives, but some linguists (for example, Sapir, 1921) have speculated that the ability of words to deal with what is not is one of the central functions of language. Pictures, I shall argue, cannot deal with what is not. That is, they cannot represent, portray, symbolize, say, mean, or indicate things equivalent to what verbal utterances of the type "This is not a..." or "It is not the case that..." can do.

On a trivial level, we can construct picture symbols or signs with negative meanings that resemble language, as do some parts of Egyptian wall paintings or other hieroglyphic forms; "languages" for traffic signs and advertising have been developed that have wide use across verbal language groups. A red crossbar across an image means "forbidden" or "do not," so that a crossbar across an image of a car means "no cars," and so on. These uses in posters, traffic signs, and even price tabs are not pictorial but rather linguistic uses of visual forms that become sign elements in a special language. They differ from what Gombrich (1961) calls a schema for picturing. In that sense, we are talking about ways of picturing, ways of structuring the universe through visual symbolic forms. In the former, trivial, sense we are talking about specific pictures or visual forms to which we assign some particular lexical meaning or function. The crossbar becomes a stimulus sign to which birds, dogs, and other animals, as well as humans, can be conditioned to respond.

In some sense, also, every positive or existential statement carries along with it the statement that it is not any other. The statement "This is a cow" or "I am a man" carries within it the conventional understanding that "This is not something that is other than a cow or other than a man," or, more exactly, "This is not a noncow" or "not a nonman." So also does a picture of a cow or of a man carry along with it the knowledge or understanding (in this culture at least) that it is not a picture of something else. Again, I believe that this aspect of pictorial negation is trivial.

However, on a value level, what is pictured is often valued precisely for what it negates by leaving out--so that in modern art it is possible to be nonrepresentational, either by being nonobjective or by being an abstract expressionist. In music, I suspect that certain notes are expected in certain codes. In earlier periods, depicting vulgar images was a rejection, and in that sense a negation, of other conventions and prescriptive rules. We therefore can, by means of our rules of picturing, accept as negations the absence of such social concepts as representation, illustration, sentiment, imitation, contrivance, vulgarity, nobility, dynamism, and so forth.[2]

Pictures Can't Say Ain't   99

I have introduced the value level not because I wish
to make a point of evaluation, but to make a point about
"meta" levels of interpretation. When we make judgments
about what a picture maker did not do, as well as upon what
he did do, we make a judgment based upon our knowledge of
choices that the picture maker had available to him, both as
psychological individual and as a member of a society performing a social act. We do not, however, make these judgments based solely upon what is in the picture itself. For
example: in looking at The Raft of the Medusa, we "know"
that Géricault could not picture "I am not at home in my
comfortable easy chair." He could paint the picture he did
and expect us to recognize that, but everything else is not
happening on the Raft of the Medusa. A picture maker cannot specify, out of all the things that his picture does not
show, which he means to say are not the case. There is
no pictorial means that a painter has of indicating that a
color, a shape, or an object is not something, or anything,
else. All that pictures can show is what is--on the picture
surface.

It is for that reason that it seems reasonable to argue
that True-False criteria cannot be applied to pictures and
that, further, pictures cannot be said to "make" propositions.
We say of verbal statements that they are "not true" or are
"false," or even are "full of baloney." We rarely if ever,
in ethnographic fact, talk that way of pictures.

Let us then first examine what we do say of pictures
on a continuum of correspondence to something called "reality." On one end of this continuum we have the motion-
picture/television image, a supposed correspondence to reality, in color, with motion and sound. At the other end we
have the picture of the abstract expressionist or perhaps even
that of the conceptual artist who uses only words and produces
no picture at all. In between, we have paintings in a variety
of styles and conventions, such as caricatures, cartoon strips,
or the sort of abstractions produced by Picasso and Braque
that imply some correspondence with the "real" world but
portray that correspondence in nonrepresentational ways, or
in less representational ways than do photographs or movies.

Let us also examine how people actually talk about
hand-produced, as opposed to machine-made, pictures. At
one end of the continuum of hand-produced pictures--the abstract, nonrepresentational spectrum--a viewer not versed
in conventions of abstraction might say that such pictures are

"silly," "make no sense," "are not understandable," and so on. Our unsophisticated viewer will almost never say that a Picasso is false or that a Phillip Guston (in his abstract-expressionist period) is false. Hand-produced pictures, a viewer "knows," are somehow supposed to correspond to some concept he has about reality. If pictures do not correspond or are not judged similar enough to this "reality," the picture maker is judged to be inept, a child to be humored, a "modern" artist to whom attention need not be paid, or some other form of incompetent or deviant. Rarely, however, is such a person considered to be a liar. Rarely is he understood to be deliberately trying to lie to the viewer. Unlike words, pictures may be thought to show it the way it is, but pictures are rarely thought of as telling lies in the way that words do.

The cliché has it that pictures cannot lie, and this is, even today, a largely acceptable statement, albeit with confusing counterexamples that lead to all sorts of angry responses that I shall deal with below.

In the case of [abstract-expressionist painter] Jackson Pollock, the unsophisticated viewer makes judgments of both deviance and incompetence, often saying, "He's crazy!" and, "Why, he can't even draw a face!"

In machine-made pictures--photography and film--we have supposed a value-free picture producer. It (the machine) tells neither truth nor falsehood but, again, tells it "like it is." The machine is to be trusted to produce an image that corresponds to that portion of the world to which it is pointed. What happens when you see a photograph of a familiar face and you fail to identify the subject of the photograph? Contrary to how you would act if it were a painted portrait, you do not doubt either your ability to identify the face nor the honesty of the photo taker who said that this was a photograph of someone you know. You blame "reality," "the photographer," or the machine and the process. In the first case (let us say it was a photograph of your friend) you might say, "She doesn't look like herself these days," or "From that angle (in that light), she just doesn't look like herself." If you blame the picture taker, you might assign some of the same reasons as his fault: "You should know better than to take a picture of Mary from that angle." The comment, "It's so underexposed that you can barely see anything" is another way that the picture taker receives the blame when instant recognition does not occur. In the last

case, when the process is at fault, you may get comments
ranging from "What can you expect from a dumb machine!"
to "You have to spend so much time fiddling that you have
no chance to think about the person you're taking a picture
of." In some studies of home moviemaking and exhibition,
as well as snapshot albums and commentary about them,
Chalfen (1975) found that, most commonly, negative evaluations blamed the mechanical aspects of picture making, rather
than the human. If a photograph was over- or underexposed,
"that stupid exposure meter" was to blame, and if the heads
of people or other important parts of the picture are cut off,
"that stupid viewing system" or "these lousy cameras" were
to blame.

All of this is based, of course, on an assumption of
intention to portray and depict a scene that corresponds to
that which the camera was pointed at. If we assume another
intention, we have a choice of an intention to produce "art,"
or a deliberate attempt to produce a product that will fool
us.

If we ask people what a "false photograph" is, almost
everyone immediately asks, "You mean a fake?" A photograph that doesn't correspond (in the accepted way) to reality
is not a lie, because we tacitly "know" that the medium has
no conventionalized procedure for stating lies. The only way
a photograph can be understood not to correspond to reality
is when we change something in a hidden, secret, and hence
tricky, manner. If I superimpose a picture of the honest
senator who swears he didn't know the gangster upon a scene
of the gangster having dinner with his cronies, so that it appears that the senator is toasting the gangster, I have produced not a lie but a fake. The attributions one might make
from such a photograph would be empirically false, but the
picture would in all respects correspond to what it would
look like if the senator had been there. If I paint a picture
of one woman (Mrs. A) and present it to a viewer as a picture of another (Mrs. B), it is not the picture that lies, but
the picture presenter.

A movie of a boy with green hair is also not seen
as a lie, and barely as a fake; it is mostly admired as a
clever manipulation. It falls into the realm of fantasy, rather
than fake, but is not judged by criteria of truth or falsity.
In a very deep sense, I am suggesting that the real world
is symbolically inviolate. If noncorresponding messages
about it are made verbally, they are either mistakes, lies,

or false statements. If noncorresponding pictures are produced, they are "fakes" or "tricks." The real world is, and is in a sense that supersedes symbolic manipulation. We would rather change our concept of the "real" to match our images or myths, if need be, but in any event we rarely allow a conflict between a pictorial symbol and "reality" to go on for long.

If we are faced with a conflict between that which a picture shows and that which we know cannot be the case, we do not shout "Lie!" but instead say firmly, "It cannot be so." The case of the so-called "impossible figures" of Penrose and others offer us an almost perfect paradigm for how we treat noncorresponding pictures (Figure 1). They are in fact "impossible." Gregory (1970) has confounded the issue further. Almost all impossible figures are drawings. Gregory has provided us with a photograph that purports to be the figure in Figure 1. When this photograph is shown to a class of high school students who have listened to a lecture on perception, we find two responses: one is anger and the other is a happy demand for an explanation of "how that trick photo was done."

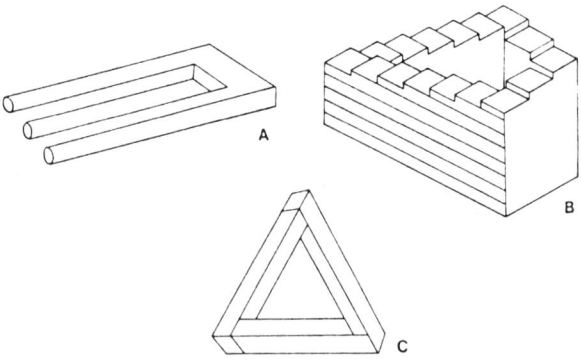

Figure 1: Impossible figures

The angry response is a common one; it is not the anger of someone who has been lied to, but the anger of

someone who has been tricked. It is an anger that I call
media rage. It occurs with greater and greater frequency
as artists in all modes of symbolic activity--painting, movie-
making, television, novel writing, and news reporting--are
trying more and more to explore the distinctions between the
real world and their symbolic world. In a movie such as
W.R.: Mysteries of the Organism, Makavejev, the Yugoslav-
ian master, uses old documentary films, current documentary
films, and old as well as current reenactments of public and
private events. He has photographs of Stalin and photographs
of actors playing Stalin intermixed and so juxtaposed with current acted and documentary footage that it is almost impossible to tell which is which. Many members of the audience,
particularly in socialist countries where such experimentation
is relatively new, become quite angry.

In America the film Medium Cool, which mixed acted
and documentary footage in ways never before attempted, created genuine rage on the part of many audiences. They felt
that this film went beyond trickery. Mixing actors and the
riots at the 1968 Democratic Convention in Chicago in a way
designed to make an acted plot seem real, or to make reality
seem like acting, was not "right." The schemata of movie
representation demands clear separation between that which
is to be thought of as acted or unacted. We want to be able
to say that an acted film was almost real enough for us to
believe, but we want a performance, not confusion. We must
be able at all times to "know" the difference.

Again, in such films as Medium Cool, the audience's
response is not that the film is, or tells, a lie, or that the
film is false. The response of many people is that the images on the screen are impossible. What they see before
them cannot be. The feeling of "cannot" is so strong that
many people move without thinking from "cannot" to "should
not." And thus, it seems to me, their anger. I have seen
the work of Escher responded to in the same way. If one
cannot take pleasure in the manipulation and the creation of
a structure that cannot be, one tends toward nonacceptance
of the medium, or genre, itself as legitimate, and thus may
become angry.[3]

Pictures, as we understand them in this culture, depict, or picture, what is. They are, in a visual mode,
somewhat similar to the verb "to be" in its existential, not
veridical, sense. Pictures, however, cannot depict condition-
als, counterfactuals, negatives, or past-future tenses. Neither

can they make passive transformations, ask questions, or do
a host of things that a verbal language is designed to do.
Pictures depict the present even when they depict fantasies,
such as fairy godmothers, myths, unicorns, and gods. When
a picture depicts the star Venus, its context (day or night)
might help us to label it the "morning star" or the "evening
star," but the classic problem of the referential meaning of
morning stars is not involved when we deal with pictures.
Instead we may wish to ask how the context of the picture
affects our labeling of that particular star. That is: how
dark or how blue must the sky be for the star to be "morning" or "evening"?

Since pictures do not have the formal capability of
expressing propositions of negation, it follows that pictures
cannot be treated as meaningful on a dimension of truth and
falsity. If pictures cannot depict the proposition that something is not so, or is not the case, it would hardly be reasonable to suggest that pictures are designed to depict only
those things that <u>are</u> the case.

What then do pictures depict? It seems that all we
can say is that what they depict <u>is. They depict events for
whose existence they are the sole evidence.</u> Pictures in and
of themselves are not propositions that make true or false
statements, that we can make truth tables about, or that we
can paraphrase in the same medium. Pictures, it must be
remembered, are not representations or correspondences
with, or of, reality. Rather, they constitute a "reality" of
their own.

But if pictures are not propositions, and not even
representations, and if pictures cannot be dealt with on True-False dimensions, how then are we to deal with them? What
is the "logic" by which meaning is interpreted from pictures?
By removing the propositional property from pictures, I seem
to have removed the possibility of grammar or syntax as we
know it.

Truth tables can only be constructed for sentences.
What are sentences in pictures? Logical syntax requires
precisely defined connectives, such as "and," "either ...
or," "if ... then." Is there anything like that for pictures?
I am suggesting that the basic difference between words and
pictures lies in the fact that our use of speech is based upon
a convention that requires a clearly defined syntax that allows
us to articulate propositions about truth or falsity, while our

use of pictures, on the other hand, is based upon conventions that, while linguisitic in nature, have no clearly defined syntax, no ability to articulate propositions (and therefore no ability to depict negation), and no ability to make "meta" statements about lower-level statements of the picture system. A picture cannot comment on itself. A picture cannot depict "This picture is not the case" or "This picture is not true."

Before continuing, I must digress, or at least stop for a moment, to consider the argument that although pictures cannot deal with negation, they can deal with something called truth. Let me briefly mention some of the arguments that lead me to feel that the subject is indeed a digression, although much attention has been paid to this issue (Price, 1949; Urban, 1939; Reid, 1964; Casey, 1970).

The theory that there is truth in pictures usually rests on the argument of correspondence, and correspondence usually means either similarity or correctness, or both. The notion of similarity rests to a large extent on the iconic-digital distinction between pictures and speech. Even linguists, in recent years, have given up their certainty about the arbitrariness of linguistic symbols (Friedrich, 1974). Semioticians, art historians, anthropologists, and psychologists have also come to realize that a "copy" theory of pictures is simplistic, misleading, and probably just plain wrongheaded. A look at Chinese painting or another look at Figure 1 should make the weakness of the copy, or similarity, theory of picture making obvious. Truth is not to be found in that direction.

Second, similarity is not, and cannot be necessary to correspondence.[4] A conventionalized code (the Morse code) can make dots and dashes correspond to letters of the alphabet, although their degree of likeness to letters is very small and their degree of similarity to the sounds of speech is almost negligible. Third, similarity is an almost impossible criterion of correspondence. Similarity, or verisimilitude, asks that we match one thing (the picture) against another. How close a match makes a match? Clearly only a picturing convention or schema can tell us whether the picture is similar to something in reality.

If we take correctness as our criterion for correspondence, we fall into a set of problems that confuse, rather than clarify, the issue. Here we usually mean scientific correctness, or accuracy. As a matter of speech, we refer to "accuracy" colloquially as "scientific truth." Science carries high status and is the closest approximation we have to a method of determining something called empirical truth. But in order to be correct, we must have a measure, a standard. We must have something to measure against. "Reality" is too vague. Do we compare with a standard of our eyes--what we see--or with our cognitive capacities--what we know? In either case we are again confronted with conventions, rules, and schemata. If we pass that problem, we find ourselves back to the problem of nonrepresentational pictures and what they correspond to. Truth, as it concerns pictures, is indeed a digression.

Pictures and speech are different precisely because pictures are not a language in the verbal sense. While words mean, primarily or basically, because of lexicon and syntax, pictures have no lexicon or syntax in the formal grammarian's sense. And yet I am suggesting that we can interpret meaning from pictures. It is clear, however, that if pictures have no grammar in the strict linguistic sense, they have something like it: they have form, structure, convention, and rules. It is clear that even though a theory of correspondence is not sufficient to deal with truth in pictures, pictures must nonetheless correspond to something. Even the most un- or nonrepresentational painting must refer to something or it would make no sense at all.

Our notions of correspondence, of similarity, and of correctness in the meaning of pictures are evidenced more in such statements as "That's a movie?!" "That's no mural!" and "I don't even call that a picture!" rather than by such statements as "That's not true," "That's a false picture," or "That pictures means that it is not about a sunset." What we mean when we say "That's not a movie" is that the articulated symbolic event before us does not correspond to our conventionalized knowledge of the way signs in movies are manipulated in our society. In effect, pictures are a mode that best communicates a dialogue with the "real" world that Picasso called "a proposition to the viewer in the form of traditional painting violated." "I want," he continued, "to give my work a form that has some connection with the visible world, even if only to wage war on that world" (New York Times, April 9, 1973). That dialogue in the form of traditional painting violated is similar to what some painters have meant when they said that painting was about painting, and what Malraux meant when he said that painters did not

copy nature: painters copied other painters. Pictures, in
this sense, picture conventions, forms, structures, and so
forth. Pictures are a way that we structure the world around
us. They are not a picture of it.

Although pictures do not have a grammar by which to
structure how the world is, they are clearly not usage. The
concept of the "language of pictures," the "grammar of art,"
the "syntax of the cinema" must be understood as a metaphor,
at best. Elsewhere I have discussed the problems of describing a film grammar and have shown that certain concepts that
make sense in speech or verbal usage are simply not used in
motion pictures. Notions of "grammaticality," "native speaker,"
"paraphrase," and grammatical or syntactic transformation,
while powerful enough to be forced into applicability in relation to almost all symbolic usage, actually make very little
explanatory sense when applied to pictures. We can always
say of pictures that grammaticality refers to that set of rules
that allows even an unsophisticated viewer to "know" that a
drawing is unacceptable because the perspective is "not right."
We can stretch the concept of grammar to say that the recognition of "impossible figures" demands a native speaker's
knowledge of the grammar of visual representation. To some
extent, of course, an ability to interpret perspective is necessary in order to infer meaning from a perspective drawing,
but it seems to me to be a distortion, or at least not very
helpful, to refer to such conventions as perspective as a language or grammar of pictures.

It seems to me rather that pictures operate both
within the framework of language knowledge within us, and
outside the framework of language in itself. That is, the
pictorial mode (from drawing to motion pictures) does not
have a rigorous set of rules employing a lexicon, a grammar,
an ability to construct paraphrases, or an ability to produce
translations within its own formal devices. But we, the viewers, do have a faculté de langage in general, about all symbolic materials, so that in motion pictures, for example,
where sequence and time become parameters to be manipulated, we can instantly bring to bear linguistic rules for implication and inference. In other research (Worth and Adair,
1972) I have shown that people who are native speakers of
Navajo will frequently use Navajo syntactic rules as justifi-
cation for the structuring of films that they themselves have
photographed and edited.

Metz (1970) has shown quite convincingly that the acceptability of film content most often depends on its adherence to film convention rather than on its adherence to "reality." For example, a shopgirl is depicted in films in a certain way. Everyone "knows" that real shopgirls do not look or act that way. If a real shopgirl were to be cast in a film, we might recognize her correspondence to life, but would reject her because of noncorrespondence to film. What we call "true to life" must be a stereotype if it is to be recognized, and therefore becomes the least, rather than the most, valued as "art."

What is communicated by pictures, then, is the way picture makers structure their dialogue with the world. What is meant by pictures, when we use a communicational strategy of interpretation, is how we should put the pieces together. First, we recognize some object, person, or event in movies. It may be a "tree" or a "man." In a painting, it may be a representational object or a color, shape, or juxtaposition of elements. We can, and many people often do, stop right there. They start attributing--putting onto and into the picture. Others, however, are able to go farther, both in the articulatory as well as the interpretive process. They recognize and can articulate structure, assume purposeful manipulation and, therefore, social behavior, and treat that manipulation as a set of instructions by which meaning may be inferred.

When people are speaking, participants are able to be speakers as well as listeners. In picture making, as in reading novels, "dialogue" or "discussion" does not exist. What we appreciate is the manipulations that the picture maker or writer performs on his materials and our ability to recognize and to understand the conventions, rules, styles, and usages within which his particular dialogue with the world has been carried out and in which we may share.

Notes

1. The full text of this paper appeared in **Versus** 12 (1975): 85-108. A later edition of it appeared in Gross, L. (ed.). Sol Worth: Studying Visual Communication. Philadelphia: University of Pennsylvania Press, 1981. Reprinted with permission.

2. For an interesting discussion of this issue see Gombrich (1963).

3. See Chukovsky (1963), who points out a similar response: the anger of adults at children's fantasy verse.

4. I have relied heavily on the excellent review of this concept that appears in Casey (1970). His final conclusions, it should be noted, differ markedly from mine.

References

Casey, Edward S. "Truth in Art." Man and World 3, 4 (1970).
Chalfen, Richard. "Cinema Naivete: A Study of Home Movie-making as Visual Communication." Studies in the Anthropology of Visual Communication 2 (1975): 87-103.
Chukovsky, Kornei. From Two to Five. Trans. and ed. Miriam Morton. Berkeley: University of California Press, 1963.
Gombrich, E. H. Art and Illusion. New York: Pantheon, 1961.
―――. Meditations on a Hobby Horse. New York: Phaidon, 1963.
Gregory, R. L. The Intelligent Eye. New York: McGraw-Hill, 1970.
Metz, Christian. "Images et Pédagogie." Communications 15 (1970): 162-168.
Price, Kingsley B. "Is There Artistic Truth?" Journal of Philosophy 46 (1949): 285-291.
Reid, Louis A. "Art, Truth, and Reality." British Journal of Aesthetics 4 (1964): 323-331.
Sapir, Edward. Language. New York: Harcourt, Brace and World, 1921.
Urban, Wilbur M. Language and Reality. London: Allen and Unwin, 1939.
Worth, Sol, and John Adair. Through Navajo Eyes: An Exploration in Film Communication and Anthropology. Bloomington: Indiana University Press, 1972.

CONVENTIONS AND MEANING IN FILM

John Carey

The conventions of film can be described as consistent patterns employed by filmmakers to communicate meaning to an audience. Conventions involve virtually any element in the control of filmmakers--for example, positioning of the camera, editing techniques, objects used in shots, lighting, dialogue, and plot structure. Conventions are consistent in the minimal sense that the particular editing technique or camera movement is used many times by one or more filmmakers to communicate a limited and identifiable set of meanings. In this sense conventions are structural elements that are present all the time in all films. It should also be noted that the term "filmmaker" is used throughout this chapter collectively to represent the director, editor, scriptwriter, or camera operator who controls the film convention under discussion.

The literature treats filmic conventions from a broad range of perspectives. Individually these perspectives can shed light on certain conventions, such as how the positioning of a camera is analogous to techniques in novels whereby point of view is communicated. Collectively, however, the breadth of discussions can muddle our understanding of meaning in films. How do audiences know what is going on when they watch a film? Where does meaning come from? In order to deal with this issue, we must first sort out some of the more common perspectives that influence how we think about films.

Film perspectives

Many popular books on film history, as well as newspaper and television critiques of movies, employ a superficial aesthetic perspective in which films are judged as good or bad against a set of standards. Often the set of standards is no more than the personal reaction of the critic. Films are generally compared with other works by the same director or films of the same genre to support arguments about the merits of the work under review. From this perspective films are judged as boring, exciting, hilarious, slow-paced, and so on. They have meritorious and notorious scenes and are surrounded by tidbits of gossip about the making of the film or the actors in it. Popular criticism does not provide an explanatory model (that is, why things happen or how they achieve meaning) nor does it consider the audience's role in the communication process. This does not mean that popular criticism should be dismissed as worthless. It is an important resource for the public in deciding what films to view and provides stories for cocktail-party chatter. It contributes, however, little to film theory.

A related but more substantial aesthetic perspective on film can be found in criticism and histories of avant-garde and "serious" films. This approach can also be found in some courses on cinema. Here careful attention is paid to details about what occurs in films vis-à-vis plot, use of the camera, lighting, and character development, among other components. These details are used to assess the film in terms of a reasonably well-defined set of standards. In addition, the set of standards is often shared by a group of scholars. Yet this perspective also has severe limitations as an explanatory model. It is concerned with "good films" --trends, consistencies or inconsistencies, breakthroughs (e.g., the first film to use a given technique), and other components that give value to a film. Typically there is a large conceptual gap between filmmakers and audiences. Indeed, the communication process through which a filmmaker exchanges meaning with an audience may be treated as a taboo and inexplicable sacred ground. That is, many high-status film critics treat communication processes as a mysterious element that renders film an art form and that cannot be deciphered.

Trade practices, as taught in professional film schools and described in literature about film techniques (e.g., Reisz and Millar, 1968), deal explicitly with rules and procedures that the filmmaker should follow in creating a film. In some instances a technique is characterized as correct practice, without any consideration of its meaning, such as how to use a cutaway in order to achieve continuity of action. In other instances meaning is assigned to a technique in an invariable manner: cutting for a medium shot to a closeup to communicate greater intensity, for instance. Further, trade practices are more concerned with how things are done, not how they came to be done in a certain way.

Trade-practice literature does provide voluminous source material for researchers who wish to analyze conventions and meaning, by describing many conventions with precision. Theory about conventions, however, does not generally flow from those who write trade literature.

Another group approaches film from a language perspective. Bazin (1967: 23-40) speaks of a film "grammar" and a "syntax of film." This is an enticing perspective, one that has permitted much useful work in the description and analysis of film structure. It has, however, seduced many down one of two paths, each of which is distinctly limited. The first path involves the application of linguistic structure to film and the search for linguistic equivalents in film structure--the search, for example, for morphemes and phonemes in film and the grammatical connections among them. But there are too many elements present in film that are not comparable to linguistic structure, and vice versa. The result can be an inadequate grammar of film that is applicable to a limited set of issues.

The other language path that is paved with gold for a short distance is the transfer of structural principles discovered in relation to the theater and novels. There is strong evidence that filmmakers have borrowed many conventions from both media. Balázs (1970: 143) comments about some early films:

> When a director wants a change of scene but does not want to show intermediate scenes, he often uses a curtain of shadow, technically termed a "wipe," drawn across the picture. In other words, he begins a new scene by means of a device borrowed from the stage.

Though this perspective is useful in understanding some conventions in film, it is important to know when this line of investigation has reached its limit and when one is forcing film structure into a literary or theatrical mold.

Many scholars have applied communication theory to film. Two distinct points of view, however, are represented among this group: those who believe that film has innate universal properties that dictate the structure of conventions, and those who believe that film conventions are largely created by filmmakers over time and learned by audiences. Indeed, the heart of the issue is reflected in alternate words used by the groups when discussing filmmakers and conventions. Do filmmakers create or discover, invent or make use of conventions? Did D. W. Griffith create or discover parallel montage (a technique to communicate that two actions are occurring simultaneously in different places). One can argue that he discovered a property innately related to the film medium, or, alternately, that he created a convention that audiences had to learn.

Some scholars treat filmmakers like chemists, who discover properties of an element and then use them according to laws given by nature. Arnheim (1957, 1966) makes strong theoretical arguments for this viewpoint. He holds that there is a physical order and visual reality to which we are biologically and perceptually attuned and to which we can respond instantly. For Arnheim, a visual stimulus has a character of its own and contains objective properties that guide the organizational system in our brains. This relationship determines the form and meaning of specific structural elements in a film. From this point of view, film conventions are manifestations of the film medium itself and the physiological makeup of viewers. Further, the properties of film are universal and static. They do not vary in relation to those who make and view films, or change over time.

While Arnheim argues that meaning is rooted in biological processes, Sol Worth (see the preceding chapter in this volume) argues that it is rooted in social-communication processes and the relationships between those who use images to convey meaning and those who view and interpret those images. From this point of view, filmmakers may be said to create conventions and audiences to learn them. Both, however, share a body of knowledge and experiences based upon other films, paintings, and visual elements in everyday life, as well as conventions rooted in the novel, theater, and many other media. This amalgam of shared knowledge and experiences provides the fabric for and sets limits upon the conventions that are likely to emerge in a given period. Within this perspective one must understand audiences as well as filmmakers to account fully for film conventions and their meanings. In addition, it is a fluid model, in which conventions change, audiences vary, and multiple meanings or interpretations of a convention are possible. Yet, if conventions emerge from complex interactions among many elements, they are nonetheless knowable and subject to analysis.

If one were to simplify all of the perspectives described above, it would appear that film conventions may represent: 1/ artistic processes that can be observed but not really understood; 2/ trade practices that do not require any further analysis; 3/ the visual equivalent of linguistic structure; 4/ borrowing from other genres, such as theater or the novel; 5/ a static system of rules determined by the visual reality to which we are biologically attuned; or 6/ mechanisms created by filmmakers and learned by audiences, based upon schemata that they share and therefore likely to change over time and across cultures.

Temporal and spatial transitions in film

In order to evaluate the perspectives on film, we shall analyze a set of conventions that are present in a large corpus of films. This set includes those mechanisms or techniques used in films to communicate spatial and temporal transitions --that is, the ways in which a filmmaker communicates that the shot or scene we are viewing is at a different point in time and/or space than the previous shot or scene. For example, if we are watching a scene that depicts an airport in Atlanta, and the filmmaker wants to follow this with a scene that depicts an airport in Paris two weeks later, how is this transition communicated to us? Such transitions, and therefore transition conventions, are present in nearly all full-length fiction films.

Broadly considered, conventions of temporal and spatial transition make use of dissolves, fades, wipes, traveling masks, and straightforward cuts from one scene to another. In addition, they include a large set of insert shots between scenes. These may involve a card with writing to tell us that a scene is about to change, or symbolic visuals, such as calendar pages flipping off a wall, a ship crossing the ocean, or a clock whose hands rotate before our eyes.

An examination of a large group of full-length fiction films from the early 1920s through the 1970s provides evidence about the structure of conventions and how they communicate meaning.[1] It reveals marked changes in the mechanisms for accomplishing temporal and spatial transitions over time, and yet a consistency in the pattern of using these mechanisms within any period. Filmmakers observe the conventions used by their contemporaries, not a set of invariant rules. Further, variations from contemporary conventions are themselves patterned, so as to teach audiences what they mean. These patterned variations also provide a means for conventions to change over time.

To consider simple transition conventions with one element (e.g., one scene dissolves into the subsequent scene, or a simple fade down on one scene and fade up on another, with no inserted cards or shots within the transition): analysis reveals heavy use of the fade during the 1920s and 1930s; moderate use of dissolves; and occasional use of a wipe or traveling mask. In the 1940s and 1950s there is a significant shift, in which use of the fade is reduced sharply. Dissolves become the dominant transition convention during this period, and the wipe or mask is rare. In addition, a new convention emerges: the straight cut from one scene to another. During the 1960s and 1970s use of the fade is further reduced, the wipe remains rare, dissolves are less common, and the straight cut becomes the dominant convention. These patterns are consistent for comedies, adventure films, and other film categories during each period.

If we examine the number of multiple-element transitions (that is, where one or more shots, such as calendar pages flipping off the wall, is inserted within the transition itself) against the total number of transitions in a film, we find a marked dependence on multiple-element transitions during the 1920s. Approximately two-thirds of all transitions during the 1920s used insert shots within a transition. The number of multiple-element transitions levels off to about twenty-five percent from the 1930s through the 1950s. They drop off sharply to less than five percent during the 1960s and 1970s.

The length of viewing time occupied while making a transition also changes markedly over the history of film. During any given period transition times in films are remarkably consistent. Considering all types of transitions, single-element and multiple-element, the mean time for completing a transition declines steadily from over six seconds during the 1920s to less than half a second in the 1960s and 1970s. For example, a film made in the 1920s typically faded down from one scene (1 second), showed the audience a card that described what they would see next (4 seconds), then faded up on the new scene (1 second). A typical film in the 1940s slowly dissolved from one scene to another (3 seconds). A 1960s film might dissolve quickly from one scene to another (1 second) or employ a straightforward cut (0 seconds).

When a filmmaker varies from the conventions of the period in which the film is made, the variation is likely to carry additional meaning. Thus a film in the 1960s that uses a three-second dissolve is likely to carry some expressive meaning beyond the simple message that a transition is occurring. For example, A Man for All Seasons (1966) uses "overlong" dissolves when there is a temporal-spatial transition during moments of heightened dramatic tension.

During the 1930s and 1940s there were a number of conventionalized insert shots during transitions--a clock with rotating hands, a ship crossing the Atlantic, a train going around a mountain bend, a flower blossoming, and so forth. A filmmaker who drew upon such a conventional symbol could expect that the audience would infer what was meant without additional information. The audience could refer the symbol to its knowledge of other films where that symbol had a particular meaning, and thereby know what was intended. Filmmakers, however, could also employ symbols that were not conventionalized, to help communicate a transition. In these instances they instructed the audience as to the meaning of the new convention. For example, in Lloyd's of London (1936), a shot of a ship's bell is used throughout the film to communicate a temporal-spatial transition. The first time the bell is used in the film, we see its full context, and this teaches us what it means. It is an old ship's bell in a tavern. When news comes in about missing ships, the bell is rung and the news is posted on a blackboard. Later in the film the bell is used without its full context to signal a transition in time and to fill in news. Viewers can then refer the shot to its full context (which they experienced early in the film) and thus understand its meaning, just as they do by referring a conventionalized transition mechanism to the larger context they have learned from watching other films.

Changes in transition conventions over time are instructive about the evolution of communication between filmmakers and audiences. In the 1920s title cards inserted between scenes told audiences explicitly that a transition was occurring. The filmmaker could, simultaneously, use the title card to comment about the story. That is, while the 1920s' filmmaker was stepping outside the story to make a temporal-spatial transition, that occasion would often be used to tell the audience some detail about a character or the action that the audience could not or might not have inferred from the film. In The King of Kings (1927) the inserted title card is sometimes a quote from the Bible, so the moral message of the scene is explicitly reinforced. Thus the filmmaker employed verbal information, completely external to the visual action, to communicate statements about the transition and commentary about the scenes. During the 1930s the title-card convention was often replaced during a temporal-spatial transition, by inserts, of a newspaper headline, a note written by one of the characters, or some other verbal statement that emerged from a scene in the film. For example, a scene in an office dissolves to a newspaper headline "Strike Vote Due Tomorrow"--which dissolves to a subheadline "Violence Is Predicted"--which dissolves to a scene outside a factory with workers and police about to confront each other. By the 1940s we still see a few inserts of verbal information during transitions. A greater number of inserts, however, are symbolic visuals: a wornout boot, a bottle that is nearly empty, a ship sinking. By the 1950s inserts within transitions carry less information. It appears that dramatic tension and other expressive messages are communicated merely by the use of the multiple-element transition form. The filmmaker does not have to insert an explicit visual to imply dramatic tension. The transition structure itself appears to communicate expressive meaning. In A Hatful of Rain (1957) a multiple-element transition occurs when Eva Marie Saint is going home to tell her husband (a drug addict) that she is leaving him. The visual inserts within the temporal-spatial transition are neither dramatic nor are they necessary to give the viewer information about the transition. This transition structure, rare both for the late 1950s and this film, serves to heighten the tension of the expected confrontation.

To summarize, the communication that filmmakers attached to title cards in the 1920s moved to a newspaper headline or telegram in the 1930s, a visual symbol in the 1940s, and a visual structure in the 1950s. By the 1960s the use of inserts within transitions was rare. Indeed, most temporal-spatial transitions involved a straightforward cut from a preceding scene at one point in space and time to another scene somewhere else and at a different time. An important question arises here. If a cut from one scene to another is identical to a cut, within a scene, from one camera angle to another, how do audiences know when a temporal-spatial transition has occurred? And how can a filmmaker communicate expressive messages about the action while signaling a transition?

By the 1960s a transition was signaled by a structural or symbolic relationship between visual information contained within shots immediately preceding and immediately succeeding the transition: shots that are part of the ongoing film. In Planet of the Apes (1968) the camera pans up to the sun during a scene. There is a cut to another shot of the sun from a slightly different angle. The camera pans down to another scene at another point in time and space. In both scenes the visual object (the sun) and the camera movement serve a role in the ongoing action. They also, however, communicate additional meaning by virtue of their structural relation to each other. Filmmakers and audiences know that this pattern signals a temporal-spatial transition.

The changes in transition conventions over time demonstrate, first, that film conventions are not a static system of invariant rules. Temporal and spatial transitions have evolved in a direction away from explicit verbal information and toward symbolic visual information. Audiences witnessed the use of external title cards in the 1920s evolve to visual objects with verbal information (the newspaper headline), which evolved to visual object-symbols (a ship crossing the ocean), then to visual structure alone (a dissolve), and, more recently, to a visual relationship that the audience must infer from objects or camera movements in scenes before and after the transition. All along, the conventions have become more efficient in the sense of accomplishing the transition in less time. More of the meaning in a convention is related to visual structure and less to explicit linguistic or pictographic encoding. This suggests that audiences have grown in their level of understanding filmic communication. Not only have they adapted to changes in transition mechanisms, but they have learned to perceive and understand conventions of a more symbolic nature, in considerably less time.

This process of change from explicit verbal statements

toward symbolic visual information has parallels in other
media. Pre-Renaissance paintings often contained words to
tell viewers about the purpose or meaning of the painting.
Similarly, magazine advertising in the United States changed
drastically between 1950 and 1970 in its reliance on words to
convey meaning. During the 1950s nearly every ad was filled
with paragraphs of print information. By the 1970s many ads
contained either a simple slogan or no copy at all. More of
the meaning was encoded in photographic techniques and symbolic visual associations.

As audiences grew in their understanding of a wide
range of transition conventions, filmmakers made use of the
knowledge in viewers' minds to build associations between
current films and earlier films. Thus The Sting (1973), a
film about an earlier period in American history, made use
of transition conventions from that period (title cards inserted
between some scenes) to communicate a feeling of the period.
Similarly, a grade-B western made in the 1970s, but following the typical story line of a 1940s western, may employ
inserts of newspaper headlines or "wanted" posters, to identify with the form of the earlier films.

Conventions and meaning

What does all this tell us about film conventions? The conventions examined here are clearly not static, as literature
about trade practices suggests. Further, the evolution of
temporal-spatial transition conventions does not support arguments that film structure is bound to some innate visual reality, as Arnheim suggests. It does appear that some early
conventions borrowed elements from the theater. Yet such
borrowing from a genre that audiences in that period understood well is but one piece in the overall structure, not an
explanatory model of conventions and meaning. Similarly,
linguistic analogies may be useful, but a language model does
not seem appropriate to film conventions.

The analysis of temporal-spatial transitions supports
the model suggested by Worth (in this volume) and other communication theorists (such as Bateson, 1969) that visual conventions are social pacts negotiated between those who create
communications and those who receive them. This model
accounts for consistent patterns at a given point in time,
with changes over time. It also permits patterned variations

from conventions by individual filmmakers. The model can be tested further. If it is correct that conventions and their associated meanings in a film do not represent the surface manifestation of an innate and universal visual reality, then it would follow that they are learned. Moreover, naive film viewers today must learn a greater number of conventions than their counterparts in the 1920s, since today they must view and understand films made throughout the history of film. Finally, naive film viewers will encounter very quickly a level of visual convention (in modern films) that is more symbolic than was encountered by their counterparts in the 1920s. One can therefore expect either 1/ terrible confusion on the part of modern children, since everything is thrown at them at once, or 2/ some mechanisms in films and television aimed at children that teach them about film conventions and bring them up to speed.

An examination of television cartoons and children's films made during the 1970s and 1980s reveals a structure that is similar to many films made for audiences in the 1920s and 1930s. Children's TV cartoons employ slow dissolves, wipes, and masks to communicate temporal-spatial transitions. Typically a half-hour cartoon show employs one standard temporal-spatial transition throughout the program. For example, it will use a two-second dissolve each time the filmmaker wishes to communicate a transition. Often the convention incorporates a well-known symbol that represents the hero of the show. The Batman cartoon program employs a traveling mask in the shape of Batman's cape each time a temporal-spatial transition occurs. Freedom Force employs a triangle mask (their symbol), and Plastic Man, a swirl of plastic between scenes. In addition, each of these cartoons consistently uses a standard sound effect to support the visual convention. The traveling-mask convention in cartoon shows requires about three seconds to complete.

In many films for children the temporal-spatial transition is reinforced by a verbal statement. The statement may come from a character in the scene just before or subsequent to the transition, or from a narrator. The narrator's function in children's films is similar to the title card in films from the 1920s. For example, in Scruffy, a full-length animated movie, an unseen narrator speaks at selected points to tell the audience that a temporal-spatial transition is happening and comment on the action.

These characteristics of cartoons and films for children--time required to complete the transition; reinforcement of the message in more than one channel; more consistent use of one convention in each program; and support from external verbal statement--suggest that children are being introduced to visual conventions at an early point in their development and that mechanisms to teach them about conventions are present. In addition, the structure of transition conventions in children's films demonstrates that conventions do vary in relation to the intended audience. Thus an understanding of the processes at work in film communication requires a model that treats the relationships between a source or creator of information and those who receive it. Conventions represent a relationship between filmmakers and audiences.

A working model

The examination of a narrow set of conventions--temporal and spatial transitions--reveals principles that can be used to construct a more general, although tentative, model of conventions and meaning in film.

Those who make films share a large body of knowledge and experiences with those who watch them. Some of these experiences are largely physiological (e.g., color perception) and therefore relatively static. Most shared experiences, however, are part of the social world: speeches by politicians, family dinners, and gossip with friends. Also, many of our shared experiences involve media: magazine photographs, television commercials, and, most importantly for our model, films. Clearly these shared experiences and the knowledge that flows from them are not consistent for all filmmakers or all members of all audiences. Nonetheless, these fluid and variable schemata, together with all of the elements available in the film medium, provide components for the construction of meaning in a film convention.

A filmmaker who wishes to communicate some meaning to an audience, whether it be a feature of action or the location of a scene, employs words, actions, costumes, and sets, along with such filmic elements as camera angles and editing techniques to imply meaning. Rarely, if ever, is the presentation in a film a true correspondence to something in the real world: it is a construction that may contain some elements from the real world. These elements, however, are organized according to patterns that are related to film conventions. The patterning transforms them and gives them meaning in a film context.

When people watch films, they can treat what they see as part of the real world and interpret it accordingly. Indeed, it is reported that in the early days of film a member of the audience occasionally stood up and shouted at a character on the screen. Yet it is more likely for individuals to interpret certain aspects of a film, under specific conditions, in terms of real-world criteria and thereby bypass the inferences they would otherwise make if they applied film conventions. For example, a Vietnam veteran might infer different meaning from a scene in <u>The Deer Hunter</u> (1979) than was intended by the filmmaker.

It would be chaotic if all meaning in a film were open to broad interpretation, based upon each viewer's real-life experiences. We may enjoy debating the personality of a film character with another person who has seen the film. It would, however, be disturbing if a companion interpreted a film as a western in the old tradition while we understood it to be a science-fiction tale about the twenty-first century. Film conventions appear to be powerful tools that reorganize and transform elements from the real world and render them part of the film world. In addition, they steer or guide audiences to a more limited range of interpretations about a film, based upon what they have learned by watching other films that have employed these same conventions. In this sense there are two components to a film convention: a signal and a referent. To imply meaning a filmmaker must communicate a signal (e.g., a dissolve) and a referent that tells viewers where to go in their body of stored knowledge about films in order to understand its meaning. For example, if one sees a film today that has a shot of calendar pages flipping off a wall (inserted within a temporal-spatial transition) and one recognizes that the film was made in the 1930s, one will likely infer that it is a perfectly reasonable transition. If something in the film suggests that it was produced in the 1950s, the referent context would suggest that the calendar-pages shot is incongruent. If something in the same film referred to a 1960s context, one might laugh <u>at</u> the filmmakers if one felt that they intended a nonexpressive transition, and <u>with</u> them if one assumed that the convention from the 1930s <u>was</u> intentionally employed for a comical effect.

More generally, filmmakers must communicate to the audience (through camera angles, lighting, sound) that they

Conventions and Meaning of Film 123

are adhering to the viewers' patterned expectations about film conventions for the period of time when the film was made; deviating from those conventions toward another set of conventions the audience knows; or deviating in a new way, in which case they must not only teach the audience the new convention but build a referent context that will give the convention a meaning the filmmakers intend when the audience encounters it again in the film or in some future film.

Conclusion

This examination of conventions and meaning in film provides some evidence in support of a theoretical model. However, a more complete understanding requires a good deal more investigation, particularly in relation to audience interpretation of many types of films and the social contexts in which films are viewed. Many of the articles in this volume contribute substantively to these areas.

Consider the opening sequence in The Empire Strikes Back (1980), where the filmmaker relies upon audience knowledge of conventions for movie serials. The audience reads a scrawl of print that identifies the film as "Chapter Six." This mechanism refers the film to a 1940 movie-serial context and allows the viewer to infer that Empire is part of a long series, not merely a sequel to Star Wars (1977). Further, Star Wars must have been Chapter Five, since its story line flows directly into Empire. Did everyone who watched the movie make this inference? Perhaps some missed the reference completely but learned the information from TV commentaries and discussions with friends about the movie. What are the roles of these information channels--TV talk shows, movie ads, discussions with friends--in audience interpretation of meaning in films? It appears to be the case that many movies in the 1980s rely upon a great deal of knowledge by audiences about films in order to understand a particular sequence in a film. For example, the opening sequence in Airplane! (1980) employs a music convention from Jaws (the music that signaled the shark's approach) to produce a comical effect. Presumably a viewer who had not seen Jaws would not understand the parody. An alternate explanation, however, is that nearly all potential American viewers would have heard the Jaws music somewhere, say, on radio ads or TV skits about the movie, and could infer the meaning intended by the producers of Airplane!. These other channels of information about conventions and meaning in films are likely to help shape the knowledge that people apply when they watch films.

It appears that many conventions are attached to, or associated with, certain categories of film, westerns for example. What are the logical types of films, as understood by filmmakers and audiences? Are "chase films" or "Burt Reynolds films" logical categories of film with associated conventions? Do The French Connection (1971) and The Blues Brothers (1980) share a set of conventions? Investigation is likely to reveal that logical typing is not a one-dimensional phenomenon and that any given film employs film conventions associated with two, three, or several logical categories.

Finally, the discussion here has been limited to fiction films that are commercially produced. If one were to include documentaries, docudramas, or home movies, real-world strategies for judging events come into more direct competition with filmic conventions in steering viewers' interpretations of what they see on film. These areas of investigation reinforce the need for a communication model of film in which audiences as well as filmmakers participate.

Notes

1. Much of this discussion draws from John Carey, "Temporal and Spatial Transitions in American Fiction Films," Studies in the Anthropology of Visual Communication 1, 1 (Fall 1974).

References

Arnheim, Rudolf. Film as Art. Berkeley and Los Angeles: University of California Press, 1957.
―――――. Toward a Psychology of Art. Berkeley: University of California Press, 1966.
Balázs, Béla. Theory of the Film. New York: Dover, 1970.
Bateson, Gregory. "Communication." In The Natural History of An Interview, edited by Norman McQuown. Chicago: University of Chicago Press, 1969.

Bazin, André. <u>What Is Cinema?</u> 2 vols. Berkeley and Los Angeles: University of California Press, 1967.
Reisz, Karel, and Gavin Millar. <u>The Technique of Film Editing</u>. New York: Hastings House, 1968.

HOME MOVIES AS CULTURAL DOCUMENTS

Richard Chalfen

Scholarly attempts to understand home movies as a form of social communication are virtually nonexistent. The failure of film scholars to examine the structure and significance of the home movie is particularly strange. With increasing frequency professional filmmakers "use" authentic and fabricated models of home-movie style and content for a diversity of reasons.[1] The fact remains: the annual production of home movies far outstrips that of professional documentary films. Home moviemakers unquestionably value their own movies much more than examples of "significant cinema." How, then, can this authentic vernacular form be understood as a cultural document embedded in a process of visual (pictorial) communication?

Home movies as visual communication

One starting point is the understanding of home movies as a symbolic form, as a genre of film, and as a type of pictorial communication. Film communication is a social behavior that manipulates a recording on film for the purpose of articulating some meaningful content. The message of film communication results from the human construction and interpretation of content and patterned structure of the film. A film (or group of films) is a symbolic form that is produced and viewed within social and cultural contexts. Behavior surrounding filmmaking is promoted, limited, or restricted primarily by social norms rather than by technical variables.

Film communication can thus be studied as the creation, manipulation and interpretation of symbolic events that occur in, and as, a series of social "performances." Within this conceptual framework the form "home movie" is considered as one genre of film communication.

Home movies belong to yet another large collection of symbolic behavior, one that I have called "the home mode of visual communication" (Chalfen, 1975a, 1975b). All products of this mode of photographic representation are characterized by the nonprofessional use of communications technology for private "documentary" purposes rather than for public or "artistic" use. Home-mode imagery is conceptually and pragmatically distinct from the professionally produced forms seen in advertising, photojournalism, art or museum exhibitions, feature films, education, film festivals, and the like. Home-mode imagery is generally produced by nonprofessional photographers using inexpensive, mass-produced cameras. However, the sophistication of the camera or the cameraman is less significant than the communicative use of the imagery. Social characteristics of the communication process take precedence over its technical features.

Other visual products of the home mode are family-album snapshots, wallet photographs, wedding albums, travel or baby photographs, photographs displayed on household walls, on television sets, furniture, and the like. Each of these items can be studied as cultural documents in their own right; this chapter will focus on how the home movie, as a product and process of visual communication, is amenable to traditional anthropological inquiry.

Home movies as cultural documents

It is not enough simply to say that home movies qualify as cultural documents because all human products can be recognized and understood as such. Three points deserve attention. First, we must understand that home movies are products of an often unrecognized set of human decisions. Moviemakers must decide who, where, when, and what to record on motion-picture film. Determination of the style or manner of the visual recording and the reasons for making the movies--the "how" and the "why"--also are often taken for granted.

The second point is related to a search for patterns of shared beliefs and behavior. We are not examining instances of idiosyncratic picture-making behavior. Previous work has shown that there is a great deal of similarity in the home movies produced by members of the same society[2] --people who have never met one another and who certainly have not discussed what "should" or "should not" be filmed (Chalfen, 1975a). In other words, certain characteristics of "culture," such as shared knowledge, tacit consensus, informally learned behavior, models for appropriate behavior, and structured patterns of interpretation, are all relevant to the construction and use of this visual genre and, therefore, to our consideration of home movies as culturally structured documents.

The third point focuses on a distinction made by Worth when he discussed the significance of pictorial symbolic forms as products <u>about</u> culture and as products <u>of</u> culture. One can use <u>photographs</u> to collect "evidence" and data about "what's there." Photographs and films, however, also represent the way something was looked at. Photographic images offer information on the culturally structured ways of seeing things with cameras. Thus the latter orientation, "<u>of</u> culture," assumes significance alongside the more frequently considered "<u>about</u> culture." In this context Worth urges the coordination <u>of</u> "what the members of a society made pictures of, how they made them, and in what contexts they made and looked at them" (1980: 18). The proposed scholarly attention to home movies will be much indebted to this perspective.

Two topics central to contemporary visual anthropology will help clarify the relationship of home movies to cultural documents: the approach summarized by Mead and Metraux (1953) as "the study of culture at a distance"; and the research on the indigenous production of pictorial forms. Let us now review both areas, with specific reference to better incorporating home movies as a subject of study.

The study of culture at a distance

In 1953 Margaret Mead outlined a plan for analyzing cultural regularities of societies that were inaccessible to direct observation. Certain societies could not be visited for geographic or political reasons, such as active warfare, or travel and research restrictions, or because a particular society no longer existed. Martha Wolfenstein (1953) applied "the study of culture at a distance" to film analysis, citing work by John Weakland, Jane Belo, Geoffrey Gorer, Margaret Mead, and Gregory Bateson.

John Weakland has spent considerable time analyzing feature films produced in various parts of China and shown in both China and the United States. Weakland offers the following rationale for incorporating the study of feature films into anthropology:

> The most important point about anthropological film analysis is that, despite its apparently special object of study, this work relates clearly to the mainstream of traditional anthropological concerns. In projecting structured images of human behavior, social interaction, and the nature of the world, fictional films in contemporary societies are analagous in nature and cultural significance to the stories, myths, rituals, and ceremonies in primitive societies that anthropologists have long studied [1975: 240].

> The most basic premise is that any film (or group of films from a single cultural source) will, like a culture, constitute in some form and to a significant degree an ordered whole, will exhibit a pattern made up of recurrent thematic elements related in characteristic, recurrent ways. This premise is based on the general scientific aim of building as orderly a view of the world as possible ... [1975: 242].

Substituting "home movie" for "fictional film" in the first quotation, or including "home movie" in the ranks of "any film" in the second, exposes an unexamined wealth of cultural and ethnographic significance.

As with the study of feature films, one primary task in analyzing the cultural significance of family films is to discover a pattern of content, to understand how an "orderly view of the world" has, unconsciously, <u>both</u> organized the home movie <u>and</u> appears in the films. This patterned content is distinguished by a limited number of people participating in a confined array of places and events (Chalfen, 1975a,

1975b) and the redundant quality of a family's collection of
personal imagery, including snapshots and family albums, as
well as home movies. One pattern is that we generally do
not find unfamiliar people or even disliked family members
central to the image. Home moviemakers prefer to record
and celebrate births rather than deaths, the early years of
life rather than the last years, weddings rather than divorces,
vacations rather than vocations, and so on. We also do not
often see people arguing with one another, using the bathroom
(other than children playing in bathtubs), vomiting, engaging
in sexual intercourse, and the like. The home-movie pattern
has been much more consistent through time than we would
discover for feature films. Thus the case is easily made
for what Weakland refers to as "a pattern made up of recurrent thematic elements related in characteristic, recurrent
ways."

Weakland's notion of abstracting "an orderly view of
the world as possible" (1975: 242) is relevant to the study
of home movies. Anthropological fieldwork has always sought
to understand the ways people from different societies construct meaning, world view, and ideas of reality. Home movies are particularly interesting in this respect. We must not
assume that people look at everyday life, or at their environment, in exactly the same ways that they look through their
cameras when they produce home movies. The relation between the two "looks" or "constructions" is problematic.
Home-movie content, however, reveals a carefully constructed
and orchestrated view of a relatively happy and successful approach to life. In a sense, we have a native model of the
way life should be. A culturally determined bias has selectively retained or eliminated specific people, places, events,
and things to produce "an orderly view of the world."

Home moviemakers and audiences value these films
precisely because they show people, places, events, and
things "just as they were in real life." A frequent comment
is that "we want to remember just how we looked" or "how
things looked" at a certain point in time. To most people
home movies are untampered, unmanipulated visual recordings of real life. Readers should be alert and critical of the
sometimes naively accepted notions of "untampered" and "unmanipulated" recordings. By their very nature, conception,
and construction all symbolic forms are tampered with and
manipulated in some way. Yet home moviemakers tend to
overlook the selective argument and consistently reveal a culturally structured and persistent belief in the objective powers
of the camera.

Weakland discusses the selective quality of feature films:

> There are several basic reasons why fictional films should be especially useful in the study of general patterns of culture. In the first place, they are useful precisely because they are not factual. Instead, they tell a story; that is, they represent an interpretation of some segment of life by selection, structuring, and ordering images of behavior.... Yet we may recognize that even real life involves the conceptualization, organization, and punctuation of experience, and compared to daily life a fictional work represents a more highly ordered and defined unity, whose premises and patterns can be more readily studied [1975: 246].

Weakland thus introduces a rationale for studying fictional treatments of "real" life. He cites characteristics of feature films as significant for cultural analysis: they have a storylike quality; illustrate a segment of life (that is, not all of life); present an interpretation of human behavior; offer a structured and ordered set of images; and present a "defined unity." When home movies are understood as visual symbolic forms, all of these qualities become relevant to the study of film as a culturally structured document. In this context it is clear that home movies do not record all of personal and social life. Equally evident is that home moviemakers have independently reached a consensus on what segments of daily social life warrant filmic treatment. It is this process--the selection of items from an infinite number of possibilities--that produces an interpretation[3] of the way things appear and happen. Thus, in two separate but related senses, "home movies show us how we looked."

One last point comparing the analysis of home movies and feature films: two problems that hinder the study of feature films as cultural documents involve the problematic relation between the small number of film producers and the large number of film viewers, and between the content of feature films (themes, plots, structure, narrative style) and the culture of the people who produced and viewed the films. Readers should realize that producers of feature films are a special kind of collective, what might be described as a "media elite." Studies of "popular culture" have the problem of ascertaining the relation between the "speakers"--members of the relatively small and unelected elite--and the "spoken to"--the heterogeneous collection of people who comprise the mass audience.[4] Powdermaker emphasizes the studying of feature films from both functional and historical perspectives: the anthropologist "must analyze the movies themselves, study the audience, and learn about the conditions under which the pictures are made" (1947: 81). According to Weakland, the ideal situation occurs when

> one can study how films are related to their makers, to their audiences, and to their depicted subject matter.... The situation is simplest when the filmmakers, viewers, and subject matter are all similar [1975: 245-246].

When one is studying feature films produced by societies that are geographically or temporally inaccessible, valuable information may not be available on either the moviemakers or the movie viewers. Sociocultural dimensions of the producer-viewer relationship have to be reconstructed and continually subjected to the validity of hypothetical inferences.

Home movies allow us to approximate Weakland's "simplest situation," that is, "when the filmmakers, viewers, and subject matter are all similar." We know that the home moviemakers (not a corporate entity as in many forms of mass communication) produced a filmic representation of important aspects of their lives, and that the intended audience consisted of people either related to or known to the filmmaker. The home movie provides a simplified and fertile starting point for studying the relation of photographic symbolic forms and culture.

Indigenous forms of film communication

The second important tradition in anthropology focuses on indigenous autobiographical statements. Primary attention has usually been given to the verbal elicitation of life histories (Langness, 1965). It is also acknowledged that the natives "speak for themselves" through a variety of symbolic forms, such as religion, myth, folklore, art, and music. In all of these cases the report is produced by a member of the society being studied.

More and more societies are able to "speak about" themselves and "speak to" themselves in <u>visual</u> (specifically photographic) modes of communication. Research projects have supplied people with cameras to produce photographic, filmic, or video forms of communication for the first time. Fieldworkers try to elicit kinds of ethnographically significant information that might not be revealed through verbal techniques, seeking to understand how the structure of both the content and the social organization responsible for the production are related to other characteristics of the culture. Examples of this research are Worth and Adair's biodocumentary film research on the Navajo reservation (1972); Bellman and Jules-Rosette's film and video research among the Kpelle and the Baposto peoples of Africa (1977); Carpenter's introduction of filmmaking equipment, as well as tape and video recorders, in New Guinea (1972); Downey's video recordings made with the Yanomano; and my own sociodocumentary research projects involving groups of Philadelphia teenagers (1972).

In all of these examples a camera was put into the hands of a native by an outsider. The image-making subjects/students were not making photographic pictures before the instructor/researcher arrived, and, possibly, they will never make films after the project is completed. This point receives additional significance when we introduce and compare the notion of a home movie as a related object of study.

Home movies represent a special kind of artifact and process of communication because home moviemakers are not coerced, instructed, paid or persuaded by outsiders to produce their films. Home movies have been generated under "natural" conditions--that is, with neither the intervention nor observation of some kind of investigator. In one rare example David Sudnow relates the study of home movies to his ethnomethodological interests as follows:

> You can look at films that are made by the member [of a particular society] in a variety of actual natural circumstances and treat this director's productions as data. In this regard, what I have been trying to work with are home movies where we can see the varieties of the ways in which the filmer of the home movies attempts to structure the final product in accord with his conceptions of the phenomena and the interest that the phenomena would have for later recall, later use, and so on [Hill and Crittenden, 1968: 55].

The study of the actual film is fully justified in many circumstances, but researchers should take advantage of easy access to living home moviemakers and viewers. The opportunity to find a body of film produced under undisturbed and uncoerced conditions thus gains greater significance and should further our understanding of film as a culturally structured process of visual communication.

Readers should also recognize a theme mentioned earlier in this chapter, a theme that unifies much of the research cited above. In Worth's terms the production and use of pictorial forms are being studied as data of culture. We are not concentrating on the context of the imagery for what it might show about culture. The significant context of this analytic approach is guided more by a notion of culture than one of film.

Furthermore, the emphasis is placed on understanding home movies as structured expressions of culture. Worth constantly reminds us that pictorial forms are an organized and structured way of looking at the world, rather than merely some kind of evidence or "true" image of the world. For Worth a photograph or film is "not a copy of the world out there, but someone's statement about the world" (1980: 20, Worth's emphasis). Home movies should be understood as an indigenously produced "statement about the world"--a statement that belongs alongside other verbal and visual reports about human existence.

Conclusion

This chapter has focused on how the home movie, as a form of symbolic visual communication, can be studied as a cultural document from several perspectives. Home movies are a significant type of pictorial communication. They provide people with a means of presenting themselves through the mediation of symbolic visual forms, with a means of showing what they want to show about themselves to themselves.

Attempts to understand what these artifacts represent and how home movies work as a system of communication will become increasingly important to students of visual anthropology and to visual studies in general. Worth writes:

> It is not unreasonable to expect that the New Guinea native, the American Indian, the Eskimo, the peoples of developing and developed states in Africa

and Asia, as well as various segments of our own
society, will soon be able to make moving pictures
of the world as they see it and to structure these
images on their own way to show us the stories
they want to show each other, but which we may
also oversee [1973: 346].

A sense of urgency is introduced as Worth goes on to
consider how we teach and study substantive problems in visual anthropology:

and more importantly, what problems have we to
set before our students now that will, at the least,
not hinder them from coming to an understanding
of an age in which man presents himself not in person but through the mediation of visual symbolic
forms [1973: 347].

The home movie has been described "not as a record
of some datum of culture, but as a datum of culture in its
own right" (Worth, 1973: 359). The significance of this approach will become clearer as scholars begin to treat unstudied pictorial forms in contexts of culture and visual communication.

Anthropology should be a disciplined perspective, a
way of looking at, asking about, understanding, and explaining any product and process of human behavior. This chapter
has applied a particular perspective to the home movie as a
seemingly trivial cultural artifact. It is hoped that certain
characteristics, hitherto taken for granted, of this kind of
film can now be seen as worthy of analysis and as culturally
variable, and that this analysis will eventually produce a
better understanding of the social and cultural significance of
the home movie and related pictorial forms.

Notes

1. An abbreviated review of this diversity includes the
    following categories.
    (1) Several Hollywood feature films have incorporated
    home-movie scenes, as in Up the Sandbox (1972) and
    The Apprenticeship of Duddy Kravitz (1974).
    (2) A popular trend in creating an autobiographical style

in documentary and art films is to use sequences of authentic home-movie footage, as in Amalie Rothschild's Nana, Mom and Me (1974), Alfred Guzzetti's Family Portrait Sittings (1975), or Jerome Hill's Film Portrait (1965-71).
(3) In other examples the entire film has been edited from authentic home-movie footage, as in Frederick Becker's Heroes (1974), Sandy Wilson's Growing Up at Paradise (1977), or Barry Levine's Procession (1980).
(4) In a closely related category of use home movies are treated as "found footage" and subsequently edited, manipulated, and incorporated into another type of film exemplified by Victor Faccinto's Sweet and Sour (1976).
(5) Several acknowledged members of the New American Cinema have created artistic versions of home-movie style and content; examples are films by Jonas and Adolphas Mekas, Pola Chapelle, and Stan Brakhage.
(6) Home movies are also incorporated into films that either compare them with other professional recordings, as in Six Filmmakers in Search of a Wedding (1972) or The Nitake Films (n.d.), by Don and Sue Rundstrom, or attempt a socio-cultural-folkloristic overview, as in Zeitline and Star's Home Movie: An American Folk Art (1975).
(7) In yet another form the idea of using family members, at home, in familiar home-movie activities is "played with" visually, as in Dana Hodgdon's Reflexfilm/Familyfilm (1979) or Ed Emshwiller's videotape Family Focus (1975).
(8) And, finally, we are seeing celebrity home movies put in archives or on television, as in the films of Adolf Hitler, the Kennedys, and the like. Many of these films are discussed by Small (1976), Weiss (1975), and Katz (1978).

2. David MacDougall goes farther, claiming that "home movies tend to look similar in all societies" (1969: 30). However, there is no evidence for this claim, even if we could decide what "tend" means and what characteristics of the genre were being compared.

3. John Carey offers valuable insights in his review of The Interpretation of Cultures, by Clifford Geertz: "Geertz is suggesting that the great need of the social

sciences ... is the creation of a theory of fictions. Fiction is used here in its original sense--fictio--a "making," a construction. The achievement of the human mind and its extension in culture ... is the creation of a wide variety of cultural forms through which reality can be created (1975: 189).

4. This relationship is easily oversimplified. Herbert Gans offers an interesting analysis of British vs. Hollywood filmmakers and their respective constituencies when he explains the popularity of "Hollywood Films on British Screens" (1962).

References

Bellman, Beryl L., and Bennetta Jules-Rosette. A Paradigm for Looking--Cross-Cultural Research with Visual Media. Norwood, N.J.: Ablex, 1977.
Carey, James W. "Communication and Culture." Communications Research 2, 2 (1975): 173-191.
Carpenter, Edmund. Oh, What a Blow That Phantom Gave Me! New York: Holt, Rinehart & Winston, 1972.
Chalfen, Richard. "How Groups in Our Society Act When Taught to Use Movie Cameras." In Through Navajo Eyes, edited by Sol Worth and John Adair. Bloomington: Indiana University Press, 1972, pp. 228-251.
_____. (a) "Cinema Naivete: A Study of Home Moviemaking as Visual Communication." Studies in the Anthropology of Visual Communication 2, 2 (1975): 87-103.
_____. (b) "Introduction to the Home Mode of Visual Communication." Folklore Forum 13 (1975): 19-25.
_____. "Tourist Photography." Afterimage 8 1-2 (1980): 26-29.
_____. "Redundant Imagery: Some Observations on the Use of Snapshots in American Culture." Journal of American Culture 4, 1 (1981):106-113.
_____, and Jay Haley. "Reaction to Socio-Documentary Filmmaking Research in a Mental Health Clinic." American Journal of Orthopsychiatry 41, 1 (1971): 91-100.
Gans, Herbert. "Hollywood Films on British Screens." Social Forces 9 (1962): 324-328.
Hill, Richard, and Kathleen Crittenden (eds.). Proceedings of the 1968 Purdue Symposium on Ethnomethodology. Institute Monograph Series No. 1, 1968.

Katz, John Stuart (ed.). Autobiography--Film/Video/Photography. Ontario: Art Gallery of Ontario, 1978.
Langness, L. L. The Life History in Anthropological Science. New York: Holt, Rinehart and Winston, 1965.
MacDougall, David. "Prospects of the Ethnographic Film." Film Quarterly, 23, 2 (1969): 16-30.
Mead, Margaret, and Rhoda Metraux (eds.). The Study of Culture at a Distance. Chicago: University of Chicago Press, 1953.
Musello, Christopher. "Studying the Home Mode: An Exploration of Family Photography and Visual Communication." Studies in Visual Communication 6, 1 (1980): 23-42.
Ohrn, Karin B. "The Photoflow of Family Life: A Family's Photograph Collection." Folklore Forum 13 (1975): 27-36.
Powdermaker, Hortense. "An Anthropologist Looks at the Movies." Annals of the American Academy of Political and Social Sciences 154 (1947): 80-87.
―――. Hollywood--The Dream Factory. Boston: Little, Brown, 1950.
Small, Edward S. "The Diary-Folk Film." Film Library Quarterly 9, 2 (1976): 35-39.
Weakland, John H. "Themes in Chinese Communist Films." American Anthropologist 66 (1966): 477-484.
―――. "Real and Real Life in Hong Kong--Film Studies of Cultural Adaptation?" Journal of Asian and African Studies 6, 3-4 (1971): 238-243.
―――. "Feature Films as Cultural Documents." In Principles of Visual Anthropology, edited by Paul Hockings. The Hague: Mouton, 1975, pp. 231-252.
Weiss, Elisabeth. "Family Portraits." American Film 1, 2 (1975): 54-59.
Wolfenstein, Martha. "Movie Analysis in the Study of Culture." In The Study of Culture at a Distance, edited by Margaret Mead and Rhoda Metraux. Chicago: University of Chicago Press, 1953, pp. 267-280.
Worth, Sol. "Toward an Anthropological Politics of Symbolic Forms." In Reinventing Anthropology, edited by Dell Hymes. New York: Pantheon, 1973, pp. 335-364.
―――. "Margaret Mead and the Shift from Visual Anthropology to the Anthropology of Visual Communication." Studies in Visual Communication 6, 1 (1980): 15-22.
―――, and John Adair. Through Navajo Eyes: An Exploration in Film Communication and Anthropology. Bloomington: Indiana University Press, 1972.

FILMIC OBJECTIVITY AND VISUAL STYLE

Warren Bass

The usual approaches to visual style in film are to relate a film to a genre or aesthetic movement (surrealism, expressionism, cinéma vérité, and so on); to analyze formally the time/space or communicational structures; or to view style as an organized system of techniques (such as moving camera versus static camera).

Without excluding any of these approaches I have found it useful to think of visual style in terms of the stance of the filmmaker in relation to the world-in-front-of-the-camera-- whether objective, subjective, interpretive, or reflexive. This has been particularly useful in my own filmmaking as a means of clarifying attitudes and relationships. This approach looks at style as an essential, relational core rather than as an ornament, polish, or mannerist façade.

Even as a viewer it can be revealing, when analyzing style, to examine at least the appearance of these attitudes as they manifest themselves in a film. We may not know the filmmaker's actual attitude (nor may he or she be aware of it). All we may have to go on are appearances, but in terms of style appearances are everything. Every film (even a bank-surveillance film) allows us to posit at least an indirect presence of a filmmaker. Someone must have set up the camera and devised a system for turning it on.

By chance, design, or default some kind of relationship between the filmmaker and the world-in-front-of-the-camera is represented on the celluloid. This, I suggest, is an essential aspect of style. It is from this perspective that we may examine the concept of filmic objectivity and its alternatives.

Objectivity

Film has an undeniable recording capability, and under limited circumstances we can attribute factual relevance to data recorded by the camera as we can to data recorded by a seismograph or Geiger counter. Yet objectivity is not an automatic result.

The camera is inherently an interpretive tool. Film is biased to record external behavior expressed through action or change. The camera frames experience into a hard-edged rectangle, its color determined more by Eastman Kodak than by nature. The camera interprets visual data into pointillist fields of silver halide or dye particles, reducing time/space continuity into twenty-four discrete two-dimensional tableaux per second. The most realistic image we see on the screen is at best a limited representation with some degree of abstraction. There is no way around it: film distorts. Even modern physics has had to come to terms with the fact that all instruments have inherent limitations, biases, and eventual levels of uncertainty, and the very act of recording can affect the phenomenon being recorded.

Another barrier to objectivity is the human factor. Pressing the camera's ON button is an act involving an interpretive choice, as is the choice of camera position, field and angle of view, type of lens, film stock, lighting, exposure, and where to cut. These decisions are necessary in the production of a film, and to the degree that they are interpretive (and to the degree that the camera itself colors our perceptions) they work against pure objectivity.

We are locked into our subjective selves. Our views of the world are colored by our thoughts, experiences, levels of awareness, and individual biological processes of perception (which in themselves are internal, private, inferential, and uncertain). In a sense, all experience is subjective, and such concepts as objectivity are merely states of subjectivity. If "filmic objectivity" is to be a useful term, it must be recognized as relative objectivity within the inherent limits, distortions, and conventions imposed by the film medium and our own inescapable subjective spheres.

"Filmic objectivity" can be defined as the least biased representation of the object or event in front of the camera that the medium will allow. It is accomplished by an act of will in which the filmmaker submerges expression of the self (to as great a degree possible), defers this expression to the object of the film, minimizes distortions inherent in the medium, and directs his or her faculties toward honestly recording that object or event. The camera is used as a recording tool rather than a tool for formative or self-expressive purposes. An objective style is oriented toward the world-in-front-of-the-camera; as viewers we are relatively unaware of camera or filmmaker.

An objective style means framing action so that essential information is not excluded and so that the bias of the frame itself is minimized. This may result in a tendency toward full-figure shots. Camera movements are justified by this policy of nonexclusion of essential information; they follow rather than lead or seek out. If the camera is static, it justifies its position by the appearance of its neutrality and noninterference in the event, yet supplies us with a view that does not exclude essential information. Such a view tends to have neutral angles that neither aggrandize by looking up nor diminish by looking down upon a scene and uses normal lenses that neither compress nor expand space. Objective style tends toward long takes of "real time" governed by the duration and structure of events in front of the camera, and tends to allow a context (determined by the nature of the event-in-front-of-the-camera) that minimizes biased perceptions.

I am suggesting only tendencies. It is dangerous to make rigid categorical assumptions--such as long shots are objective and close-ups are interpretive--because so much depends on context. For example, close-ups can easily abstract and interpret. They exclude as well as include. The Indian parable of the blind men and the elephant, in modern media terms, can be taken as the parable of the close-up. Each blind man comes into contact with a different part of the beast and assumes that he has encountered a snake or a tree, or comes to some other conclusion based on inadequate information. But it is possible, given the right context, to employ close-ups in an objective manner or long shots in a subjective manner. A close-up of a festering pimple may be objective in the context of a film on dermatology, while the identical shot would be highly interpretive

in a film on punk rock. Film is not capable of recording
the totality of experiential reality. Any one framing, any
one camera distance, records some data at the expense of
other data. Thus the long shot may offer an objective view
of an overall action and its relationship to its environment,
but it may be quite mysterious in terms of subtle detail, such
as nuances of facial expression or surface texture.

Even a disadvantaged camera--one that is locked into
its vantage point by circumstance--can evoke a sense of
objectivity if the immediacy and primacy of the event in front
of it justifies the disadvantaged position. In fact, a highly
advantaged camera may be suspect in terms of objectivity.
This factor appears to work against the principle of inclusion
of essential information. However, the use of a disadvantaged
camera is a piece of information itself: it says that the filmmaker is not in collusion with the event in front of the camera.
In recent years the plausibly disadvantaged camera striving to
observe essential information is one of the stylistic codes we
read as the difference between documentary fact and cinematic
fiction (whether it is or not). It is the essence of the visual style
of filmmakers like Richard Leacock, D. A. Pennebaker, and
Robert Drew.

We have defined filmic objectivity as being a necessarily relative term. The obvious question is, relative to
what? A more complete definition must explore the alternatives to filmic objectivity. Objective and Subjective have existed as polar concepts since the philosophical dualism of the
Greeks. Because the purpose here is to make distinctions,
I shall suggest Reflexive and Interpretive as additional postures.

Interpretive style

An interpretive style uses the aesthetic variables of the medium to establish a privileged view of the object- or event-in-
front-of-the-camera. As viewers we may feel that a camera
or a formative force is relating to the event, but not to the
degree that we experience the person behind the camera.
Leni Riefenstahl's Triumph of the Will chronicles a real event,
the 1934 Nazi Party Congress in Nuremberg. The result is
so highly selected and controlled that the event is cinematically interpreted into a deification of Adolf Hitler. We can
have interpretations of real events or fictitious ones. For
example, in the fiction film Citizen Kane, when the camera
moves through the El Rancho sign, over the roof of the night-

Filmic Objectivity and Visual Style 143

club, and down through the skylight, we are aware of our privileged view. But we are not overtly aware of Orson Welles or Greg Towland as being attached to the camera, and we certainly do not read the shot as signifying the reporter's entrance path into the nightclub. It is a highly interpretive shot.

Renoir, on the other hand, creates the appearance of relative objectivity while subtly manipulating the mise-en-scène into interpretive stances. In <u>Grand Illusion</u>, for example, using a series of full-figure, eye-level shots, he follows the characters Mareshal and Rosenthal as they travel perilously across wartime Germany. As the two come to the verge of a violent falling out with each other, their path has taken them to the edge of a great precipice, where the camera frames them. Certainly a fiction film is not and cannot be a record of objective reality, but since film is, ultimately, appearances, it can appear to be more or less objective within the codes we accept for fiction. (Moments within <u>Grand Illusion</u> may look objective relative to <u>Citizen Kane</u>, but we do not mistake it for a documentary.)

In communication, punctuation creates clarity, emphasis, and nuance. Through editing and selection the interpretive style punctuates the filmed event and thereby structures our impression of it. In contrast, an objective style may let the event punctuate itself in its own scale and its own tempo, allowing viewers to come to their own conclusions, within the limits of the medium.

Subjectivity

A subjective style exhibits self-expression. It gives the impression that the film's view of external reality is private to a particular observer in the way that thoughts and dreams are. As viewers we have a sense of a personality behind the camera, which the personality uses to represent its way of seeing. The subjective stance is personal, intuitive, and possibly mystical. It emphasizes introspective data.

In Hollywood terminology a point-of-view shot (referred to as a p.o.v.) is an <u>illusion</u> of subjectivity. It is possible for each of these stances--objective, subjective, interpretive, or reflexive--to be an actual view (within the limits of relativism) or an illusion. In a point-of-view shot we have the <u>illusion</u> that we are looking through the eyes of a character in the film. In an actual subjective stance the filmmaker merges his or her own fleeings and attitudes with the object of study to the degree that the resultant film is felt as a personal view. Many of the films of Stan Brakhage exhibit this attitude, particularly Dog Star Man and The Art of Vision.

The difference between an interpretive style and a subjective one is exemplified by the stage director who puts talent and energy into interpreting a play versus the director who uses the text as a point of departure. The interpretive director does not change a line but within the latitude of the script adds emphasis, color, concreteness, clarity, and distinctive visual form to bring the play to life on the stage. Every choice is made in terms of whether it serves the play, in much the same way a classical musician interprets Bach with great latitude but will not violate the primacy of the score--a distinctively different intention from the improvisational musician.

Reflexivity
―――

The reflexive stance attempts demystification by creating awareness of the medium itself. As viewers we are distanced in the Brechtian sense so that we may have a perspective on the relationship of the filmmaker to the medium or to the event-in-front-of-the-camera. Reflexivity reveals the filming process and admits that the medium is a medium. In a sense, this appears to be a superobjectivity.

Reflexivity may help us strip the medium of its stale myths, particularly that of the implied invisibility of the camera common to many films of the 1960s Direct Cinema movement. For example, Allan King's A Married Couple documents its subjects through bedroom scenes and embarrassingly frank arguments using the nonreflexive style of Direct Cinema. The couple never acknowledge the camera in such intimate situations where a camera otherwise could never be. If the participants pretend that the camera is not there, then one wonders what other actions in the film might also be pretend. Outstanding examples of reflexive films where the viewer is for the most part aware of the filmmaker's presence are Jean Rouch's Chronicle of a Summer, Michael Rubbo's Waiting for Fidel, and Timothy Asch and Napoleon Chagnon's The Ax Fight.

Although it has its roots with Dziga Vertov in the

Filmic Objectivity and Visual Style 145

1920s, Reflexive Cinema is a relatively recent movement and offers some new approaches to consciousness. But it also has limitations. A reflexive stance gives us a perspective on what we are watching, but what gives us a perspective on that perspective? Absolute demystification is no more possible than absolute objectivity; Heisenberg's Uncertainty Principle explains this inevitability (nothing is certain but uncertainty).

The infinite regress of a perspective on a perspective on a perspective and so on will never totally demystify the filmmaker, the filming process, or the event. There is even the danger of the mystique of reflexivity itself: like the serpent eating its tail, the medium consuming itself to the exclusion of other content can be a very mystic experience. We must also consider such films as Gino's Pizza and No Lies, which look like documentaries but in reality are scripted fiction affecting a reflexive style. Thus it is possible to have the illusion of reflexivity. Gino's Pizza and all other mock documentaries point up the danger of uncritically accepting filmic appearances as actuality.

Simultaneous modes

In conclusion it must be noted that the possible relationships of filmmaker-to-material are often very complex. Most films exhibit a variety of stances, at times objective, other times interpretive, subjective, or reflexive. These modes should be seen as a continuum with Objective at one pole, Subjective at the opposite, and Interpretive balanced in between. If we were to make a graphic representation of this continuum, Reflexive might be placed at right angles to the line established by the other three, situated as an extension of the Objective end. This would signify the place apart that the Reflexive stance must take to have a perspective on the others. There are an infinite number of points along this continuum, and any one point represents the relative mode discernible from one context of viewing.

An overt example of how complex relational attitudes within a film can be for both filmmakers and observers alike is The Ax Fight, by Timothy Asch and Napoleon Chagnon. In part one we witness a brutal fight in a South American tribe, unedited as the filmmakers saw it. In part two it is analyzed with slow-motion and freeze frames, in part three explained as a chart, and in part four shown as an edited sequence in the style of a typical documentary. Our perceptions change remarkably with each part.

We may have a different attitude toward the actual event, the event-as-captured, and the capturing process employed by the filmmaker, and thus may have multiple perspectives on any one moment in the film. Even the simplest film embodies more than one relational mode depending upon the viewing context. The Lumière Brothers' 1895 film <u>The Practical Joke on the Gardener</u> is an <u>interpretive</u> performance of a practical joke (by most standards of performance a rather poor acting job), but it is an <u>objective</u> record of that poor acting job. To a degree, all <u>films have</u> some objective content, in that every frame is a documentary record of a phenomenon that occurred on the emulsion, and by inference some substantive phenomenon had occurred in front of the camera.

Since experience can be placed in multiple simultaneous contexts, the initial question in analyzing reflexivity, objectivity, interpretivity, and subjectivity in style is not whether the film or even a single shot is in one style or another but rather what <u>aspects</u> of the film or the shot are in what mode and in what context? A full viewing of a film involves examination through every relevant context.

These four categories are not the only aspects of style that can be read as the relationship of the filmmaker to the world-in-front-of-the-camera. They are simply one matched set of possible relationships, one paradigm. Camera styles can also be characterized as voyeuristic, respectful, indifferent, assaultive, hostile, sympathetic, seductive, shy, aggressive, etc., limited only by the range of perceptible relationships one human being can have to the world at camera distance. All of these possibilities ought to be considered in an analysis of style. They add important distinctions to our original analysis of objectivity and its alternatives.

GENRE FILM:
MYTH, RITUAL,
AND SOCIODRAMA

Vivian Sobchack

Myth fulfills in primitive culture an indispensable function; it expresses, enhances, and codifies belief; it safeguards and enforces morality; it vouches for the efficiency of ritual and contains practical rules for the guidance of man. Myth is thus a vital ingredient of human civilization; it is not an idle tale, but a hard-worked active force; it is not an intellectual explanation or an artistic imagery, but a pragmatic charter of primitive faith and moral wisdom [Malinowski, 1926: 19].

What anthropologist Malinowski says of myth in "primitive" culture can also be said of the genre film in twentieth-century America. All those groupings of popular movies--the western, the gangster film, the musical, and so on--narratively function as myth. Long the staple product of Hollywood, the genre film differs from other fiction films in that it follows codified narrative patterns, uses stereotypical characters, and communicates through certain repeated formulas and clusters of action and imagery. The experience of genre film is a familiar one, built upon audience expectations that are satisfied not through novelty but through imaginative repetition of known stories. These stories express sacred cultural values, perpetuate moral norms, and practically and painlessly instruct each of us in the viewing audience in the rules that govern ideal social behavior. The movie theater has replaced the campfire, and the distinctive genre forms have replaced more obvious ritual activity. Gunfighters, private eyes, and dancers have replaced the gods, animals, and humans who interacted in, and acted out, the archetypal conflicts of venerable mythology. And yet, like the sacred myths of other and earlier cultures, the stories of such popular figures function beyond their mere secular capacity to entertain us like folktales or to aggrandize history like legends. Those surfaces to which we respond so casually disguise a deeper structure and a greater social purpose, and fulfill a larger cultural need. The narrative of genre film is mythic, and its various forms of expression in the individual genres are comparable to the discrete rituals through which myth is often articulated.

  The purpose of myth, Lévi-Strauss tells us, "is to provide a logical model capable of overcoming a contradiction (an impossible achievement if, as it happens, the contradiction is real) ..." (1972: 193). The genre film achieves the impossible. Together, the mythic content and the ritual form of the genre film function magically, effortlessly, and therapeutically to transform, to dramatically resolve, and to celebrate and sanctify the irreconcilable contradictions inherent in our lives as simultaneously individual and social beings. Conflicting values are embraced equally in the ritual dramatization of mythic narrative. As Schatz points out, "genre films tend to treat various sets of oppositions or cultural conflicts which, through feats of narrative illogic and emotive resolution, tend to be masked and thus celebrated coterminously" (1977a: 48). These sets of oppositions, finding expression in certain forms of dramatic conflict, enable us to distinguish among the genres, to see them as separate from each other by virtue of their respective differences in subject matter, thematic concerns, characterizations, plot formulas, and visual settings (Sobchack and Sobchack, 1980: 190). However, the conflicts presented by each genre, the different sets of oppositions, can be subsumed by one major conflict, one major opposition always presented and resolved in the genre film as it never is in real life. No matter what differences of form and emphases of content mark the individual genres, all are variations upon a single basic theme and all perform the same function. They simplify, dramatize, and resolve the archetypal conflict between Nature and Culture--in less abstract and more dramatically realizable terms, the conflict between the individual and the community, between personal desire and social law. Genre films celebrate <u>both</u> individualism and social integration within the very play of their conflict (Schatz, 1977a: 48).

Like myths, genre films put the conflict between Nature and Culture into supportable form. The person hearing the myth, going to the movies, is presented with a narrative that does not announce itself as didactic and that does not bring the archetypal conflict to its audience unmediated. Rather, both myths and genre films bring "down a vague but great apprehension to the compass of a trivial, domestic reality" (Malinowski, 1926: 77). Thus we need not deal directly and anxiously with the worrisome conflicts and paradoxes of our own social lives. Our surrogates on the screen can do so for us--and within the safety and disguise of a closed narrative form seemingly far removed from serious social problems. Whether horror film or disaster movie, whether western or family melodrama, genre films offer viewers a social equivalent of the personal catharsis provided by psychodrama, that form a therapy in which patients act out scenarios related to their psychic problems. Watching genre films, moviegoers achieve social catharsis, vicariously identifying with the action of mythic figures in a scenario, a "sociodrama" related to their own, usually suppressed, crises of faith and action as social beings. As Thomas Sobchack observes, genre characters act as we would like to:

> They can pinpoint the evil in their lives as resident in a monster or a villain, and they can go out and triumph over it. We, on the other hand, are in a muddle. We know things aren't quite right, but we are not sure if it is a conspiracy among corporations, the world situation, politicians, our neighbors down the street, the boss ..., but whatever it is, we can't call it out of the saloon for a shoot-out or round up the villagers and hunt it down. Genre characters inhabit a world which is better than ours, a world in which problems can be solved directly, emotionally, in action [1977: 46].

The genre film is therapeutic on a grand, if unacknowledged, scale.

These claims for the genre film may seem extravagant. Nowhere in the annals of Hollywood history appears evidence that the studios and filmmakers involved with making genre films deliberately produced movies bent on "overcoming" contradictions in the culture, aimed at resolving the irreconcilable oppositions that structure our behavior as individuals and members of society. Rather, genre films were considered by both Hollywood and viewers as action-packed, escapist fare that had nothing to do with controversial issues, social problems, or messages. That old Hollywood dictum, "If you want to send a message, call Western Union," was certainly applicable to genre films. Gangster movies, musicals, and adventure movies were supposed to "entertain" viewers, not provoke them. Genre films were made to make money, not myths. And yet, by definition and function, both myths and genre films are popular. They appeal to people, touch them and engage them in ways that are familiar and satisfying. They do entertain. Thus, in the case of a modern mythology that involves great sums of money, viewers have signaled their approval of westerns and horror films by buying tickets, by collectively contributing to the development and continuation of genre films through economic sanction (Wright, 1975). A certain kind of film may first be produced and offered to the public because it appealed to a few individuals (also social beings part of the common culture) who thought it seemed like a good story or a vehicle for a particular performer, or it seemed to promise a high return on a small investment. If the public responds favorably, if the film sells tickets and turns a profit, then the consumer-oriented business enterprise that is Hollywood will attempt to repeat its success. It will make the same story with variations again and again--the repetition creating a recognizable genre, functioning "to make the structure of the myth apparent" (Lévi-Strauss, 1972: 193). Conscious myth-making is less at issue, is indeed beside the point, than is the fact that the myths are made and responded to.

Consider, for example, two traditional horror films: The Wolf Man (1941) and The Cat People (1942). Both were made on low budgets and most likely with no other intention than to entertain people by mildly and safely scaring them a little. This does not mean, however, that the films were trivial. Right there on the screen--directly perceptible in The Wolf Man and suggested in the shadows of The Cat People--was particularized the brute and sexual animal that threatens to escape its containment beneath our civilized, socialized exteriors. Larry Talbot, a nice guy who wears suits and asks for dates, turns into a monster, bristling with hair and violence, erupting from his clothes like some primeval force. Irina, in The Cat People, fears her own sexuality with good cause; her passion and sexual jealousy when unleashed turn her from a timid young newlywed into a feline predator, a leopard who stalks the edges of the screen and the night for victims. In these films sexuality is never addressed directly. The individual libido, with its antisocial desire for immediate satisfaction, is only a covert character in the drama. Watching such films, we have no need to recognize consciously that what is being played out before us is a mythic ritual that celebrates both sexuality and the condemnation of sexuality, that allows us to acknowledge and identify with both the protagonist and his or her obsession, and the society that must be protected from such an unruly libidinal attack. The filmmakers may have thought they made, and we may have thought we were watching, two instances of inconsequential escapist fantasy. And yet both they and we may have also had our inarticulate individual conflicts and fears transformed from the horror of personal nightmare into the calm resolution of a depersonalized and collective myth (Sobchack and Sobchack, 1980: 241). It is no accident that horror films have traditionally appealed most to a teenage audience. Playing out the very real and potentially painful drama of puberty in a culture that values sexual attractiveness and potency but that must also suppress it within appropriate institutions, adolescents can identify with the ritual drama before them on the screen. And they can do so never once having to recognize overtly or articulate the real basis of the horror film's mythic conflict and its intimate connection to their lives outside the theater. The blatant stylization of the horror film (either traditional or modern), with its ritual form of expression, mediates between the pressing need to deal with a troubling conflict that has no resolution and the pain attendant upon a direct and isolated confrontation with that conflict. In The Language of the Rite Grainger tells us that

> the rite is the language of the un-thinkable. It is a way of "living those things which do not bear thinking." As such it is a necessary means of expression, for what cannot be thought must still, if it exists, be adequately taken into account, adequately recognized, for truth's sake. The fearful must be registered if the truth is to be lived. However, the fact remains that it is considerably easier to depict a painful truth than to contemplate the same truth [1974: 109].

The great force of the genre film is that it depicts truth without contemplating it, that it dramatizes our deepest conflicts in such a way that they are apprehended indirectly, painlessly.

It is this hidden drama that differentiates the genre film as myth from the kinds of films that directly address aspects of the conflict between self-interest and the needs of others. These other films either do not resolve the problem at all, leaving it raw and open like a wound, or they attempt to reconcile an irreconcilable conflict that has been so openly acknowledged and articulated that the resolution must necessarily seem flimsy and artificial. In either case these films force us to think about the unthinkable--and their cathartic power, their ability to make us leave the theater feeling purged and satisfied, lies more in their formal coherence, their artistry, than it does in their ability to fuse inconsistencies magically into emotional harmony, as does the genre film. The genre film is able to deal with failure in the guise of success. It is able to play out, to depict, the logical inconsistencies that plague our being, while allowing us to contemplate the successful resolution of clearly defined narrative problems. And unlike the nongenre film, which is marked by aesthetic originality, the genre film uses ritual form to disguise and stylize the painful truths of its depiction so that they can be emotionally acknowledged and dealt with without ever having to be directly confronted. The most distinctive quality of the genre film (and the one that most likely accounts for its popularity) is that it treats serious problems in a disguised manner. This is how myth operates. Lévi-Strauss has suggested as much, indicating that his work shows "not how men think in myths but how myths operate in men's minds without their being aware of the fact" (1969: 12). Neither filmmaker nor audience need think about the myth that is played out in the genre film for it to work upon them.

I have already intimated why all movies are not mythic according to the anthropological definition initially set forth. Not all films are bent on "overcoming a contradiction" or on resolving conflict. Not all films wish us to reconcile ourselves unthinkingly and emotionally to the human condition. Many films wish to point out and celebrate the cracks and chasms that underlie the edifice of civilization, society, and culture. Many want us to question openly the beliefs, morality, and rules by which we have been instructed to live. Myth is reactionary, and some art attempts the revolutionary. A film like Apocalypse Now (1979) does not function as traditional myth and does not classically function as a genre film. A film like Air Force (1943) is a genre film. Both movies focus on war and base their narrative movement on the accomplishment of a mission, but whereas the former is constantly and overtly emphasizing the moral inconsistencies by which civilized people live, the latter is disguising them. Some films deal with our deepest conflicts not only overtly but by appealing to our reason; they are attempts to allow us to understand ourselves and the human condition, to explain the basis upon which we live for ourselves and for others. These films, too, are not mythic. As Malinowski says:

> Myth ... is not an intellectual reaction upon a puzzle, but an explicit act of faith born from the innermost instinctive and emotional reaction to the most formidable and haunting idea.... [Myths] never explain in any sense of the word; they always state a precedent which constitutes an ideal and a warrant for its continuance, and sometimes practical directions for the procedure [1926: 33].

A horror film like Psycho (1960) pokes fun at the notion of explanation as a way of allaying "the most formidable and haunting idea" of madness and violence that threatens social order. Hitchcock, a master of genre film, ends Psycho with a lengthy and dry psychiatric explanation of the mad Norman Bates's behavior--but the explanation is mocked for its irrelevance to the force and truth of what we have previously witnessed. The last shot of the film returns us to Norman's face, which still holds its mysteries intact. The shot implies that if madness cannot be explained than neither can sanity; the latter thus rests finally upon faith rather than knowledge. If genre films explain things about ourselves and our irreconcilable conflicts, they tend to explain them away-- to the subliminal level of the dramatic narrative. The mutant monster in the science-fiction film may be overtly explained as the accidental result of atomic radiation, as some inhuman thing that mindlessly stomps cities and that bears the responsibility for destruction. This explanation on the dramatic level is satisfyingly glib, but inaccurate. It functions not really to explain but to explain away the human responsibility for destruction that arises not from mindlessness, but from reason itself--a reason that spawned the potentially monstrous power of nuclear energy and that used it not accidentally but deliberately. On another level the monster is a mythic figure that ritually articulates reason run amok, that plays out a drama in which the very institutions that create culture also destroy it.

As myths refuse to explain the key inconsistencies

with which we must live, Malinowski also observes that myths present an ideal, an a priori value system that is never questioned and that often provides models for behavior. This, too, seems descriptive of the genre film. Consider, for example, the large genre of adventure films that concern group survival. Not only do war movies like Battleground (1949) and The Dirty Dozen (1967), or disaster films like Flight of the Phoenix (1966), The Poseidon Adventure (1972), and The Towering Inferno (1974) invariably assert as given the ideal of social order, the primacy of group survival over individual survival, but they also provide the viewer with practical directions on how to behave in a crisis, dramatizing in the most palatably didactic way the "do's" and "don'ts" that constitute laudable social action. Nongenre films, however, usually ask more questions than they answer. They are not so didactically sure of themselves, nor so quick to label behavior black or white. Instead they may bring out into the open the irreconcilable conflict between the value we all place on our own lives and the value we are supposed to place on the lives of others. A nongenre film may be overtly sympathetic to individuals who save their own necks by refusing to observe the "do's" that preserve society and culture, or it may suggest that the rules that govern ideal social behavior are not to be taken as given (see, for an example of both, a film like The Americanization of Emily, 1964). The genre film does not question cultural values even when they contradict each other. Rather, it reaffirms them and presents the troubling play of their conflict, mediating their brute reality through various forms of dramatic ritual.

It is this ritual form that most characterizes the genre film. It is the way in which the myth (and its variations) achieves expression. The presence and mode of presentation of what Lévi-Strauss has called "slated structures" are repetitively employed so that we are attuned to the fact that a myth is being told (1972: 193). We "know" what a western or a musical or a horror film looks like, and we have a pretty clear idea of what will happen within the films of each genre, as well to whom and when it will happen. Certainly some of our knowledge of narrative and dramatic structure is drawn from our experience of American cinema in its entirety. That is, we do not have to be in the presence of a genre film ritually dramatizing a myth to know that in every film we are likely to see a narrative that has a beginning, middle, and end, that has a protagonist and antagonist, that is based on conflict of some sort, and that moves structurally toward some climactic peak and final resolution. We are also sure

that no matter what sort of film we see, it will usually be
edited in some fashion and that it will use, in various ratios
to each other, combinations of long shots, medium shots, and
close-ups, and static and moving camera. However, in all
films we cannot predict the kinds of narrative elements and
the structures through which they will find expression so
sharply as we can in the genre film. There are the barroom
sequences of westerns, the shootouts. There is the dark at
the top of the stairs, which exists nowhere so darkly and yet
so clearly as in horror films. There is the strange way that
lovers singing in musicals face us as much as they face each
other. There are clusters of characters in adventure films
whom we know intimately the moment we meet them, know
what they will do and when they will die and who will survive.
There are objects that take on a totemic significance they
would not have in less strictly structured and repetitive forms:
clothing, the stagecoach, French windows in a horror film,
even a specific performer like John Wayne. These narrative
structures, and the images and action through which they are
realized within the films of each genre, are secular, but
nonetheless sacred, rituals.

A ritual is a system of actions that are symbolic, that
encompass and express in an obvious though metaphorical
manner some abstract belief--whether religious, social, or
personal. Ritual and myth are to a great degree interdependent; the "ritual actions, and the narrative framework that
supports and interprets them--and is itself supported and interpreted by them--evolve as partners together" (Grainger,
1974: 157). The myth provides the ritual (action that is symbolic) with the content that is to be symbolically enacted. It
is useful to remember that drama first arose within a religious context, isolated and repetitive action giving physical
realization to abstract concepts based not on certain knowledge
but on faith. Indeed, the rigid structure and repetitive nature of ritual may be said to lend faith a surety, a perceptible bedrock, it might otherwise not have; the closure of
such form, its clear isolation from the random appearance
of "real" action, gives belief the appearance of knowledge.
In a like manner, the values transmitted through the ritual
form of the genre film are lent an _a priori_ facticity they
would not have dramatized in a looser structure. Myth and
ritual thus work in concert for the benefit of culture. Grainger usefully summarizes their relationship:

> ... the myth _always_ has a social purpose, in that
> it provides an over-arching truthfulness which is

> able to relate contrary elements--positive and negative, purposeless and purposeful, productive and sterile--within a single universe, a single socio-religious system. Ritual demonstrates and embodies a completeness which can be understood only as a religious phenomenon, in religious terms. Myth and rite present the whole picture of man's life in the world in a way that makes sense to those involved in it. The picture is necessarily an idealized one, because, outside this ritual universe and the religious awareness that it expresses, the world remains existentially unintelligible, or at least disturbingly inconsistent [1974: 92].

While the genre film is certainly not openly religious (except in the case of some horror films), it does function in relation to sacred social content. Myth, the logical model that overcomes contradictions, is a creation of a culture perpetually in conflict with itself and its members, and myth in turn creates a social faith that overrides the inconsistencies and conflicts of social life to celebrate unreasoningly and subsume values that are arbitrary beliefs. Ritual, in its repetitive and closed activity, disguises the arbitrary nature of belief and the solely emotional underpinnings of faith. It gives to both a formal certainty that hides the existential uncertainty to which both respond.

Although there are some recent exceptions (Schatz, 1977a, 1977b; Altman, 1977; Sobchack and Sobchack, 1980: 240-243), studies of genre film have not directly seen the formal articulation of their narratives as related to ritual. The formal and repetitive structure of the <u>individual</u> genres has been discussed in terms of formula, convention, and iconography. The term "formula" denotes a fixed and conventional set of rules or methods for achieving a predictable end result. A formula plot provides the basic structure of the ritual drama that is the genre film. It is a series of related actions that lead to a familiar and predictable narrative conclusion. The basic dramatic conflict, the general movement of what happens in the film, the roster of characters and their activities, roles, and relationships to each other, the resolution of the narrative problem, are all known from previous films within a given genre. Rather than surprise us with novelty, genre films satisfy us with repeating what we already know. Suspense is artificial, except for our lack of specific knowledge about the particular variations worked upon the formula in each film. Certain formulas tend to provide the framework for certain genres, each genre generally based on a discrete set of plot episodes and character configurations different from those of other genres. The adventure film, for example, is usually constructed so that it begins in a normal context in which people take themselves and their social roles for granted. A random grouping of such people is collected spatially (in an army unit, on a hunting expedition, in an office building, on an oceanliner), and then is subjected to some catastrophe that will isolate this random group and force its members to form a cohesive unit able to overcome the obstacle with which it is faced. Given this formula, we know that various sequences will involve tests of individual character, conflicts between an individual's self-interest and his or her interest in the group. The characters themselves are familiar in their large number and their stereotypical dispositions, ethnic backgrounds, and occupational status (the Coward, the Comedian, the Black, the Jew, the Intellectual, the Auto Mechanic). Thus in each genre, through a specific formula and its attendant characterization, a specific set of relationships between individual and society, and self and other, is articulated and played out. The formulas that provide the dramatic structure of the western and the musical, the numbers and configurations and stereotypical force of their characterizations, are different from those that inform the adventure film. What is true of rite, then, is also true of formula: "It employs a certain number of fixed actions, each one of which transmits a single, more or less definite meaning. Change the actions, or the order of the actions, and the rite's meaning is completely changed" (Grainger, 1974: x).

Whereas a ritual or formula is an entire structure or series of actions resulting in a predictable end, a convention is a customary and recurrent unit of action in genre films. The barroom brawl or the shootout in the western and the love song between the protagonists in a musical are such units of action; they are repeated so often within the films of a given genre that they acquire the force and power of a tradition and they offer the viewer the comfort and security of the familiar. Conventions, however, need not simply concern the customary action of characters. The manner in which these actions are cinematically presented may also be a convention of the genre. The lighting and angles of a horror film, long shots by an objective camera showing monster and urban landmark together in the same frame, the entire editorial pattern of a western shootout in the town's streets, are all examples of cinematic conventions affixed to particular genres (Sobchack and Sobchack, 1980: 198-199).

Although the smallest ritual unit of the genre film, the icon is perhaps the most powerful and compressed. In an already symbolic activity (in the genre film, the ritual dramatization of the myth that has already disguised the real social conflict in the costume of narrative) the icon symbolically contains the ability to evoke--simply through its presence--the entire ritual with which it has become associated. Certain kinds of dress, objects, landscapes, and performers have become so familiar that they signify events in the plot that have not yet occurred, the very character and moral stance of people in the film with whom they are connected. Such icons as the railroad in a western, a trench coat in the detective film, the foggy cemetery of a horror film, or John Wayne in a western or war movie all accumulate tremendous significance and emotional weight from their repeated use and similar meaning throughout films of the genre. They communicate enormous amounts of narrative information to the audience and indeed are so evocative that they are often highlighted in advertisements to signal just what kind of ritual, which genre, the viewer will find in the theater (Sobchack and Sobchack, 1980: 200-203).

Each film genre has its own sets of rituals, its own system of formulas, conventions, and iconography. On occasion some of the components of the ritual may be shared among genres. Sword fights and dance sequences in musicals are very much alike, both in their treatment by the camera and in their pattern of insertion into the narrative. Recently the work of filmmakers who grew up watching genre films has led to a deliberate mixing of generic elements (Star Wars, 1977), an exaggeration of them into parody (Blazing Saddles, 1974, and Young Frankenstein, 1975), or a subversion of them (McCabe and Mrs. Miller, 1970, and The Long Goodbye, 1973). These kinds of homage to, or subversion of, a generic ritual attest to its distinctiveness and its familiarity. One could not successfully mix conventions, exaggerate them, or subvert them unless they were first part of common cinematic knowledge, unless the audience knew the way the genre film "should" tell its story, each variant form of the underlying myth (the reconciliation of Nature and Culture) possessing its own particular ritual activities and each clearly recognizable.

These sets of rituals that provide the formal markers from genre to genre are not just of aesthetic interest. They perform the more important function of providing different sets of activities that symbolically focus on a particular aspect of the basic myth that underlies all genre films. Each genre, through its different rituals, acts out a different set of social relationships, presents its own permutation of the conflict between individual and community in its own disguised fashion. As Grainger tells us:

> The grammar of ritual is the relationship of personages within the rite itself. Because it makes use of living personages ... ritual is always a language about society, an existential language about the experience of relationship, rather than a language for the transmission of ideas in the abstract [1974: 10-11].

Certainly it is possible to catalog the specific units of generic ritual. A great deal of genre study has done so, describing and isolating the formulas, conventions, and iconography that characterize the Western (Kitses, 1969; Ryall, 1970; Cawelti, 1971), the gangster film (Warshow, 1971; McArthur, 1972; Shadoian, 1977), the musical (Scheurer, 1974), and other genres. The ritual, however, is not just a structure that elaborates upon a theme; it also performs a cultural function, relieving an unarticulated tension through its performance of a crucial conflict. Each genre, constituted by myth and regulated by its rituals, is "a laboratory, a melting-pot, an arena; which is why so many rites are stylised battles of some kind or another" (Grainger, 1974: 12). What is of interest beyond the catalog of ritual activity and narrative theme is the particular aspect of the basic myth that each genre addresses through its ritual dramatization--what relationships and conflicts between the individual and society are played out, what culturally real and irreconcilable contradictions are narratively reconciled within each generic model.

Each genre seems to explore the conflict between the individual and his or her culture in relation to a particular social institution or its conceptual superstructure. In addition, each genre seems to affiliate itself with another genre that addresses that same institution or social idea from an opposing position. Although both genres resolve their conflict on the side of culture, the one tends to do so with a minimum of ambiguity, while the other tests the limits of social obligation and pushes the force of the individual as far as it can go without destroying the institutional edifice with which it is concerned. For example, the musical and the screwball comedy are both rituals of courtship, concerned with kinship systems and, most particularly, with the institution of marriage. Both play out the conflict between individual expressions of spontaneous emotion and the social need to domesticate those expressions in the institution of marriage. In the musical, spontaneous emotion is expressed and contained by the formal articulation of song and dance--individual desire and social need are reconciled from the beginning of the musical and its conflicts are few. In the screwball comedy, however, spontaneous emotion is expressed but not contained by the unpredictable and inventive antics of the protagonists. In the musical, marriage is the end result of a movement from disorder to order, from literal disharmony to harmony. The show is slowly put together and goes on, the lovers come together as the most nimble and compatible partners and dance. The form of the musical is smooth, propelled toward integration, and certainly not anarchic. The screwball comedy, on the other hand, is not smooth and progressive. Marriage is more the result of exhaustion and capitulation than a fusion of individual and social desire. Although the lovers are finally integrated into the culture and the institution of marriage is triumphant, the progress of the screwball comedy is from order to disorder. The established order of the social world is disrupted by individual expressions of love and courtship; one thinks of the escaped leopard in Bringing Up Baby (1938) or the disrupted wedding ceremonies of It Happened One Night (1934) and The Philadelphia Story (1940). Where the musical generally represents the society's position vis-à-vis the conflict between individual and social emotional expression, the screwball comedy represents the individual's position. As genre films, myths that bind wounds, both the musical and screwball comedy end by upholding the values of culture over those of the individual, but the ritual dramatization of each gives expression to the conflict itself.

One can find similar social and individual emphases in relation to a particular institution in the pairings of the western and the private-eye film; in the two manifestations of the adventure film, the survival film and the swashbuckler; in the science-fiction and horror film; or in the gangster film and the family melodrama. The western and the private-eye film ritually dramatize the relation between personal codes of conduct and social, legal codes of conduct--the institution of law. Although generally nostalgic and regretful at the passage of personal autonomy and individual codes of honor, the western advances society's position. (This is not true, of course, of those recent films that self-consciously use genre traditions to expose the real conflict that underlies the myth.) The march toward civilization is seen as inevitable, and, as in the musical, individual and social needs come together when personal law and social law conjoin in the person of a sheriff or marshall. If they cannot be integrated, then the gunfighter or outlaw must die or ride off into the sunset of history. The private-eye film also addresses this conflict between individual and social code, but here the individual code is usually represented as superior to the social institution, even though, again, society is triumphant at the end. Sam Spade's moral code is far superior to those of the legitimate detectives in The Maltese Falcon (1941), and society itself is shown to be full of corruption, yet at the end Sam's code coincides with the law and he turns in the murderess he loves.

The survival film and the swashbuckler, two major ritualizations of the adventure genre, both focus on political institutions, on the creation and maintenance of the body politic. The survival film focuses on the formation of a microcosmic and democratic society. The hero emerges from the group but is no braggart; he has crucial survival and organizational skills but lacks style, which might make him too individual. A hero like James Stewart in Flight of the Phoenix (1966) does what needs to be done to integrate the disparate members of the group and to return them to mainstream society, but he is willing and eager to mutter "Aw, shucks" at praise and transform himself back into an "ordinary," "average" guy. On the other hand, the swashbuckler follows the exploits of an individual who strives to bring down an undemocratic and corrupt aristocracy. However, the hero is often an aristocrat himself and is not a revolutionary; his aim is to restore equity, justice, and benevolence in the person of a good king or territorial governor. The swashbuckler focuses on the individual, and personal style is thus seen as a value rather than as the sin of pride. But despite all the skills that differentiate the swashbuckling hero from his less able peers, he is at heart a democrat. Errol Flynn in The Adventures of Robin Hood (1938), Gene Kelly in The Three Musketeers (1948), and Stewart Granger in Scaramouche (1952) are men who take pleasure in their grace and skill, who often brag--yet their final allegiance is not to themselves but to their society.

The science-fiction film and the horror film also seem affiliated, approaching the institutions of science and religion, the social issues of knowledge and doubt and faith, with different emphases. The science-fiction film generally focuses on the corporate, social effort to deal with the unknown. Since it takes the side of society, the genre usually does not burden the culture with the responsibility for its scientific mistakes. The mutant monster created by atomic radiation is an accident and not the result of an error of institutional judgment. In contrast, the horror film plays out a dramatic ritual in which the individual desire for knowledge is pursued, in which social good is not at issue for the protagonist. A lone, obsessed scientist or social outcast is caught in a Faustian drama in which he challenges not only the intellectual academy but also divinity. His work must be destroyed, the institutions of society revered and maintained.

Finally, both the gangster film and the family melodrama can be viewed as ritual dramas that revolve around conflicts prompted by economic institutions and the world of work and business: ambition, social mobility, power, success. Each of these genres allows the viewer to experience vicariously the personal preeminence of its protagonists and also their justly negative deserts. Ambition and success are laudable, but they must also be held in contempt, for though they ultimately advance culture, they threaten social cohesion by marking some individuals as more obviously equal than others. The gangster film emphasizes men's business, the corporate world of crime, which mirrors its legitimate counterpart in approved society. The viewer is thus able simultaneously to applaud and experience the drive toward success and condemn it as antisocial. The family melodrama functions similarly, but it emphasizes women's business, the domestic arena and its environs. The films focus on women who may as well be gangsters, for they seek illicit self-realization beyond the home or they strive after social mobility as if it were a promotion. The protagonists of <u>Little Caesar</u> (1930) and <u>Stella Dallas</u> (1937) both must pay a dear price for their ambition and success, for their attainment of autonomy and power. One is a gangster and dies at the end of the film--gunned down, alone, in the end a failure. The other is a woman and an outcast at the end of the film-- viewing her only child's wedding from a distance, alone, the preservation of her individuality finally meaningless. Although the rituals of both genres play out a drama in which the conflict is experienced from the individual's point of view, again the films end by reaffirming, enhancing, and safeguarding social norms.

As mythic rituals, genre films are a great deal more complex than this brief summary suggests. The conflicts

between the individual and society and its institutions within
each genre and across genres are expressed in ways, however disguised and displaced, that echo the complexity of the
inconsistent values we all must embrace. The multiplicity
of relationships, the subtlety of the delicate balance in which
contradictions are held, or the intricate ways in which they
are resolved can only be touched upon here. The basic aim
of the genre film, however, is to resolve logically these contradictory values, to ease the personal and social tension
that we all must experience if not confront, to make us feel
safe and secure in our world. The major characteristics
of ritual all contribute to this sense of order and social wellbeing.

Ritual is, of course, repetitive. Its power is also
cumulative, action building serially upon action, gathering
emotional weight as it grows. Ritual is symbolic and employs
various simple objects to evoke complex associations. It
celebrates tradition and the status quo. It is oriented toward
the past and what has been done before that ought to be done
again: it is nostalgic. Ritual is simple, too, acting through
patterns that are easily recognizable and often dualistic: light
is in conflict with darkness, good with evil, the hero with a
villain of equal stature, and so on. Most comforting, ritual
is predictable. We come to know what is going to happen
next and how it will end, and such knowledge is pleasurable
rather than boring. Finally, ritual serves a function. It
provides its audience with respite from social anxiety, with
a sense of belonging to a group that suffers the same conflicts and has homogenous goals; it celebrates the bonding of
individuals into an ordered community (Altman, 1977: 38-41;
Sobchack and Sobchack, 1980: 242-243).

The rituals of the different genres are distinct, but
all are dramatizations of the same basic myth and all function as ritual to perform a crucial social function. As
Grainger notes:

> The instinct which finds expression in corporate
> rituals, which chooses rituals as its proper way of
> expressing itself, is the instinct of society, the
> movement on the part of individuals to establish
> social identity and social belonging. It is man's
> need to demonstrate and present himself in relation; to demonstrate this fact about himself, that
> he lives in relation; to present himself as himself,
> in a meaningful and explicit action; to reassure

himself in the demonstration of inter-dependence and co-inherence; to define his own limits and the limits of his world ... [1974: 21].

Each genre and its defining ritual acts out before us a different set of social relationships that establish social identity and social belonging. In this sense, all the genres from the horror film to the musical are systemically connected. The social relationships played out within them, and the rituals that give that play form, fit together into a single system that communicates the fundamental moral of the myth they all dramatize, the myth in which Nature and Culture are forever at war and forever in harmony. This moral, common to all genre films, is that "self-interest is the source of all evil" (Leach, 1976: 88). Providing us comfort and a place to act out surreptitiously our antisocial fantasies of individual preeminence, genre films are necessary--even sacred--social constructs.

References

Altman, Charles F. "Towards a Theory of Genre Film." Film: Historical-Theoretical Speculations. The 1977 Film Studies Annual: Part Two, 1977, pp. 31-43.
Cawelti, John. The Six-Gun Mystique. Bowling Green, Ohio: Bowling Green Popular Press, 1971.
Grainger, Roger. The Language of the Rite. London: Darton, Longman & Todd, 1974.
Kitses, Jim. Horizons West. Cinema One Series. Bloomington: Indiana University Press, 1969.
Leach, Edmund. Claude Lévi-Strauss. New York: Penguin, 1976.
Lévi-Strauss, Claude. The Raw and the Cooked: Introduction to a Science of Mythology. John and Doreen Weightman (transl.). New York: Harper and Row, 1969.
_____. "The Structural Study of Myth." In The Structuralists from Marx to Lévi-Strauss. Richard and Fernande DeGeorge (eds.). Garden City, N.Y.: Doubleday, 1972, pp. 169-194.
McArthur, Colin. Underworld USA. Cinema One Series. New York: Viking, 1972.
Malinowski, Bronislaw. Myth in Primitive Psychology. New York: Norton, 1926.
Ryall, Tom. "The Notion of Genre." Screen 2, 2 (1970): 22-32.

Schatz, Thomas G. (a) "New Directions in Film Genre Study (A Response to Charles F. Altman)." Film: Historical-Theoretical Speculations. The 1977 Film Studies Annual, Part Two, 1977, pp. 44-52.
_____. (b) "The Structural Influence: New Directions in Film Genre Study." Quarterly Review of Film Studies 2 (1977): 303-312.
Scheurer, Timothy E. "The Aesthetics of Form and Convention in the Movie Musical." In Film Genre: Theory and Criticism. Barry K. Grant (ed.). Metuchen, N.J.: Scarecrow, 1977, pp. 145-160.
Shadoian, Jack. Dreams and Dead Ends: The American Gangster/Crime Film. Cambridge: M.I.T. Press, 1977.
Sobchack, Thomas. "Genre Film: A Classical Experience." In Film Genre: Theory and Criticism. Barry K. Grant (ed.). Metuchen, N.J.: Scarecrow, 1977, pp. 39-52.
_____, and Vivian Sobchack. "Genre Films." In An Introduction to Film. Boston: Little, Brown, 1980, pp. 189-248.
Warshow, Robert. "The Gangster as Tragic Hero." In The Immediate Experience. New York: Atheneum, 1971, pp. 127-133.
Wright, Will. Six Guns and Society: A Structural Study of the Western. Berkeley: University of California Press, 1975.

Part III

THE AUDIENCE

TO WHAT EXTENT DOES
ONE HAVE TO LEARN
TO INTERPRET MOVIES?

Paul Messaris

The film theorist Béla Balázs tells a story of an English colonial administrator in the early part of this century who lived for many years in places cut off from the Western technological developments of the period. One of these developments was film. Although he had read about it in newspapers and magazines received from home, the Englishman had never seen it. When he finally returned home, he eagerly went to the movies for the first time; but, although some children sitting near him clearly had no trouble following the picture, he himself found it utterly impossible to understand (Balázs, 1970: 34). This story and many others like it (e.g., Wilson, 1961; Worth and Adair, 1972: 130-131) have been used to support the notion that the interpretation of film requires a special set of skills, which viewers have to learn. The purpose of this chapter is to examine the degree of validity of this notion. It will be argued that the extent to which film content can be interpreted by analogy with its real-life counterpart is probably greater than frequently assumed, and that the popular notion that viewers must learn a special "language of film" may be, in certain respects, an overstatement.

Before we begin this examination, it must be emphasized that by "interpretation" what is meant here is only the identification of what it is that a film represents. Other kinds of interpretation, such as the extraction of a moral, the abstraction of a metaphor, or the aesthetic assessment of a nonrepresentational film, are not our concern, and they would certainly not come under the kind of argument that will be developed in the following pages.

The case of still pictures

It will be convenient, for reasons that will become apparent later on, to begin this discussion with a look at still pictures (photographs, cartoons, etc.) before turning to film itself. As with movies, so also with photographs and some kinds of drawings. There are many stories about people who, on encountering them for the first time, reportedly had a lot of trouble understanding them (Herskovits, 1948: 381; 1959: 56). Stories of this kind are often cited as evidence supporting the argument that even photographs cannot be interpreted correctly without a certain amount of prior experience and learning. In theoretical terms the argument usually goes something like this: Clearly, photographs--and even the most "faithful" handmade pictures on a flat surface--are not exact copies of the things they represent. Nor can they be exact copies of the appearance of these things, except in a very limited sense: for our normal view of the world (whether we are looking at it with two eyes or with one) involves countless shifts of perspective accompanying even our slightest movement, whereas a still picture can give us only a single view of whatever it depicts. Therefore, the argument goes, even the most realistic picture presents our eyes with slightly different information from that which the "real thing" would have given us, and we must therefore learn to make the leap from the picture's information to the correct identification of the things that it represents.

Put in this way the argument seems to make perfect sense. However, it has a flaw. It fails to take into account a critical fact about the way in which we interpret the visual world, namely, that we rarely process visual information very thoroughly, so that incomplete or "imperfect" information may not constitute an obstacle to interpretation so long as a reasonable estimate of what it represents can be made from it. This point has long been a cornerstone of the psychology of perception (see Neisser, 1967). The more general point is this: our normal perception of the objects and events in our environment can be said to be a series of guesses, drawing on available information only so much as is needed to form a guess that reasonably corresponds to our expectations of what is there (Gregory, 1970). So, for example, mistyped words are read "correctly" as long as we do not look carefully enough to spot the error. In the case of pictures, then, it can be argued that our ability to make the necessary leap from the incomplete/incorrect information that they give us to an accurate "reading" of their referent is part of our normal perceptual apparatus and need not involve any special set of skills (Hochberg, 1972; see also Gibson, 1971; Kennedy, 1974: 42-64). Nor need it involve any special kind of learning.

Several studies have investigated various aspects of this issue, and there is a variety of evidence in favor of the argument we have just gone over. Among these studies the one that deals with the issue in the most direct way was performed by Julian Hochberg and Virginia Brooks (1962) with their son as subject. This child was brought up from infancy in almost total isolation from any kind of pictorial material and with no instruction whatsoever, direct or indirect, on the meaning of a picture. Halfway through his second year the child began spontaneously to name the objects of the rare pictures that his parents were unable to prevent him from seeing. At that point Hochberg and Brooks conducted a careful series of tests in which the child was shown a variety of pictures (photographs and cartoons) to see if he could correctly identify what they represented (faces of familiar and unfamiliar people, various toy objects, etc.). Almost without exception the child gave accurate identifications without difficulty.

This kind of study is obviously difficult to do with human children, but relevant information has been obtained in several experiments in which animals were found to be able to recognize pictures (not just photographs but also line drawings) without previous training (Hayes and Hayes, 1953; Herrnstein and Loveland, 1964; Zimmerman and Hochberg, 1963). In the case of animals, of course, the criterion of recognition is not the verbal labeling of a picture (except for some of the apes who have been trained to "speak") but, rather, the correct performance, in the presence of a picture, of discrimination tasks previously learned in reference to real-life objects.

From what has been said so far it seems reasonable to conclude, for both theoretical and practical reasons, that the ability to interpret ordinary still pictures is not a special skill that viewers have to learn to perform. With this idea in mind we can now turn to moving pictures and resume our examination of whether their interpretation requires specific learning.

From stills to single-take (unedited) motion pictures

On the basis of what has been said about still pictures, especially photographs, it seems reasonable to make the following extrapolation about movies: if viewers do not have to learn to interpret a still picture, they should not have to learn to interpret a moving picture either, so long as the picture is unedited and the action in it flows without interruption, as it would in reality. The reasoning here is that a moving picture of this kind (uninterrupted by editing of any sort) is, if anything, closer to the appearance of the real world than a still picture can ever be. And since we have argued that our habits of processing real-life visual information are readily transferable to stills, the same should hold for unedited motion pictures (i.e., single unedited shots).

There does not seem to be any systematic evidence on this issue, although it is worth noting that one of the first images that the child studied by Hochberg and Brooks labeled spontaneously was a television picture. Nevertheless, relevant information is contained in surviving accounts of audience reactions to the first movies ever made, which were of the kind we are considering at this point, namely, single shots. (The duration of these early films was typically only a few minutes, and the subjects were such things as dancing girls, street scenes, comic skits, and nature scenes.) Although there are several firsthand reports, from newspapers or private correspondence, of the reactions of "first-night" audiences (including the writers themselves) to these early movies (see Ramsaye, 1926: 129-130, 196-197, 204-205, 227-228, 240-241; Kauffmann and Henstell, 1972: 3-4), there is not a single instance, in these accounts, of reported incomprehension or even of difficulty of comprehension. On the contrary, the recurrent theme in most of these accounts is admiration at how true-to-life the images appeared to their audience (even though, with a few exceptions, these images lacked color and sound). For example, an account of the first public film exhibition in Richmond, Indiana (the date: October 29, 1895), in the Richmond Telegram explained that the new device gave "a complete picture, with the changing expression of countenance and every movement of the figure just as in life" (Ramsaye, 1926: 196); while a New York Journal story about Thomas Edison's first public demonstration of a film projector (on April 3, 1896) says that the screen figures (of dancing girls, etc.) "all of life size, seemed to exist as realities on the big white screen" (Ramsaye, 1926: 228). Even the occasional reports of viewers panicking at the sight of a train headed toward them as it entered a station (Ceram, n.d.: 150) or ducking to avoid the spray from the Dover surf (Ramsaye, 1926: 232) are not, as is sometimes claimed, proof of misinterpretation (in the sense in which we are using the term here); for, while such reports do indicate an incomplete adjustment to the degree of reality of the image (a reaction one can still see, for example, in audiences at 3-D movies), they also clearly indicate that these viewers' interpretation of the image (a train coming at them; a seascape) was correct. The same can be said of the classic apocryphal story about African tribesmen throwing spears at filmed images of elephants.

Naturally, anecdotal information of the kind we have just examined is no substitute for systematic evidence. It doesn't tell us, for example, what difference a moving camera makes to audience comprehension (since the early film camera was almost always fixed), nor does it indicate the role of prior "training" with photographs and various optical devices (see Ceram, n.d.) in preparing early audiences for the acceptance of movies. Consequently, we have to say that we do not yet have completely satisfactory evidence on the question we are examining at this point, namely, whether single, unedited shots require special interpretational skills that a viewer would not have developed anyway in learning to deal with the real visible world. Nevertheless, as we have seen, it is possible to construct a good argument on this point by analogy with what we know about still pictures; and the available data do support this argument. Therefore the tentative conclusion that viewers do not have to learn to interpret the content of most single shots seems to be within the bounds of prudence.

How does editing affect comprehension?

Very few present-day films--or even scenes within films--are constructed entirely of one shot. Let us move on, then, to what seems to be the next logical step in this discussion. What happens when we add editing to the picture? How much does the introduction of editing change a film's visuals from the kind of visual information that is available to us in our "real" environment? The answer to this question depends on the kind of editing one is talking about. Some kinds of editing result in a sequence of images that is similar to "ordinary" visual experience in the real world. For example, if the camera cuts back and forth between two people talking without changing its position (in other words, simply by changing angle with each shot), it is doing what a human spectator might well do in such a situation. (As you will see if you try this yourself with two objects in different parts of a room; you do not normally notice any blur as your eyes switch back and forth, and the film will not contain one if cuts are used.) On the other hand, there are many kinds of editing that put images together in a way vastly different from any real-life experience, sudden changes in location being a good example. If we continue the line of argument that we have used so far, it seems reasonable to assume that the extent to which the interpretation of any particular kind of editing requires a <u>special</u> set of skills (different from the visual perceptual skills one uses in the real world) must depend on how much that kind of editing departs from everyday visual experience. We should expect, in other words, that some kinds of editing (such as the manner of filming a conversation described above) should require little or no adaptation on the part of the audience, whereas others, such as abrupt changes in location, should require much more. The notion we will be dealing with here, then, is that the various types of editing can be arranged along a <u>continuum,</u> according to the degree to which film-specific rules are required for the interpretation of any particular type.

Evidence concerning this notion comes from several studies of the difficulty with which children of various ages interpret various kinds of editing. Two studies of children's comprehension of editing styles will be discussed here. The first of these was conducted by Bianka Zazzo, a French film scholar whose subjects were the pupils of the six grades of a French secondary school (Zazzo, 1952). Zazzo's question was precisely the general one we are asking here: do viewers (in this case, young children) have to learn to interpret a film adequately? Zazzo's method was to show the children a five-minute segment of a standard commercial movie and then to test their comprehension in various ways. The movie contained a confrontation between two rival gangs of youths, a brief scuffle between the leaders, a scene of one gang pursuing the other, and, finally, the restoration of order by the police. An important component of this movie, from the point of view of our immediate concern with editing, was the

presence of the following editing devices: first, a pair of
shots in which the camera cuts from the point of view of one
of the gang leaders to the point of view of the other; second,
a scene in which one of the gangs is barricaded in a hut and
the camera cuts back and forth between interior and exterior;
third, a time lapse at the end of the movie, between the ar-
rival of the police and the conclusion.

The reason these sequences are important for our purposes is that, although they all represent standard examples
of Hollywood editing, by the criteria we have used here they
depart considerably from the possibilities of real-life visual
experience. Although a Hollywood editor might argue that it
is "natural" to want to see each of the gang leaders as the
other sees him at the moment of confrontation (cf. Pudovkin,
1970: 54-121; Bazin, 1967: 23-40), nevertheless this alternation of subjective views is a complete physical impossibility;
likewise, while one might wish that one were able to jump
instantaneously back and forth between interior and exterior
views of the cabin so as to witness all aspects of that confrontation, there is not really anything in real life that could
approximate that experience; and the same goes for the time
lapse at the end of the film. Except for these three segments the rest of the film was edited in a more "realistic"
style--that is, without any other time lapses and with much
less dramatic shifts in point of view. In testing the children's comprehension Zazzo was careful to distinguish between the three "difficult" segments and the remainder of the
film. For example, she compared their performance on pic-
ture-sequencing tests corresponding to portions of the film
with and without these editing devices. What she found was
that there was a dramatic difference between the two. Almost none of the children had any trouble with the more "realistic" segments of the film; almost half failed to perform
correctly on the tests involving the "unrealistic" segments,
the proportion of failures ranging from almost all of the first-
grade children to almost none of the sixth-graders. In other
words, the departures from "realism" in the three critical
sequences of this film appear to have made those sequences
quite difficult for all but the most experienced viewers among
these children to follow (assuming, of course, that it was indeed greater film experience, rather than other developmental
differences, that accounted for the age-related trends in the
results).

Similar results were found in a second study, by Mialaret and Méliès (1954), which we shall discuss rather more

briefly. This study compared children's responses to three versions of a film: 1/ a version filmed in long shot, with very little editing; 2/ a version with greater variety in shot types (i.e., including medium shots and close-ups) and more frequent changes in point of view within scenes; and 3/ a version intended as the most "unrealistic" of the three, including much use of "subjective camera," cross-cutting between locations, and temporal discontinuity. Interestingly enough, the second version did not appear to be more difficult to follow than the first, and in fact there was some indication that the closer views aided comprehension. On the other hand, as Zazzo's study (and the argument being developed here) would have led one to expect, the more radical departure from real-life visual possibilities represented by the third version did appear to cause severe interpretational difficulties. As with Zazzo's study, too, there was an age-related trend in these difficulties.

Both of these studies support the overall argument that there is a continuum in the degree to which editing devices present an obstacle to interpretation and that the place of a particular device on this continuum depends on the degree to which it combines images in a way similar to the possibilities of real-life visual experience. Furthermore, assuming that the age-related trends in these findings are due to differences in amount of film experience (rather than other aspects of growing up), these findings round off the evidence in support of the more general notion that we have been examining here: that the amount of film experience and learning required for the interpretation of any particular editing device depends upon its place on this continuum.

Steps toward a continuum of editing types

The next question to ask is whether it is possible to be more precise about what kinds of editing belong in what position on this continuum. Unfortunately there is little systematic empirical evidence to go by on this issue, aside from the studies just cited. In the absence of sufficient evidence the best we can do is to form a tentative and necessarily crude set of guesses.

A useful distinction to begin with is the one between two overall categories of editing: on the one hand, editing within a scene, that is, editing that does not involve a change in time or location; and, on the other hand, editing that does involve such changes. We shall assume that the former general category is the more basic of the two, since it involves no break in the natural continuity of place, time, and character, although it may of course involve "unnatural" sequences of images within its single location and time period.

Within this simpler of the two categories it may be possible to make some finer distinctions. We have already discussed what is taken here to be the very simplest editing device in common use, namely, cutting to various parts of a scene from a single camera position with no change in focal length. This is also the only editing device of which it could be argued that it actually does not depart at all from the physical possibilities open to a real-life spectator. The most common devices for editing within a scene, however, both involve slight departures from this situation. These two editing devices are, first, the shifting back and forth of camera position by which conversations are usually filmed if they are not done in a single two-shot (both speakers in one shot); and, second, changes in the magnification of people and objects in a scene (e.g., going in from a long establishing shot to medium shots at the beginning of a scene or moving farther in for close-ups of speakers later on).

The first of these two devices appears to be the simpler. All available evidence indicates that, when the change in camera position involved is not so extreme as to cause an apparent reversal of the relative position of the characters in a scene, this device does not appear to offer any obstacles to interpretation, despite its "slight" violation of "naturalistic" sequences. So, for example, even studies of very young children (below school age) have not reported any degree of incomprehension associated with this device (Mialaret and Méliès, 1954; Noble, 1975; Winick and Winick, 1979). Furthermore, although the introduction of this kind of editing into the films of the first decade of this century, in place of the single-take, theaterlike scenes of the very first movies, was apparently undertaken with some hesitation by the film pioneers of the day, there is no record of audience difficulty with it or protests against it. Edwin S. Porter's The Life of an American Fireman (1903), whose three-shot climactic scene makes it the earliest recorded departure from the theaterlike style of its day, was an unambiguous success with audiences (Jacobs, 1968: 37-41); while D. W. Griffith, who liked to boast about resistance to his many innovations in film structure, appears not to have encountered any obstacles in his initial moves to break scenes down into shots (beginning with For Love of Gold in 1908; see Jacobs, 1968: 101-201).

What has been claimed to be a source of difficulty, in some of its uses, is the second of these devices (changes in magnification). In particular, transitions to a tight close-up have been said to disorient inexperienced viewers. This kind of disorientation has been reported in accounts of the introduction of close-ups into early movies. There are many stories of audience members protesting against them (e.g., Griffith, 1972: 86) or even being frightened by them (e.g., Balázs, 1970: 34-35). Some of these stories are clearly mistaken in their premises. For example, it is sometimes claimed that a famous close-up of an outlaw in Porter's The Great Train Robbery (1903) terrified audiences because they interpreted it as a disembodied bust. Yet equally tight close-ups (from the chest up) had been in use in film since its very first days (e.g., Fred Ott's Sneeze, made by W. K. L. Dixon in 1893, and The Kiss, an Edison film from 1896), and, as Griffith argued, all audience members must also have seen the same kind of close-up in painting and photography (Griffith, 1972: 86). Furthermore, there is a much more plausible reason for any apprehension the audience may have felt at the close-up in The Great Train Robbery: in this shot the gangster is seen firing a gun directly at the audience. Surely this was a novelty. Nevertheless, the variety of anecdotal evidence concerning audience resistance to some early close-ups makes it more than likely that at least in some cases this did happen. What must be stressed, however, is that the cause of difficulty could not have been the close-up by itself: there is no record of objection to the single-take close-up films of the 1890s (on grounds of intelligibility, that is; on the other hand, The Kiss was widely attacked for its alleged immorality; see Ramsaye, 1926: 257-261). Rather, it seems that the transition to a close-up--that is, the loss of previously available contextual information--is what may have disturbed some of these early audiences. The same conclusion is indicated by some more recent evidence: In a study of young children's preferences for various editing styles Noble found that, while older children tended to like the detail provided by close-ups, younger children tended to prefer longer views that allowed them to maintain a sense of the location of things at all times (Noble, 1975: 189-190).

Aside from these occasional difficulties reported with regard to transitions to close-up, the two editing devices we have been talking about here appear not to depart sufficiently from realistic sequence to cause any interpretational problems, even among the most inexperienced viewers. Among the common devices for editing within a scene it would appear that it is only the more extreme departures from realism, such as the alternation of subjective viewpoints studied by Zazzo, that are serious obstacles to interpretation. Since there is no further systematic evidence on these issues, beyond that already examined above, a more detailed discussion of within-scene editing will not be attempted here.

Instead, we will now consider the other overall category of editing devices--transitional editing--in which there is some discontinuity in time, place, or both. It was argued earlier that this kind of editing is more complex than the kind of within-scene editing we have just discussed, since transitional editing violates realistic sequence more than within-scene editing does. In other words, transitional editing presents the spectator with time and space juxtapositions that could almost never be encountered in reality, and, for an adequate interpretation of anything but the most episodic film, the spectator must be able to weave these disparate times and places into a single, uniform "network of causality," within which the film's plot, character development, and so on acquire meaning. This point bears some emphasis. The adequate interpretation of a film is not merely a matter of correct interpretation of the action at any one point. The spectator must be able to make all the connections between one incident and another through which the world depicted on the screen acquires unity and coherence. This maxim holds true whether one is talking about the relationship between one tiny shot and the next or about the structure of an entire film; but the point that has just been suggested is that making sense of the juxtaposition between disparate times and places may be more "unrealistic" a task than piecing together the various incidents in a single time and place.

Evidence in favor of this proposition comes from both of the studies with children described earlier. According to Zazzo, the time lapse in the concluding part of the film in her study was the single most difficult feature for the children to interpret (Zazzo, 1952: 33), while the cross-cutting between locations in the third version of the film used by Mialaret and Méliès was reportedly the greatest source of difficulty for the children in that study (Mialaret and Méliès, 1954: 227). Furthermore, in a related study by Zazzo and Zazzo in which a "difficult" kind of within-scene editing--cross-cutting between subjective viewpoints--was compared with editing based on time lapses, the latter was found to be the more difficult for viewers (including adults) to interpret (Zazzo and Zazzo, 1951: 168).

In addition to these studies there is a considerable amount of other research with a less direct bearing on this point. The general finding, which any one project may approach in its own way, is that children (or even older viewers) who do not give evidence of any difficulty with the editing within individual scenes do, on the other hand, misinterpret the larger connections in a film's structure. In a study by Collins, Berndt, and Hess (1974), for example, age-related differences were found in the ability of children to make the connection between three different scenes (a crime; a subsequent attack against a witness; and the consequent arrest and trial of the criminal), even though the younger children were apparently able to report the action within individual scenes (see also Collins, 1975; 1979). In several sets of observations Noble has found that younger children were less able than older ones to determine the point at which a film's scenes added up to a completed story, whereas following the action at any one point did not seem to be as major a problem (Noble, 1975: 91-94). In a series of studies summarized in Messaris and Gross (1977) even older viewers (eighth-graders and college students) who had no difficulty with the individual incidents of a visual narrative were almost totally unable to make certain connections spanning its entire structure (see also Pallenik, 1976). Finally, a study of adult subjects by Messaris (1975) found that only experienced viewers (filmmakers and film students) were able to make competent structural connections in parts of a film involving severe departures from "naturalistic" time-space sequence.

The notion that transitions in time, space, or both constitute a particularly acute obstacle to interpretation, and require considerable film-viewing experience on the part of audience members, is also supported by the historical evidence on the introduction and evolution of such transitions in American movies. In an elegant study of this history Carey has shown how long it took before Hollywood filmmakers were confident enough of their audiences' level of comprehension to be able to dispense with lengthy transitional material (titles, shots of locomotive wheels, pages flipping off a calendar, slow dissolves) between two different space-time points in a

film. It was not until the sixties that the use of simple cuts
in these situations became a common thing (Carey, 1974).
An interesting example of the kind of early audience reaction
that was presumably responsible for this directorial apprehension over space-time transitions occurs in a trade review
(from the New York Dramatic Mirror of June 20, 1908) of
the film The Blue and the Grey. This film contains a transition from a scene in which the hero is brought before a
firing squad to be shot, to a scene in which his girlfriend
manages to secure a letter of pardon and then hurries back
to save him. What is involved here, in other words, is not
only a space shift but also a shift backward in time, so that
the two actions could climax simultaneously. This dramatic
device, rather obvious by today's standards of film editing,
was considered a case of "faulty story construction" by the
reviewer of the day, whose interpretation of the scene obviously could not accommodate the backward time shift: "The
spectator is then asked to imagine the firing squad suspending
the fatal discharge while the girl rides from Washington to
the Union camp" (quoted in Kauffmann and Henstell, 1972: 7).
Another good example of early resistance to transitions of
this sort is the classic case of D. W. Griffith's experience
in making the film After Many Years (1908). Griffith's wife
has recorded the serious objections of his associates to his
inclusion in this film of a direct cut from the film's heroine,
deep in thought, to the object of her thoughts, her husband
cast away on a desert island. In this case, however, it appears that the audience did not share these objections (Mrs.
D. W. Griffith, 1975: 66).

In general, then, there is a variety of evidence in
support of the notion that breaks in space and time violate
the inexperienced viewer's reality-based expectations of image
flow more than most kinds of within-scene editing and therefore occupy the more extreme positions on the continuum of
editing-types. Clearly, a thorough description of such a continuum would deal with distinctions among various subcategories of space-time transitions, some of which (e.g., flashforwards) depart from the possibilities of real-life visual experience more than others (e.g., transitions from the exterior
to the interior of a building). However, since the kind of
data that would be needed to support such finer distinctions
are not yet available, our construction of a continuum of editing types must necessarily stop with the tentative outline discussed thus far.

Conclusion

In this chapter we have examined a question that has long been a concern of film scholarship: is the interpretation of a film something that a viewer has to learn to do? In response to this question we developed the following argument: from what we know about human perceptual processes, visual perception is apparently not dependent on absolute accuracy or completeness of available visual information; therefore the fact that photographs and single-shot unedited pieces of film depart from the appearance of reality in certain ways need not mean that special interpretational skills must be developed for dealing with them. The introduction of editing into a film should change this situation to a greater or lesser degree, depending on the extent to which a particular type of editing approximates the kinds of combinations of images that could occur in real-life visual experience. The degree to which experience with film and special skills for film interpretation are required by any one type of editing should vary accordingly. The presentation of this argument concluded with a first attempt to construct a continuum of editing types, according to the extent of film-related interpretational experience required by each.

Several observations should be added to this summary of our argument. First, it must be emphasized again that the only kind of interpretation of concern to us here has been the identification of what a film represents, assuming that it does represent something. Our argument is clearly irrelevant to other kinds or aspects of interpretation. Second, it must also be emphasized that there are many types of editing that this discussion had to overlook for lack of space and of relevant data. Finally, it should be pointed out that our discussion has also omitted consideration of an important corollary question to the one we have been dealing with: if viewers do have to learn to interpret some aspects of film structure, how does this learning occur? While the question may seem obvious once stated, it does not appear to have received any attention in the literature on film, and the most one can do here is to acknowledge its importance.

References

Balázs, Béla. <u>Theory of the Film: Character and Growth</u>

of a New Art. New York: Dover, 1970.
Bazin, André. What Is Cinema? 2 vols. Berkeley and Los Angeles: University of California Press, 1967.
Carey, John. "Temporal and Spatial Transitions in American Fiction Films." Studies in the Anthropology of Visual Communication 1, 1 (1974): 45-50.
Ceram, C. W. Archaeology of the Cinema. New York: Harcourt, Brace & World, n.d.
Collins, W. Andrew. "The Developing Child as Viewer." Journal of Communication 25, 4 (1975): 35-44.
―――――. "Children's Comprehension of Television Content." In Children Communicating, edited by Ellen Wartella. Beverly Hills: Sage, 1979, pp. 21-52.
―――――, T. J. Berndt, and V. L. Hess. "Observational Learning of Motives and Consequences for Television Aggression: A Developmental Study." Child Development 45 (1974): 799-802.
Gibson, J. J. "The Information Available in Pictures." Leonardo 4 (1971): 27-35.
Gregory, R. L. The Intelligent Eye. New York: McGraw-Hill, 1970.
Griffith, D. W. The Man Who Invented Hollywood. Edited and Annotated by James Hart. Louisville: Touchstone, 1972.
Griffith, Mrs. D. W. When the Movies Were Young. New York: Benjamin Blom, 1975.
Hayes, K. J., and C. Hayes. "Picture-Perception in a Home-Raised Chimpanzee." Journal of Comparative and Physiological Psychology 46 (1953): 470-474.
Herrnstein, R. J., and D. H. Loveland. "Complex Visual Concept in the Pigeon." Science 146 (1964): 549-551.
Herskovits, Melville J. Man and His Works. New York: Knopf, 1948.
―――――. "Art and Value." In Aspects of Primitive Art, edited by R. Redfield, M. J. Herskovits, and G. F. Ekholm. New York: Museum of Primitive Art, 1959, pp. 42-97.
Hochberg, Julian. "The Representation of Things and People." In Art, Perception, and Reality, by E. H. Gombrich, J. Hochberg, and M. Black. Baltimore: Johns Hopkins University Press, 1972, pp. 47-94.
―――――, and Virginia Brooks. "Pictorial Recognition as an Unlearned Ability: A Study of One Child's Performance." American Journal of Psychology 75 (1962): 624-628.
Jacobs, Lewis. The Rise of the American Film: A Critical History. New York: Teachers College Press, 1968.
Kauffmann, Stanley, with Bruce Henstell, eds. American

Film Criticism: From the Beginnings to Citizen Kane. New York: Liveright, 1972.

Kennedy, John M. A Psychology of Picture Perception. San Francisco: Jossey-Bass, 1974.

Messaris, Paul. "Interpretational Styles and Film Training." Ph. D. dissertation, University of Pennsylvania, 1975.

_____, and Larry Gross. "Interpretations of a Photographic Narrative by Viewers in Four Age Groups." Studies in the Anthropology of Visual Communication 4, 1 (1977): 51-58.

Mialaret, G., and M. G. Méliès. "Expériences sur la Compréhension du Langage Cinématographique par l'Enfant." Revue Internationale de Filmologie 5 (1954): 221-228.

Neisser, Ulrich. Cognitive Psychology. New York: Appleton-Century-Crofts, 1967.

Noble, Grant. Children in Front of the Small Screen. Beverly Hills: Sage, 1975.

Pallenik, Michael. "A Gunman in Town! Children Interpret a Comic Book." Studies in the Anthropology of Visual Communication 3, 1 (1976): 38-51.

Pudovkin, V. I. Film Technique and Film Acting. New York: Grove, 1970.

Ramsaye, Terry. A Million and One Nights: A History of the Motion Picture. New York: Simon and Schuster, 1926.

Wilson, John. "Film Illiteracy in Africa." Canadian Communications 1 (1961): 7-14.

Winick, Mariann Pezzella, and Charles Winick. The Television Experience: What Children See. Beverly Hills: Sage, 1979.

Worth, Sol, and John Adair. Through Navajo Eyes: An Exploration in Film Communication and Anthropology. Bloomington: Indiana University Press, 1972.

Zazzo, Bianka. "Analyse de Difficultés d'une Sequence Cinématographique par la Conduite du Recit Chez l'Enfant." Revue Internationale de Filmologie 3 (1952): 25-36.

_____, and René Zazzo. "Une Expérience sur la Compréhension du Film." Revue Internationale de Filmologie 2 (1951): 159-170.

Zimmerman, R., and J. Hochberg. "Responses of Infant Monkeys to Pictorial Representations of a Learned Visual Discrimination." Psychonomic Science 18, 5 (1970): 307-308.

THE NATURE OF THE VIEWING EXPERIENCE: THE MISSING VARIABLE IN THE EFFECTS EQUATION

James M. Linton

The literature on "effects" comprises a large portion of the research about mass communication. Effects studies have been so prominent because the academic community has reacted to the public assessment that the mass media may have a deleterious impact on the social order. This concern with the need for the social control of popular entertainment can be traced back as far as the sixth century, but it was intensified by the change in the mode of social interaction occasioned by the introduction of the mass media beginning in the late nineteenth century (Jowett, Reath, and Schouten, 1977).

Movies were particularly troublesome in this regard because of their graphic nature and their intense appeal to children. The Payne Fund Studies were one of the earliest "scientific" responses to this concern, with a majority of their volumes dealing with the movies' effects upon children and adolescents. When television supplanted the movies as the dominant mass medium (in terms of breadth of coverage and extent of exposure), the focus of effects research shifted as well, with the portrayal of violence on television constituting the major topic of study.

This evolution of the central subject matter of effects studies was paralleled somewhat by the shift in orientation

toward the media's ability to influence audience members
(McQuail, 1976). The initial view posited the mass media
as having a direct and virtually inescapable impact. This
idea was modified on the basis of research in the 1940s that
suggested a more modest power. Later research and theorizing put forward a view that emphasized the ability of individuals to resist the media, stressing the role of social-situational factors in determining effects. Such a perspective
led some researchers in the 1960s to discount the media's
impact entirely, but a less drastic view allowed that the
media could have <u>indirect</u> effects "by shaping the materials
of knowledge, nor<u>ms, and</u> judgements which people acquire
and then apply in everyday life" (McQuail, 1976: 344). This
latter orientation, and some considerable empirical confirmation of it, has led to the almost theoretical exclusion of the
notion of direct effects. As modest as such direct effects
may appear at first glance, however, they "may be cumulative and significant in individual cases" (McQuail, 1976: 344).
The reason for this discounting of direct effects, according
to McQuail (1976: 344), is the small amount of attention that
"has been paid to sorting out and identifying the different
kinds of effect <u>process</u> which are at work, <u>the mechanisms
by which changes related to the viewing experience are produced</u>" (emphasis added).

In attempting to come to terms with the issue of media
effects we will need to explore these "mechanisms," which
in turn can only be understood in relation to the complex of
physical, social, and psychological factors that constitute the
viewing experience. It is this failure to acknowledge and
study the nature of the viewing experience that accounts in
large part for the incompleteness of most effects studies and
the unsatisfactoriness of their findings. By paying attention
to this intervening stage between the creation and dissemination
tion of media content and its resultant impact we give proper
emphasis to the <u>processual characteristics</u> of mass communication, and it becomes easier to approximate McQuail's
(1976: 346) dictum that "it is more useful to know <u>why</u> effects occur than to know <u>what</u> effects actually occurred."

Unfortunately, very few communication theorists or
researchers have paid much attention to the nature of the
viewing experience as a factor in the determination of effects.
There is no fully articulated "theory of the viewing experience." In addition, very few researchers seem concerned
about whether studies are conducted in a laboratory or natural environment; subjects are exposed to materials alone

or in groups; experimental stimuli consist of video or filmic materials; such stimuli are "artificial" creations made simply for the purposes of the study at hand and are usually extracts from actual media content or complete examples of such content; and so on. While the present study can in no way pretend to present a fully articulated theory of this phenomenon, it will attempt to identify most of the significant variables in this process and tentatively suggest the relationship among them. It is hoped that such a formulation will provide a starting point for further research and inquiry that will suggest refinements or reformulations of this tentative "theory."

Characteristics of the film-viewing experience

The viewing experience must be conceptualized as a composite of several elements: the physical characteristics of the setting, the social characteristics of the activity, and the psychological or personality characteristics of the viewer. The literature has paid some attention to those physical features of the film-viewing experience that make it different from the viewing situation of television (Cook, 1976; Noble, 1975; Taylor, 1975; Tudor, 1969). Tudor (1969), for example, notes that the darkened theater and the heightened intensity of message stimuli (due to such features as large image size, high picture resolution, and sound clarity) create an increased sense of social isolation. Combined with the relaxed posture of the viewer, these features make the message more emotionally potent and the viewer more susceptible emotionally to such stimuli than is the case with television.

     Studies have demonstrated that movie going is rarely a solitary activity, unlike television viewing; moreover, it has the aura of a special occasion about it (Jowett and Linton, 1980). Interaction does take place among members of the movie audience, but it can vary from one type of setting to another (large or small theater, drive-in or airplane) and it is more subtle than the interaction that occurs in front of the television set in the home. In fact television viewing often occurs when an individual is engaged in another activity (e.g., studying, doing housework, reading). Such differences in attention to media messages, and in audience-member orientation, certainly warrant attention when one is concerned with the impact of such messages.

     These first two variables in the viewing experience can each be classified into a small number of categories.

The third variable, psychological or personality characteristics, however, introduces the possibility of almost infinite variation. Individuals are like snowflakes, some people would contend: no two of them are exactly the same. Although this observation may be true at some levels, one can differentiate among groups of individuals in terms of their self-esteem, self-image, and sense of identity. The relevance of these and other such "self-concepts" to the viewing experience can be clarified only in terms of the interaction of the three components as described below.

The crucial question about the viewing experience, as it relates to effects, is that of the nature of the relationship between the viewer and the world presented on the screen. In films the process whereby the viewer crosses the distance from the screen and imaginatively enters the screen world has been called identification. This concept has been employed in various guises in film theory from its earliest beginnings (Dart, 1976). Unfortunately, however, "In spite of the popularity of the concept of identification, research studies throwing light onto the process are old, sparse and inconclusive" (Noble, 1975: 39) and consequently the idea "belongs more to the sphere of art than science" (Maccoby, 1968).

This widely accepted notion of identification emerges from the popular belief that in order for dramatic materials to function properly, the viewer must be made to experience vicariously the events that occur within that dramatic world. The most obvious way in which this can happen is by the viewer "putting him- or herself in the place of" or "empathizing with" one of the characters in the film. One study that attempted to examine identification empirically measured it "by indications of emotional attachment [to] or liking [of]" various characters (Clark, 1971). Two commonly recognized forms are similarity identification and wishful identification: in the former the viewer identifies with those characters most like him- or herself; in the latter the identification occurs with those whom the viewer desires to be like (Feilitzen and Linné, 1975). Noble (1975: 39) describes a third type and claims that all three have been "derived somewhat simplistically from Freud." This third type is anxiety-reducing identification, in which the viewer seeks to become like a frightening aggressor to overcome the fear engendered by that character.

Tudor (1974: 76-85) has improved upon this essentially one-dimensional conceptualization of the mechanisms involved in identification by combining two types of "star-individual identification" with two different "consequences" to produce a fourfold classification: emotional affinity, self-identification, imitation (of physical and simple behavioral characteristics), and projection. Emotional affinity is probably the most common and is the weakest form of identification: "The audience feels a loose attachment to a particular protagonist deriving jointly from star, narrative and the individual personality of the audience member: a standard sense of involvement." This style of identification is "subject to rapid and extensive variation," Tudor claims.

The next category is self-identification, in which "the audience-member places himself in the same situation and persona of the star." Imitation, the third category, is most prevalent among the young. In this form of involvement "consequences are no longer limited to the immediate cinema-going situation, the star acting as some sort of model for the audience." This category shades over into the final, most intense and diffuse form of involvement: projection. Here "the person lives his or her life in terms bound up with the favored star." The star, in effect, "becomes a receptacle for the projected desires, frustrations, and pleasures of the fan." Projection seems to be most prevalent in adolescents, a group that is "most likely to grasp at the models provided by the star system as a way of forming a sense of identity and a social reality." It also seems that this approach is more prevalent among female than among male adolescents.

Tudor observes that there are also elements of involvement with story types, although it is almost solely at the level of emotional affinity. Such involvement is realized through the existence of film genres. "To see a movie made within a clearly recognized genre, such as the western or the horror movie, is to participate in a familiar locale and development, and this familiarity facilitates easy and immediate involvement." The star (as well as story type to a certain extent) seems to be quite important in integrating the film viewer into the screen world. Although a genuine "star" is not always present in a film, that does not mean that identification cannot and does not occur. Film viewers also identify with noncelebrity actors as a result of the actor's characterization of an individual immersed in specific situations. (Quite probably there is an element of this in identifications with celebrities as well.) It is in this regard that one must study such things as point of view, since its structure "is a mechanism whereby we experience contemporaneously with a character" (Branigan, 1975: 64).

The Nature of the Viewing Experience 189

An extension of these formulations is provided by Browne (1975-76). To the triangle of spectator position, camera point of view, and a character's perspective (i.e., the normal notion of identification), one must add an identification "with a character's position in a certain situation." This means that "the way we as spectators are implicated in the action is as much a matter of our position with respect to the unfolding of those events in time as in their representation from a point in space" (emphasis added). Ultimately, Browne claims, the structures through which the spectator is so implicated in the action "convey and are closely allied to the guiding moral commentary of the film." In other words, the meaning that the film conveys operates in the moral, normative, or ideological realm.

Noble (1975) introduces an argument, based on a theory of viewing somewhat similar to the one being developed here, that questions the generalizability of the concept of identification. Film viewing has relatively isolating and engulfing physical and social characteristics when compared with television viewing. As a result film viewers tend more to "lose themselves" in the screen world through identification with one of the film's characters, while television viewers tend more to recognize characters within the drama as similar to people they know in real life. Within this kind of "screen community" television viewers tend to interact with such characters in a more detached manner, in a process that is termed "para- or pseudosocial interaction." Film viewing, then, involves an identity-loss situation. Television viewers, however, because of the more detached and self-conscious attitude involved in the recognition/parasocial interaction process, remain more critical of and less susceptible to influence.

It is perhaps pertinent to raise a number of salient points at this juncture. First, Noble is making his argument strictly in terms of the experiences of children. Second, he does allow that the mode of response to the screen is not determined strictly by the physical differences in the two media per se: "In the cinema, or alternately watching television alone at home with the light off, a viewer is likely to identify with a film character...." Third, he contends that recognition and identification can take place simultaneously and allows that "more viewers may both recognize and identify than either recognize or identify exclusively." Finally, Noble asserts that "identification is part of a developmental process which normal children eventually outgrow."

A tentative theory of the viewing experience

With these qualifiers to Noble's comparison of the film- and television-viewing experiences, it becomes possible to sketch a tentative theory of the general viewing experience. This tentative theory helps us go beyond the what of media effects to the why, as McQuail (1976) suggests is necessary, but it cannot do so completely and can only speculate about the how of these phenomena. As noted above, the viewing experience can be seen to have three components: physical, social, and psychological characteristics. The nature of these characteristics, their relative importance, and their interactions in any particular situation will determine the kinds of effects that a film or other media message will have on a viewer.

The processes at work here may best be seen by taking the two opposite extremes in terms of these three components. At one extreme we have a film shown in a large, well-designed, modern theater equipped with 70mm widescreen projection and Dolby stereo sound. The theater is empty save for our single "subject," who is consequently able to rivet attention on the screen without the distraction of comments and reactions from other audience members--which might "break the spell." Finally, this person is either a young child, an immature adolescent, or an adult with a particular type of deficiency. The psychological characteristics that these three categories of individuals share is a poorly developed sense of identity or sense of self.

Due to the intense stimulation and lack of distraction, the viewer becomes intensely immersed in the flow of the action and identifies strongly with a character in the film. The lack of detachment and lack of self-consciousness of this relationship between the viewer and the screen world causes him or her to see the activities and events portrayed as more real than imaginary. In this most extreme case of projection the individual sees himself or herself in real life as he or she pictures the favored star in the film. In other words, in this identity-loss situation the viewer assumes the identity of the character/star and will in all likelihood imitate or replicate the types of behavior that the star has been seen to exhibit. Such a phenomenon usually comes to public attention only when the imitated behavior involves antisocial activities, such as violence. This was "the case [with such films as] A Clockwork Orange, Fuzz, and La Grande Casse [and more recently The Warriors, for] certain sections of the audience, notably youth gangs, [who] were able to identify with the "heroes" of the films; without strong social inhibitions against the use of violence, the process of identification led to imitations of these models' acts of violence" (Stanley and Riera, 1977: 83).

At the other extreme we can imagine a small, poorly tuned, black-and-white television set with poor sound quality located in a brightly lighted room inhabited by a crowd of mature, well-adjusted adults who have gathered specifically to use the television program as an excuse for, and aid to, social interactions. In this type of situation the physical, social, and psychological characteristics are so arranged that identification is reduced to the level of emotional affinity or does not occur at all. Alternately, the possibility of parasocial interaction could be enhanced, although the relationship between degree of identification (as developed by Tudor) and parasocial interaction (as described by Noble) is not clear and requires further investigation. The pertinent point, however, is that this situation does not involve identity loss as the previous one did. These individuals will be more self-conscious about, and more critical in their reactions to, the material they are viewing. Imitation or replication of observed behavior will be highly unlikely (unless, perhaps, they fall prey to some sort of "mob" or "crowd" psychology). Even in this second case, however, there will probably be "effects"; it is just that they will be more indirect and positive than those of the first example. If the viewers engage in parasocial interactions with characters in the television program, these interactions allow them the opportunity to explore social roles and reintegrate themselves into a wider society, as well as see themselves with greater insight (Noble, 1975).

Most viewing situations probably fall between these two extremes. The appropriate blend of the three viewing-experience variables could lead to crazes or fads, such as the bare-chested male phenomenon that struck the undershirt trade so hard after Clark Gable appeared without his shirt in It Happened One Night (Jowett and Linton, 1980: 105-106); to a profound impression on our "visual repository," as in the case of The Wild One influencing succeeding generations of motorcycle gangs, and, more generally, the western's molding of our impression of the old West (Jowett and Linton, 1980: 111); and to our stereotyped view of groups and whole races of people on the basis of their depiction in movies. This is the reason that minorities have been so concerned with such portrayals, as evidenced not too long ago by homosexuals' vociferous denunciation of the picture painted of their lifestyle in Cruising and Chinese-Americans' anger at their treatment in Charlie Chan and the Curse of the Dragon Queen. It is in this area between the two extremes that the majority of the movies' influence on our values, attitudes, and beliefs takes place, although it is still not clear as to exactly how such "effects" occur.

The concern with explicating the nature of the viewing experience and examining its role in determining effects has perhaps overemphasized its role in this process and obscured the role of other factors. As Tudor (1969) points out, we must have some understanding of the "language" of films and the cultural conventions surrounding them, in addition to an understanding of the viewing experience, if we are to identify and "measure" effects. Although it is impossible to deal with these phenomena in the detail they warrant in a discussion such as this, there are two pertinent points that can be briefly sketched here. In terms of film "language" it is important to note that the dominance of the narrative structure as a filmic form (Linton and Jowett, 1977) meshes well with the requirements of identification. A central characteristic of narrative films is their tendency to conceal their process of narration (i.e., the stylistic means whereby the filmic story is presented) in favor of emphasizing the plot or story (Hanet, 1974-75). The aim of the narrative film is "to eliminate intrusive camera presence and prevent distancing awareness in the audience" (Mulvey, 1975: 17).

This feature of narrative films is further strengthened by a prominent cultural convention: what can be called the "movie as entertainment" ideology that pervades North American society (Linton, 1978). Films are approached as light, somewhat frivolous, value-neutral and socially innocent experiences that allow people to escape from the cares of everyday life or to find satisfaction for "various latent needs or predispositions" (Gans, 1957: 315). This ethic further reinforces the tendency of viewers to approach films in a relaxed, receptive state and, as a result, to be susceptible to new attitudes and opinions, beliefs, and values dealing with inessential or unfamiliar matters and to have strongly held pre-existing ones reinforced--both areas in which mass communications are accepted to be the most potent (Halloran, 1964; Klapper, 1960).

Conclusion

The nature of the viewing experience generally influences the kinds of effects that follow exposure to films and other media. The more that the physical, social, and psychological characteristics are arranged to engender intense identification (ideally to the point of confusion of reality and fantasy), the more likely it is that the resultant effects will be direct, in the form of behavioral imitation. Although the operation of the less intense forms of identification and of parasocial interaction require more investigation, at this stage our "theory" posits that such states will produce indirect effects on values, beliefs, and attitudes. The precise manner in which this happens, however, requires more careful study of the entire process. In all, the confusing area of film effects (and those of other media) deserves--perhaps even demands--to be better understood.

References

Branigan, Edward. "Formal Permutations of the Point-of-View Shot." Screen 16, 3 (1975): 54-64.
Browne, Nick. "The Spectator-in-the-Text: The Rhetoric of Stagecoach." Film Quarterly 29, 2 (1975-76): 26-38.
Clark, Cedric. "Race, Identification, and Television Violence." In Television and Social Behavior, edited by G. A. Comstock, E. A. Rubinstein, and J. P. Murray. Washington, D.C.: U.S. Government Printing Office, Vol. V, pp. 120-184.
Cook, Bruce. "Why TV Stars Don't Become Movie Stars (And on the other hand, some movie stars don't do too well on television)." American Film 1, 8 (1976): 58, 60.
Dart, Peter. "The Concept of 'Identification' in Film Theory." Paper presented at the Thirtieth Annual Conference of the University Film Association, Iowa State University, 1976.
Feilitzen, Cecilia V., and Olga Linné. "Identifying with Television Characters." Journal of Communication 25, 4 (1975): 51-55.
Gans, Herbert J. "The Creator-Audience Relationship in the Mass Media: An Analysis of Movie Making." In Mass Culture: The Popular Arts in America, edited by Bernard Rosenberg and David Manning White. New York: Free Press, 1957, pp. 315-324.
Halloran, J. D. The Effects of Mass Communication, with

194 FILM/CULTURE

Special Reference to Television. Leicester: Leicester University Press, 1964.

Hanet, Kari. "The Narrative Text of Shock Corridor." Screen 16, 3 (1974-75): 18-28.

Jowett, Garth, and James M. Linton. Movies as Mass Communication. Beverly Hills: Sage, 1980.

————, Penny Reath, and Monica Schouten. "The Control of Mass Entertainment Media in Canada, the United States and Great Britain: Historical Surveys." In Report of the Royal Commission on Violence in the Communications Industry. Volume 4: Violence in Print and Music. Toronto: Queen's Printer for Ontario, 1977, pp. 1-104.

Klapper, Joseph T. The Effects of Mass Communication. New York: Free Press, 1960.

Linton, James. "But It's Only a Movie." Jump Cut 17 (1978): 16-19.

————, and Garth S. Jowett. "A Content Analysis of Feature Films." In Report of the Royal Commission on Violence in the Communications Industry. Volume 3: Violence in Television, Films and News. Toronto: Queen's Printer for Ontario, 1977, pp. 465-580.

Maccoby, Eleanor E. "The Effects of the Mass Media." In Violence and the Mass Media, edited by Otto N. Larsen. New York: Harper and Row, 1968, pp. 118-123.

McQuail, Denis. "Alternate Models of Television Influence." In Children and Television, edited by Ray Brown. Beverly Hills: Sage, 1976, pp. 341-360.

Mulvey, Laura. "Visual Pleasure and Narrative Cinema." Screen 16, 3 (1975): 6-18.

Noble, Gordon. Children in Front of the Small Screen. Beverly Hills: Sage, 1975.

Stanley, Paul R. A., and Brian Riera. "Replications of Media Violence." In Report of the Royal Commission on Violence in the Communications Industry. Volume 5: Learning from the Media. Toronto: Queen's Printer for Ontario, 1977, pp. 57-88.

Taylor, John Russell. "Movies for a Small Screen." Sight and Sound 44, 2 (1975): 113-115.

Tudor, Andrew. "Film and the Measurement of Its Effects." Screen 10, 4/5 (1969): 148-159.

————. Image and Influence: Studies in the Sociology of Film. London: Allen and Unwin, 1974.

FILM EFFECTS AND ETHNICITY

Gorham Kindem and
Charles Teddlie

Hollywood protrayals of ethnic minorities have aroused public interest and concern since at least 1915, when a group of black Americans in Boston rioted in protest of D. W. Griffith's Birth of a Nation (Cripps, 1971: 118-124). Many groups are still angered by stereotypes presented in Hollywood films today. Native Americans, Italian-Americans, and Chinese-Americans have protested revived stereotypes of Indian savagery, mafia brutality, and Charlie Chan "fortune cookie" logic. This antagonism is based at least in part, upon the assumption that a film can positively or negatively affect the ethnic attitudes of audience members. But how can we know this? How can we measure the impact of films upon American society?

Social scientists have since the 1930s been studying how and to what extent films affect people's ethnic attitudes. In the early thirties psychologist Lewis L. Thurstone tested the effects of several feature films, including Birth of a Nation, upon the ethnic attitudes of white school children (Thurstone, 1931; Charters, 1935: 18-25). He discovered that Birth of a Nation significantly increased their antiblack prejudice (Hoban and Van Ormer, 1951: 5, 13-14; Charters, 1935: 21). In the late 1950s sociologist Russell Middleton tested the effects of Gentleman's Agreement (a film about prejudice against Jews) upon the anti-

Semitic attitudes of white college students. He discovered that this film significantly reduced their anti-Semitism (Middleton, 1960: 679-784). Of course, these two films have drastically different ideological perspectives in their content. Thurstone's and Middleton's experiments, as we shall see, provide only partial answers; recent research sheds more light upon these problems. But before we examine this research in greater detail, we must understand the general theoretical context within which cognitive film-effects research has taken place.

Theories of film effects

The field of film (and general mass media) effects is crowded with theories, many of which contradict each other. These theories try to explain film and mass-media effects by focusing upon one or more of the following aspects of the communications process: 1/ source, 2/ message form and content, 3/ channel, 4/ receiver, and 5/ social context (McGuire, 1973: 223-240). The "source" is the person or persons emitting the communication. The "message form" defines the way the message is structured (e.g., comic versus serious), and the "message content" is the substance or meaning of the message. The "channel" is the mode or medium of presentation (e.g., direct face-to-face conversation). The "receiver" is simply the recipient of the message, and the "social context" defines the particular social situation within which the transmission and reception of the communication takes place (in a crowded theater with strangers or at home with a few family members in broad daylight, and so on).

The crudest theories of film effects--the hypodermic theory and the theory of selective perception--focus upon the "message" and "receiver" variables, respectively, to the exclusion of all other aspects of the communication process. The hypodermic theory suggests that films are injected into people's heads and affect everyone in the same manner and to the same degree. The hypodermic theory offers a simplistic stimulus-response model, assuming a one-way form of communication from communicator to receiver (Tudor, 1974: 30-39). At the opposite extreme resides the theory of selective perception, which suggests that the receiver determines what, if any, effects a film has, and that the message received is necessarily consistent with the receiver's prior attitudes, needs, and beliefs. The hypodermic theory implies that film and other mass media are all-powerful and that their effects are universal and inevitable; the theory of selective perception suggests that the receiver is all-powerful, and that evoking attitude changes (and other effects) through films is virtually impossible (Jarvie, 1970: 102-103).

Several theories concentrate upon the "social context" within which communication takes place. The theory of two-step flow (Katz and Lazarsfeld, 1955) attempts to explain mass-media effects on the basis of "opinion leaders," the more influential members of society who mediate between the communication message/channel and its receivers. Opinion leaders can reinforce, deny, or change messages and determine their impact, according to this theory. It seems doubtful, however, that all film messages are in fact mediated through opinion leaders.

Also focusing upon the social context is the theory of subcultures (Gans, 1957). This theory suggests that filmmakers have an imagined audience with which they communicate (hence communication is not a one-way hypodermic injection), and that the audience for one type of film differs from the audience for another (Jarvie, 1970: 104-105). Film subcultures are groups of filmmakers/films/audiences, which remain independent of each other for the most part. The effects that any one film can have are largely restricted to and limited by its specific subculture. This theory also implies that there is little chance that a film produced for a specific subculture will change attitudes to any significant degree, since it is unlikely that a subculture will form around films, filmmakers, or film genres that contradict many of its basic attitudes.

The dependency theory (DeFleur and Ball-Rokeach, 1975: 261-280) offers a complex model that suggests that mass-media messages will maximize their range of effects when media systems "serve many unique and central information-delivery functions" and "when there is a high degree of structural instability in society due to conflict and change." In other words, the dependency model argues that the precise effect of a film is determined by the degree to which people are dependent upon film for information about a particular subject and the relative degree of stability in their society at the time the film is seen (DeFleur and Ball-Rokeach, 1975: 263).

Mass-media social psychologists, unlike mass-media sociologists, have concentrated their theories upon the source, message form and content, and receiver variables in the communication process, rather than the social context. Some psychologists have suggested that the message form (humor versus serious address, say) and order (primacy versus recency) are important determinants of attitude change (McGuire, 1973: 232-237). Theories of persuasibility provide explanations of the differential effects of certain types of messages on different demographic groups or personality types. A number of theories focus upon source-receiver and message-receiver discrepancy, like the previously mentioned theory of selective perception, as well as the assimilation-contrast theory, which suggests that people have individual latitudes of acceptance for views that differ from their own and that the amount of change that takes place varies with the individual's latitude of acceptance (McGuire, 1973: 240). In short, mass-media social psychologists offer us a different perspective on film effects. They accentuate the importance of individual differences in determining the impact of messages and suggest that certain kinds of film messages will be more effective with one type of person than another.

Early research in film effects and ethnicity: theoretical contexts

The experiment of Thurstone either implicitly or explicitly reinforces the hypodermic theory of mass-media effects (Tudor, 1974: 92-99). That the films under study significantly changed the overall score of entire groups suggests that they can have extensive general effects (reinforcing the popular concern about the powerful and deleterious effects of mass media in general). But when we look more closely at Thurstone's experiment, we discover that he selected young subjects who rarely saw films at all and had little or no personal knowledge of or interaction with blacks (Hoban and van Ormer, 1951: 5, 13). If we apply the dependency theory to Thurstone's experiment, our hypothesis might be that the students' dependency upon film for information about blacks during an unstable economic period (the Depression) increased the possibility of significant attitude change. A theory of persuasibility suggests that schoolchildren are more impressionable than adults, and that age alone (Thurstone did not differentiate subjects on the basis of age even though he used students in many different grades; Hoban and van Ormer, 1951: 5, 13) is responsible for the significant change in their attitudes. Finally, the particular form of the message (a serious fictional drama) may be significant. Thurstone's exploratory study did not really control for message form and content variables. He simply pretested hundreds of films until he found a few that appeared to have significant attitudinal effects on the group as a whole, and these films became the focus of his study (Charters, 1935: 19-20).

Middleton's experiment concentrated upon receiver persuasibility. He examined the effects of *Gentleman's Agreement* upon college students who had different demographic and personality characteristics: sex, home residence, degree of personal anxiety and social isolation, socioeconomic status, status concern, conservatism, authoritarianism, religious orthodoxy, and initial degree of anti-Semitism (Middleton, 1960: 681). The film was marginally more effective in reducing the anti-Semitism of women than that of men, but the only truly significant receiver variable in terms of persuasibility was the initial degree of anti-Semitism. Middleton's attitude-measurement scale had certain inherent problems that made it difficult to draw definite conclusions. However, Middleton found that the amount of attitude change that took place was related to the receiver's recognition of the specific theme ("that people who are chiefly to blame for the persistence and growth of anti-Semitism are the decent, intelligent individuals who are not anti-Semitic but who remain passive and take no militant steps to stamp out prejudice") and the general theme ("Jews suffer injustice as a result of anti-Semitic prejudice") of the film. The fact that low initial levels of anti-Semitism were positively correlated with a recognition of the specific and general themes of the film led Middleton to conclude that the film was more effective in changing the attitudes of initially low-prejudiced receivers than those of initially high-prejudiced receivers (Middleton, 1960: 682-686).

The measurement of ethnic stereotypes and prejudicial attitudes

The assessment of film effects upon ethnic attitudes has depended upon the development of accurate and reliable measurement techniques. Thurstone developed his own attitude scales for his film experiments. These scales were composed of positive and negative statements concerning various ethnic groups. The students' responses to these statements before and after viewing a specific film could be compared and the general film effects assessed. Thurstone's were among the most widely used attitude-measurement techniques, until the relatively recent development of many alternative scales and indirect methods of attitude assessment (Summers, 1970).

Recent research in social psychology has examined the connection between ethnic stereotypes and more general ethnic attitudes (Brigham, 1971). Assessing changes in ethnic stereotypes has provided a means for evaluating the changes that occur in prejudicial attitudes after viewing a film.

Ethnic stereotypes

According to Brigham (1977: 15), there has been considerable ambiguity in the conceptual and methodological areas of ethnic-stereotype research. Lippmann (1922) broadly defined stereotypes as having three characteristics: 1/ they are factually incorrect; 2/ they are produced through illogical reasoning; and 3/ they are rigid. The broadness of this definition has led to several directions in stereotype research and an increasing confusion about what actually constitutes a stereotype.

One area of controversy centers on Lippmann's contention that stereotypes are factually incorrect. La Piere's (1936: 232-237) study of Armenian laborers is often given as evidence for this position, since the stereotype for Armenians did not fit the characteristics that La Piere observed. Support for the "kernel of truth" hypothesis has mounted over the years (Campbell, 1967: 817-829), however, and Brigham (1971: 15-35) concluded that stereotypes do have some truth, since there is agreement between several groups as to the traits that characterize a particular object group.

Brigham (1971: 15-35) attempted to clarify some of the conceptual ambiguity in the area by redefining stereotypes as follows: "An ethnic stereotype is a generalization made about an ethnic group, concerning a trait attribution, which is considered to be unjustified by an observer." The key word in this definition is "unjustified," which has two distinct interpretations according to Brigham: 1/ a stereotype may be unjustified when it does not correspond to the facts; and 2/ a stereotype may be unjustified when it serves as a rationalization for prejudicial or discriminatory social practices, which themselves may be unjustified. This definition encompasses the contradictory findings of the "kernel of truth" hypothesis.

The methodological problems inherent in measuring and evaluating ethnic stereotypes have been difficult to resolve. In 1933 Katz and Braly established a research paradigm that has become the most frequently used device for stereotype research. They asked college students at Princeton University to select traits that were the most characteristic of each of several ethnic groups. The respondents showed a high level of agreement.

Katz and Braly's paradigm suffers from a number of methodological problems. First, it allows for no assessment of the degree to which a subject feels a trait applies to an ethnic group. For instance, a subject may feel that "intelligent" and "materialistic" characterize most Jewish Americans and would list them both using the Katz and Braly technique, but the subject may also feel that "intelligent" is a more common characteristic of Jewish Americans than "materialistic." The Katz and Braly technique fails to make this distinction. Similarly, it does not allow for differentiation of positive and negative characteristics. In the example above, the stereotype of "intelligent" is qualitatively different from that of "materialistic," since the former has a generally positive connotation, while the latter has a generally negative one.

Mann (1967: 235-245) and Brigham (1971: 15-35) have made two improvements upon the original Katz and Braly paradigm. First, instead of simply listing traits for each ethnic group, subjects are asked to assign a percentage estimate (0%, 20%, 40%, 60%, 80%, 100%) of the number of ethnic-group members who possess a specific characteristic or trait. This change allows for an assessment of the degree to which a subject stereotypes an ethnic group. The second change involves an assignment of positive or negative values to the particular trait under study. Typically a subject is asked how positive or negative a characteristic or trait appears to be at the same time that he or she is assigning that trait to an ethnic group. This methodological change allows for the differentiation of positive and negative stereotypes. These two improvements upon the Katz and Braly paradigm allow a researcher to evaluate the strength and direction of an individual's stereotypes. It may be that an extreme percentage, like 80% or above for a negative trait or 20% or below for a positive trait, can then be defined as a strong negative ethnic stereotype (Brigham, 1971: 32-33).

Ethnic stereotypes and prejudicial attitudes

Brigham (1971: 34) has demonstrated that significant statistical relations exist between ethnic-stereotype attributions (Katz and Braly, 1933) and general ethnic attitudes or prejudices, as measured by other widely used and validated attitude-measurement techniques. Attitudes have cognitive, affective, and conative components. "Cognitive" refers to the aspect of the attitude that is measured by a checklist of traits for a particular ethnic group. A stereotype is thus a component of an attitude. "Affective" refers to the liking a subject has for a particular ethnic group. Finally, "conative" refers to the aspect of the attitude that has to do with the subject's behavioral intentions toward an ethnic group. Research has shown that these three components are closely related to each other (McGuire, 1973: 219-220). This relationship suggests that measuring one component of an attitude, like the cognitive component of ethnic stereotypes, provides a strong indication of an individual's overall attitude, like the overall attitude toward that ethnic group.

Recent research in film effects and ethnicity

A recent study by Kindem and Teddlie (1979) extends the earlier work of Thurstone and Middleton. Kindem and Teddlie examined the effects of two films, Blazing Saddles (1974) and Nothing But a Man (1962), on the ethnic stereotypes and prejudicial attitudes of white college students at a major southern university. They used a modified form of the Katz and Braly paradigm (discussed above) to measure ethnic attitudes and compare pretest (prefilm) and posttest scores for attitude change. Their study extends the research of Thurstone and Middleton by examining both message form and receiver variables in the same study. Thurstone operated within the context of the hypodermic theory, which stresses message variables (different films), while Middleton worked within the context of the theory of selective perception, which concentrates upon the receiver variables that affect persuasibility. Kindem and Teddlie examined the separate and joint effects of message form (comic satire versus serious drama) and receiver variables (initial prejudice level, academic achievement, and sex) on the change in subjects' ethnic attitudes.

Method

The subjects for this study were seventy students enrolled in a survey course in broadcasting and film for nonmajors, taught at the University of North Carolina at Chapel Hill

Film Effects and Ethnicity 203

during the spring semester of 1979. The students were asked if they had ever seen Blazing Saddles or Nothing But a Man and were then divided into two groups of first-time viewers for the two films.

Two experimental sessions were held for the subjects: 1/ the first occurred one week before the film screening and consisted of the administration of the pretest questionnaire; and 2/ the second session was devoted to observation of the film and administration of the posttest questionnaire (identical to the pretest questionnaire).

The pretest and posttest questionnaires comprised items that asked students to estimate the percentage of each of three ethnic groups (Jewish Americans, black Americans, and white-Christian Americans) to which specific terms, like "aggressive" or "very religious," applied. The students were also asked to rate these terms on a five-point scale ranging from very negative (-2) to very positive (+2) on the pretest questionnaire. By multiplying the rating of each term and the percentage of each ethnic group to which this term applied, and summing up the total, the researchers computed an overall attitudinal score toward each ethnic group for each subject. By comparing the pretest and posttest scores, they made an assessment of attitudinal changes that occurred as a result of watching the films.

Results

Two analyses were performed to ascertain the impact that message form and receiver variables had, separately and in conjunction with one another, on the ethnic attitudes of subjects. The first analysis examined the impact of three independent variables: 1/ type of film--Blazing Saddles (comic satire) or Nothing But a Man (serious drama); 2/ initial prejudice level of subject--high, medium, or low; and 3/ academic achievement of subject--high, medium, or low. Film type (comic satire versus serious drama) was a message-form variable; prejudice level and academic achievement were receiver variables. Prejudice level of subject was determined by subtracting the individual's attitude score toward blacks from his or her attitude score toward whites on the pretest questionnaire (0 or less = low prejudice toward blacks; 2-18 = medium prejudice toward blacks; and 20 or more = high prejudice toward blacks). Subjects were divided into high, medium, and low academic achievers according to their grade-point averages (low = under 2.5; medium = 2.6-3.0; and high = 3.0 and above).

Academic-achievement level was not found to have a significant impact on attitudes. However, there was a significant interaction between the film factor and the prejudice level of the viewer on change in attitude toward blacks. As Table 1 indicates, Blazing Saddles was most effective in positively changing the attitudes of medium-prejudiced subjects towards blacks; Nothing But a Man was most effective in positively changing the attitudes of low-prejudiced subjects toward blacks. The serious dramatic film was thus the better manipulator of attitude for a receptive audience (this study reaffirms Middleton's conclusions concerning the effects of Gentleman's Agreement), while the comic film works better for a slightly prejudiced audience.

TABLE 1

Means for change in attitude toward blacks depending on film viewed and subject's prejudice level.*

	Blazing Saddles	Nothing But a Man
Low Prejudiced	-11.53	14.54
Medium Prejudiced	10.75	0.75
High Prejudiced	1.27	6.00

*Larger numbers indicate more positive change in attitudes towards blacks from the pretest to the posttest.

These differential effects can be understood in more detail by observing the mean scores for attitudes toward blacks on the posttest questionnaire (see Table 2). The interaction between film and prejudice level of viewer was marginally significant on this variable. Middle- and high-prejudiced subjects make approximately the same ratings of blacks whether they observed Nothing But a Man or Blazing Saddles. Low-prejudiced subjects, on the other hand, rated blacks more positively after watching Nothing But a Man than they did after watching Blazing Saddles. A serious, realistic treatment of blacks resulted in a more positive reaction from low-prejudiced subjects than a satiric presentation did.

TABLE 2

Means for the posttest measure of attitude toward blacks depending on film viewed and subject's prejudice level.*

	Blazing Saddles	Nothing But a Man
Low Prejudiced	59.4	69.1
Medium Prejudiced	54.4	54.1
High Prejudiced	47.6	44.7

*Larger numbers indicate a more favorable attitude toward blacks.

    The present study thus extends earlier work in the area by demonstrating not only significant effects for the message form (films) and the receiver variables (prejudice level), but also an interaction between the two. In order to explore further the interaction between message form and receiver variables, a second analysis was undertaken. Film was again included as the "medium form" variable, and sex of subject was included as a receiver variable. This second analysis yielded a significant sex effect, but no significant effect for film and no significant interaction between sex and film. The significant sex effect indicated that women's attitudes toward blacks improved more significantly than men's regardless of which film they observed. This result parallels Middleton's previous findings and reinforces the theory of differential persuasibility by sex.

Conclusion

These results suggest that a serious drama will be more

effective at reducing the ethnic prejudices of low-prejudiced subjects than medium-prejudiced subjects, but a comic satire will be more effective at reducing the ethnic prejudices of slightly more prejudiced people. Both types of film appear to be somewhat less successful in terms of reducing the ethnic prejudice of highly prejudiced subjects. Finally, women will be more profoundly affected by both types of criticism of ethnic prejudice.

If the results of this experiment are generalizable to the social context within which films are commercially viewed, the differential effects of the films in the laboratory should be indicative of its potential social effects upon American society. In short, among a college audience we should expect that these films have had a positive effect in terms of reducing the ethnic prejudices of certain types of people. Although provisions were made to make the viewing setting much like the social context within which films are viewed on campus, caution must be exercised in assuming that the laboratory experiment is a complete analog of normal viewing conditions. Taking surveys undoubtedly sensitizes students to certain contents of the films, which may be more readily ignored in the commercial marketplace, and the sensitization to ethnic prejudice stimulated by the initial questionnaire may have affected the results. Nonetheless, this experiment gives us some means of specifying the effects that feature films can have upon our ethnic attitudes, and it builds upon and extends the previous experimental research of Thurstone and Middleton.

The effects that films have upon us are complex and varied. The progress of film-effects research has been to illuminate a complex web of variables in each aspect of the communication process (source, message, channel, receiver, and social context) that determines the precise effects that any film has upon us. Future research will undoubtedly reveal important new variables and determinants of film effects upon ethnic stereotypes and prejudicial attitudes.

References

Brigham, John C. "Ethnic Stereotypes." Psychological Bulletin 76 (1971): 15-38.
Campbell, D. T. "Stereotypes and the Perception of Group

Differences." American Psychologist 22 (1967): 817-829.
Charters, Werrett Wallace. Motion Pictures and Youth; A Summary. New York: Macmillan, 1935.
Cripps, Thomas R. "The Reaction of the Negro to the Motion Picture, Birth of a Nation." In Focus on The Birth of a Nation, edited by Fred Silva. Englewood Cliffs, N.J.: Prentice-Hall, 1971.
DeFleur, Melvin L., and Sandra Ball-Rokeach. Theories of Mass Communication. 3rd ed. New York: McKay, 1975.
Gans, Herbert J. "The Creator-Audience Relationship in the Mass Media: An Analysis of Movie Making." In Mass Culture, edited by Bernard Rosenberg and David Manning White. Glencoe, Ill.: Free Press, 1957, pp. 315-324.
_____. "The Relationship Between the Movies and the Public, and Some Implications for Movie Criticism and Movie Making." Unpublished. Referenced in Movies and Society, by I. C. Jarvie. New York: Basic Books, 1970.
Hoban, Charles F., Jr., and Edward B. Van Ormer. "Film Research to 1950." Unpublished. Pennsylvania State College, 1951. (Commissioned military study.)
Jarvie, I. C. Movies and Society. New York: Basic Books, 1970.
Katz, D., and Braly, K. "Racial Stereotypes in One Hundred College Students." Journal of Abnormal and Social Psychology 28 (1933): 280-290.
Katz, Eluhn, and Paul F. Lazarsfeld. Personal Influence. Glencoe, Ill.: Free Press, 1955.
Kindem, Gorham, and Charles Teddlie. "Attacking Prejudice with Comic Satire and Serious Drama." An unpublished paper delivered at the University Film Association Annual Conference, 1979. FRIP.
La Piere, R. T. "Type-Rationalizations of Group Anti-Play." Social Forces 15 (1936): 232-237.
Lippmann, W. Public Opinion. New York: Harcourt, Brace, 1922.
McGuire, William J. "Persausion, Resistance, and Attitude Change." In Handbook of Communication, edited by Ithiel de Sola Pool and Wilbur Schramm. Chicago: Rand McNally, 1973, pp. 216-252.
Mann, J. W. "Inconsistent Thinking About Group and Individual." Journal of Social Psychology 71 (1967): 235-245.

Middleton, Russell. "Ethnic Prejudice and Susceptibility to Persuasion." American Sociological Review 25 (1960): 679-684.

Summers, Gene F. Attitude Measurement. Chicago: Rand McNally, 1970.

Thurstone, L. L. "The Measurement of Social Attitudes." Journal of Abnormal and Social Psychology 26 (1931): 249-269.

―――. "The Measurement of Social Attitudes." Journal of Social Psychology 2 (1931): 230-235.

―――. "The Influence of Motion Pictures on Children's Attitudes." Journal of Social Psychology 2 (1931): 291-304.

Tudor, Andrew. Image and Influence: Studies in the Sociology of Film. London: Allen and Unwin, 1974.

THEY TAUGHT IT AT THE MOVIES: FILMS AS MODELS FOR LEARNED SEXUAL BEHAVIOR

Garth S. Jowett

In 1922 the distinguished American historian Ellis Paxson Oberholtzer, who had been a member of the Pennsylvania State Board of Censors for six years, wrote of the movies that

> we hear on all sides of us that the innocence and charm of young womanhood, the chivalry of young manhood are disappearing--that they have disappeared.... Thus do child and youth pass from one experience to another under the guidance of the picture maker and exhibitor.... Our old standards and ideals have been encroached upon, little by little, until we are now completely submerged. Here we are at this moment with a great industry clamoring, and threatening us, and intimidating us, and bribing us for continued right to go its course without restraint, while we are considered old-fashioned, or worse, for suggesting that it may not be a discreet thing to put all our children to school in the theatre [1922: 84].

Oberholtzer's views were based on his tenure not only as a censor but as one of those "custodians of the culture" so eloquently described by Henry F. May in his seminal work The End of American Innocence. May notes that "it is easier to laugh at the professional custodians of culture, a group

of men, mostly elderly, who were quite sure that they had
the precious commodity and also that it was their special
duty to dispense it.... Many must be given at least the
credit due sincerity and public spirit" (1959: 31). The movies represented for the "custodians of culture" a very distinct and dangerous rending of the cultural and social fabric;
and in no aspect of American life was this more obvious than
in the dispensation of sexual information by the new forms of
entertainment then establishing themselves.

In 1922 the public manifestations of the social and cultural transformations that had radically altered the shape of
a largely Victorian prewar America were the subjects of a
wide-ranging and intense debate. The unexpected entrance
into a largely European war, the unsatisfactory conclusion
to that war, and the decision to withdraw once again into an
insulated security had left the American people with a renewed sense of internal vitality. But the old, largely rural-based America, which represented the symbol of inner strength
and morality for the "custodians of culture," had by now been
displaced by a new social and cultural order, where the growth
of the urban, mostly Catholic (and to a lesser extent Jewish)
population caused the emergence of their culture to a position
of equal prominence. The clash of cultural value systems
was inevitable. [1]

The nature of this clash between the previously dominant Anglo-Saxon cultural and moral ideology and the values
of the urban-based immigrant groups took many forms. Some
historians have seen the imposition of prohibition in 1919 as
symbolic of this fight for dominance (Gusfield, 1963). Others
have suggested that "the place and role of the United States
in world affairs" was also a point of dispute between the
"villagers" and the "urbanites" (Baritz, 1970). However, in
any historical assessment of the manifestations of this cultural jockeying for position, the role and content of the new
forms of mass communication must receive close attention.
These new forms of information were able to bypass the traditional socializing institutions, such as the school, the
church, and the family, and establish direct contact with the
individual. Today the study of the "effects" of communication
has achieved a level of sophistication and understanding that
informs us that "direct contact" does not necessarily mean
"direct influence." Nevertheless, the concern was that the
information being disseminated by newspapers, magazines,
movies, and, later in the twenties, radio was not subject
to the usual strictness associated with normative socialized

behavior. (See DeFleur and Ball-Rokeach, 1975, on the concept of "direct-influence.")

One aspect of this "socialization by entertainment" issue aroused the ire of the culture custodians above all others, and this was the imparting of sexual information, especially in the guise of commercial entertainment. Much of the concern stemmed from a value system based upon the lingering combination of obsolescent Victorianism and the vestiges of Puritanism that even condemned the study of sexuality as being itself an aberrant form of behavior.

Even today the question of sexual socialization is largely unanswered. As one prominent source has noted: "That we know so little about human sexual behavior and its socialization must be attributed to the sexual taboos of our society and to their being especially severe in relation to children" (Zigler and Child, 1969: 517). What we do know from studies of intersocietal and intrasocietal studies of the variations in adult sexual behavior is that specific differences in sexual socialization do play a significant part in the existence of such variations. What is of special interest in this study are the findings that the rise in sexual interest, as the individual enters adolescence, is more the result of sociocultural influence than of hormonal or other physiological changes. Clearly then, sexual behavior is largely due to socialization; but where do children learn sexual behavior?

The question of formal socialization of sexual behavior has received much attention from anthropologists, especially in their studies of "primitive" societies. We do know that in the United States methods of formal sexual socialization are extremely rare; most of the information is imparted in the haphazard, informal manner. Where much of the socialized information is obtained by discussion with peers, equally ignorant, the need for specific instruction is increased. In the eighties there is an abundance of such material available to any who look for it; but in the period 1920 to 1950 such opportunities were not as frequent, and adolescents, and even adults, were forced to use other sources for the modeling of their sexual behavior.

The movies have always been a potent source of information, especially in areas where the audience has very little prior information, or where the audience may be actively seeking such information. It is therefore only natural to suggest that during the period of their greatest acceptance as the premier medium of entertainment, 1920-1950, the movies did act as a major source of socialization of sexual conduct. It is acknowledged that the content of films during this period was not as sexually explicit as that available today; however, the form of sexual behavior we may turn our attention to here is "courting"--male-female romantic attitudes in the premarriage situation. Essentially we are concerned with what was learned from the movies about how to be "romantic" with the opposite sex. This is a significant question, because in the absence of any formal socialization, courting behavior in the movies became the most powerful role model for two generations of American adolescents and has had a significant influence on current attitudes of romantic and sexual love.

The evidence for concern

In 1915, in his pioneering book on juvenile delinquency, The Individual Delinquent, William Healy noted that attendance at moving-picture shows were often a factor in many of the case histories he described. In particular he was concerned by the opportunities presented by the darkened movie house for the kinds of sexual activities that, in that prewar era, were still considered to be physically and psychologically harmful. Healy noted in case #225:

> We have had much evidence, sometimes in remarkable ways, that moving pictures may be stimulating to the sex instinct. We should expect pictures of love-making and similar scenes to have this effect on young adults or older adolescents, but we have strikingly heard of it in children. The effect is not only felt at the moment, but also there is the establishment of memory pictures which come up at other times, such as when the individual is in bed. We have found that bad sex habits sometimes center around these pictures. In some instances a very definite mental conflict ensues, with production of delinquency along other lines [1915: 308].

Healy then goes on to make his most telling point:

> No one considering the effect of moving pictures can neglect the possibilities for bad behavior which occur through the darkness of the hall in which the pictures are shown. Under cover of dimness evil

> communications readily pass and bad habits are
> taught. Moving picture theaters are favorite places
> for the teaching of homosexual practices [page 308].

These were the thoughts of a highly regarded psychologist, and his condemnations were widely accepted. In all fairness to Healy, however, he did recognize that some individuals were more "susceptible" to such influences than others; but what is even more remarkable is that in a later 1925 study Healy and Bronner claimed that only one percent of the four thousand cases they examined were motivated to sexual misconduct through the influence of moving pictures. (This latter study did not receive the same kind of public attention as the former had.) By 1925 Healy had clearly begun to understand how the movies could influence, and he was able to see such influence in the context of other societal factors (Healy and Bronner, 1926: 281).

The sight of the darkened room where the sexes truly intermingled without the usual chaperones was one that did not please parents, especially those whose own experiences were of Victorian America. Coupled with the largely "antisocial" content of much of what was seen on the screen, whether it be criminal "chase" sequences or flirtatious behavior, it is not surprising that the movies incurred the wrath of the "custodians of culture." The motion picture presented a unique new social problem, for unlike burlesque, its contemporary and rival for the entertainment dollar, it was openly frequented by children; in fact every major study of audience composition in these early years stressed that children under the age of sixteen made up the bulk of the audience during the course of the week. It was this fact, together with the "fear" of the unknown power of the movies and the increasingly bold use of sophisticated sexual content, that proved to be a potent and volatile source of irritation for the reform-minded groups.

The influence of the movies as an impetus toward the development of a new sexual ethic can be gauged by this innocuous-sounding comment taken from the pages of sociologist Donald R. Young's useful book <u>Motion Pictures: A Study in Social Legislation</u>, published in 1922. He noted:

> There is an undoubted effect on standards of conduct resulting from the fact that the audience, often young boys and girls, are packed in narrow seats, close together, in a darkened room. New words

and phrases are coined to meet new situations; and it is significant that the phrases, "movie masher" and "knee flirtation" are coming into use [page 6].

What better example could we have of the expansion of the language to meet the changing demands of social behavior? Similar points were made by others who claimed to observe a boldness in adolescent sexual expression that apparently had not been there before. Here, of course, it is difficult to separate out the distinctive contribution of the movies to these alterations in acceptable behavior, expecially when considered in comparison with other factors, such as the increase in urban living, which allowed young people to have greater access to each other, and the more open forms of behavior exhibited in the city, as opposed to the more clandestine activities in the barns and haystacks on the farm.

Whatever the reasons for this apparent shift toward a more sophisticated adolescent sexuality, the fact remains that the movies took the brunt of the criticism for having precipitated it. Study after study (none of them very scientific) emphasized how much sexual content the movies contained. The Chicago Board of Censors in the period November 1917 to December 1918 ordered more than 960 cuts in films submitted to them; more than fifty percent of these were offenses against "sexual standards" (Young, 1922: 21). In his study of movie content Edgar Dale found that in 1920 fifty-eight percent of movies had "sex" or "love" as their central themes. By 1930 these two categories had declined to forty-five percent, but the loss was entirely from the "love" category (Dale, 1935: 17).

Thus there is very little disputing of the fact that sexual activity, albeit in a watered-down version, was a staple form of content in American films and that younger children were being exposed to it as never before. Not only the frequency but the very nature of the filmic experience suggests that some lessons were being learned in the "darkness of the movie hall."

The evidence for socialization

The problem for social historians dealing with the problem of movie influence is to separate the often irrational rhetoric of those who were concerned with the "evil influence" of the motion pictures from the few attempts to undertake serious examinations of the role of the movies in bringing about important changes in American social interaction.

One major study of American society that has withstood half a century of scholarly analysis is Middletown (actually Muncie, Indiana), by Helen and Robert Lynd. They saw the radio, the automobile, and the movies as equal partners in making Middletown part of an increasing mass society. Even for the Lynds, however, the movies had a special place of importance. So powerful was the role model that the medium provided that its influence on the lifestyle of Middletown adolescents was quite obvious.

On their first visit to Middletown in 1925 the two researchers noted:

> ... while managers lament that there are too few of the popular comedy films, it is the film with burning "heart interest" that packs Middletown's motion picture houses week after week. Young Middletown enters eagerly into the vivid experience of Flaming Youth.... Meanwhile, Down to the Sea in Ships, a costly spectacle of whaling adventure, failed at the leading theater "because," the exhibitor explained, "the whale is really the hero in the film and there wasn't enough "heart interest" for the women" [Lynd and Lynd, 1929: 266].

The Lynds continued their examination of the influence of the movies by questioning educators and parents. They noted:

> Some high school teachers are convinced that the movies are a powerful factor in bringing about the "early sophistication" of the young and the relaxing of social taboos. One working class mother frankly welcomes the movies as an aid in child-rearing, saying, "I send my daughter because a girl has to learn the ways of the world somehow and the movies are a good safe way" [pages 267-268].

When the Lynds returned to Middletown in the early thirties to undertake the research for Middletown in Transition, they found that the Depression had wrought many changes; but the movies were considered to be more of an influence than before. The advent of the talkies and the use of more sophisticated themes meant that the movies played an even greater role in the adolescent sex education of what was a very conservative midwestern community. The Lynds note that a confidential study indicated that seven out of ten "business-class persons" past their twenties have had sexual relations prior to marriage. They contrast this finding with the point that

> sex education in Middletown is not in terms of such practice. On the formal side, the schools do very little, for the obvious reason that is a city whose adults maintain a position of official silence as regards sex, a public agency tends to play safe.... The librarian at the Middletown public library was asked where people in Middletown could get information on sex, and the reply was, "Not here!"
> ... one got in 1935 a sense of sharp, free behavior between the sexes (patterned on the movies), and of less disguise among the young [Lynd and Lynd, 1937: 169-170].

The Lynds find that in a world changing with bewildering swiftness the adolescents of Middletown were confused about which value system or role models to adopt. The bold actions of these individuals are "patterned perhaps not so much upon the lives of their own cautious parents as upon one or another of these alternative other worlds about them." The significance of the movies is made perfectly clear in this socializing and acculturizing process: "... where local patterns are not clear, the sharp figures on the silver screen of the movies are always authoritatively present with their gay and confident designs for living"[2] (Lynd and Lynd, 1937: 176).

All through the twenties study after study confirmed that so-called "love movies" served as popular guides to adolescents, and even adults. As an example, one of the better, more "scientific" studies of the period, conducted by Alice Miller Mitchell for the Wieboldt Foundation, indicated that while the preference for movies with love interest was highest among girls, "some of the older boys look upon the romance movie as a sort of 'Guide to Young Men in Love'" (Mitchell, 1929: 97). Mitchell quotes several students on the subject, including one girl who liked love movies because they showed how "a girl can pull things over a man," or "because they show the different ways that people love one another and how some are crooks" (page 99). This cynicism was not universal, however, and for the most part "girls also use the romance movie as a training course in the delicate art of loving and being loved. One girl says that she prefers romance plays to all others because they 'give me an idea of love,' and still another likes a 'romantic picture' best 'because it sets a person to thinking of the future'" (page 99).

The famous series of studies undertaken for the Payne Fund, known as "Motion Pictures and Youth," gave the first reasonably reliable confirmation of the extent to which the movies had become an essential ingredient in the socialization of the American adolescent. While many of these studies have rightly been criticized on methodological grounds, there is also an unfounded hysteria that seems to permeate much of their historical assessment. The Payne Fund studies may have been set up as a deliberate provocation to the film industry, but the end product speaks for itself; the studies were accomplished using the best available social-science techniques of the late 1920s, and many innovative methods were devised to accomplish the task. The fact remains that these twelve studies still constitute the most sustained body of research on the influence of motion pictures on American society that we have. And a careful reading of their findings can be invaluable for movie historians and those interested in American social and cultural history. To dismiss them because they were badly misinterpreted by the social reformers removes a valuable clue to the evaluation of the impact of the movies (Jowett, 1976: 220-229).

As an example, Charles C. Peters's study Motion Pictures and Standards of Morality devised a unique method of "panel evaluation" to examine which aspects of movie content seemed to be either in tune with or at odds with the prevailing standards of morality in late-twenties America. One clear diversion in the accepted morality that the movies concentrated on was the aggressiveness associated with female lovemaking. Peters noted of this finding:

> But it is clear that the mores (in the sense of approved customs) cannot long lag behind practice, especially when the suggestions of skillfully constructed drama tend constantly to give sanction to the deviating patterns and thus win approval for them [Peters, 1933: 82].

Interestingly, Peters also found that "kissing in the movies" was more nearly parallel to the accepted standards of real life, although there was still some disagreement about the propriety of actually showing such kissing scenes in public. Other relevent findings of significance were that the movies were ahead of actual practice in democratic ideals and that movie parents treated their children more considerately than in real life.

The most controversial of the Payne Fund studies were the two undertaken by Herbert Blumer. In a study by Blumer and Philip M. Hauser there are detailed selections from autobiographies of delinquent girls that describe the role of the movies in providing them with role models for their own sex lives. Although these diaries are usually subjected to a great deal of skeptical examination, they nonetheless do give us a clue to the kind of influence movies could play for certain types of individuals. Obviously, not all of American youth were affected in the same way, but the following quotation is typical of those cited:

> White, 14, truant, runaway--After I come home from seeing a picture, I mean a romantic love picture like that I can't wait till I get old enough to do things like that. Of course, I'm young now, only a kid [Blumer and Hauser, 1933: 82].

Blumer and Hauser are careful to point out they are dealing with delinquents, and "in the areas of high delinquency and social disorganization, however, the parents as a rule tend to lose control over their children.... In this situation motion pictures assume more importance as an educational agency for the boy and girl, and become a significant source of many ideas and schemes of life" (page 161).

Another study by Blumer provides long and controversial sections on adolescent imitation of movie mannerisms. His book includes a section on "Imitation of Love Techniques," which again, though it can be viewed with some skepticism, yet must be considered as an overall indication of trends and practices. More than one third of his 485 respondents specifically mentioned the acquisition of "love-making techniques" as one primary function of their moviegoing habit (Blumer, 1933: 44). One twenty-one-year-old white male's comments were representative of this group:

> The technique of making love to a girl received considerable of my attention, and it was directly through the movies that I learned to kiss a girl on her ears, neck; and cheeks; as well as on the mouth [page 47].

The diary selections presented in Blumer's study are most revealing in their explicitness, revealing exactly how the techniques demonstrated on the screen are copied, tried out, and often discarded in favor of some new technique recently witnessed. The detail absorbed by those viewers eager to learn from the movies was fascinating, as the following case illustrates:

> Female, 20, white, college sophomore--But movies are a liberal education in the art of making love. Every young person probably appreciates a love scene subjectively. I never learned any ways of flirting, because flirting is against the family code. I did learn something about the art of kissing, however; that the tableau looked far more graceful if the young lady put more weight on one foot than on the other; the effect was softer. It has been helpful, too, to see how two screen lovers manage their arms when they are embracing; there is a definite technique; one arm over, the other under [page 51].

After the Payne Fund studies were published, the question of "movie socialization" seemed to be settled, for very little research of a similar nature was done in the decades to follow. The Dutch-born, British sociologist Jacob Mayer undertook a series of studies of British movie audiences in the mid-1940s; his results were remarkably similar to those found by Blumer, and they, too, furnish us with many firsthand accounts of the manner in which audiences "used" movies as part of their sexual socialization. Mayer's work contains not only examples of the acquisition of techniques of courtship but also descriptions of imitation of fashion, hygiene, language, and other mannerisms (Mayer, 1946; 1948).

The key point in all of these diary studies, and other research dealing with the effects of film, is that they clearly demonstrated that movies were an important influence in such areas as formal relations between young men and women, the methods of attracting attention, courtship, and even more intimate relations. These were likely to be novel and unfamiliar experiences to many adolescents, and movies were able to furnish knowledge of how to act in such situations. The movie acted in loco parentis as it were. The role of the movies in the years 1920-1950 as an impetus to changing mores needs much more investigation--they clearly played a significant part in shaping the nature of male-female relationships during this time period.

Notes

1. The impact of urbanization on American culture is examined (for the early period) by Schlesinger (1933). For the later period see Mowry (1965).

2. It is interesting to note the importance placed on the increasingly powerful role of women in movies of Depression America. This was reportedly upsetting to unemployed males who were suffering status loss. As the Lynds (1937) point out: "He may even have felt new inadequacies as a husband and lover in these days when grand passions are paraded nightly before Middletown in the movies" (pages 177-178).

References

Baritz, Loren. "The Culture of the Twenties." In The Development of an American Culture, edited by Stanley Coben and Lorman Ratner. Englewood Cliffs, N.J.: Prentice-Hall, 1970.
Blumer, Herbert. Movies and Conduct. New York: Macmillan, 1933.
⎯⎯⎯, and Philip M. Hauser. Movies, Delinquency, and Crime. New York: Macmillan, 1933.
Dale, Edgar. The Content of Motion Pictures. New York: Macmillan, 1935.
DeFleur, Melvin L., and Sandra Ball-Rokeach. Theories of Mass Communication. 3rd ed. New York: McKay, 1975.
Gusfield, Joseph R. Symbolic Crusade: Status Politics and the American Temperance Movement. Urbana: University of Illinois Press, 1963.
Healy, William. The Individual Delinquent. Boston: Little, Brown, 1915.
⎯⎯⎯, and J. Bronner. Delinquents and Criminals: Their Making and Unmaking. New York: Macmillan, 1926.

Jowett, Garth. Film; The Democratic Art. Boston: Little, Brown, 1976.

Lynd, Robert S., and Helen Merrell Lynd. Middletown. New York: Harcourt, Brace & World, 1929.

_____, and _____. Middletown in Transition. New York: Harcourt, Brace & World, 1937.

May, Henry F. The End of American Innocence. New York: Knopf, 1959.

Mayer, Jacob P. Sociology of Film. London: Faber and Faber, 1946.

_____. British Cinemas and Their Audiences. London: Dobson, 1948.

Mitchell, Alice Miller. Children and Movies. Chicago: University of Chicago Press, 1929.

Mowry, George E. The Urban Nation, 1920-1960. New York: Hill and Wang, 1965.

Oberholtzer, Ellis Paxson. The Morals of the Movie. Philadelphia: Penn, 1922.

Schlesinger, Arthur M. The Rise of the City, 1878-1898. New York: Macmillan, 1933.

Young, Donald R. Motion Pictures: A Study in Social Legislation. Philadelphia: Westbrook, 1922. Rpt. New York: Ozer, 1971.

Zigler, E., and I. L. Child. "Socialization." In The Handbook of Social Psychology, edited by G. Lindzey and E. Aronson. 2nd ed. Reading, Mass.: Addison-Wesley, 1969, Vol. III.

PEOPLE'S ATTITUDES TOWARD MOTION PICTURES

Bruce A. Austin

Motion pictures have drawn considerable attention from students of history, aesthetics, law, and technology. The research studies offered by scholars from these disciplines are important for anyone wishing to gain a complete understanding of cinema. For instance, one can argue that it is, prima facie, "natural" to study the creators of motion pictures. Even the most cursory search of the literature reveals a plethora of such work. Moreover, the history and institutional structure of the film industry has been and continues to be well documented. Somewhat surprising, however, is the paucity of valid and reliable research on the consumers of motion pictures.

Leaving aside for the moment the purpose and goals of social science, it would seem reasonable to presume that the "manufacturers" of the "commodity" would be keenly interested in such research, if for no other reason than economics. It would also be reasonable to presume that the world's largest and most prolific film producers--those in Hollywood--would be among the most attentive and supportive patrons, if not initiators, of film-audience studies. Yet, contrary to intuition, this has not been the case. In the 1940s, after a half a century of popular acceptance, the powers in Hollywood were for the most part antagonistic toward and disdainful of audience research.

As Handel (1946) recounts: "In 1942 there was only a handful of persons who did not reject film research outright. Most condemned it without trial even though research was an established and useful part of other businesses." Lazarsfeld (1947: 162), writing from the perspective of social-science research, noted that "mere descriptive audience research has not developed so much with movies as with the other media." Handel (1953: 310) was to reiterate his and Lazarsfeld's point in 1953: "Audience research is well entrenched in all media of mass communications except the film." Today the state of the art in film-audience research has perhaps best been summarized by Simonet (1978: 72): "Motion picture audience research has been growing as a science from humble beginnings to more grandiose beginnings. But it seems always to have been making beginnings."

This chapter will discuss the concept of people's attitudes toward motion pictures. After reviewing the social-science literature, it will conclude with suggestions for future research.

The question "Why study movies and patrons' attitudes toward them?" can be answered in several ways. One clear purpose of attitude measurement is that of predicting behavior (see, e.g., Tittle and Hill, 1967).[1] Such predictions can be advanced through an understanding of the characteristics and values individuals expect to find, or associate with, when engaging in a particular activity (e.g., movie attendance). Beyond this "waterfront" approach to the pragmatics of attitude measurement a number of other reasons for studying patrons' attitudes toward motion pictures can be identified.

The most currently available data (1976) show that while motion pictures account for only 4.12 percent of the total U.S. recreational expenditures, movies are responsible for an astonishing 53.36 percent of the total U.S. spectator amusement expenditures (Gertner, 1980: 30A)--this despite the availability of numerous alternative choices. The popularity of movies, as measured by recreational expenditures, warrants research into patrons' attitudes toward them.

Since the first systematic study of moviegoers' attitudes toward the medium was conducted in 1930 (Thurstone), the average weekly U.S. movie attendance has plummeted by more than half. In 1930 the U.S. had a population of slightly more than 123 million (Bureau of the Census, 1973: 42) and an average weekly film attendance of 90 million (Sterling and

Haight, 1978: 352). In 1970 the total U.S. population had grown by sixty-five percent to 203 million (Bureau of the Census, 1973: 42), while the average weekly film attendance had dropped by eighty-three percent (since 1930) to 15 million (reported in DeFleur and Ball-Rokeach, 1975: 59). These figures raise an important question: does the dramatic decline in attendance over the space of forty years also reflect a less positive attitude toward the cinema?

In spite of this decline box-office records continue to be broken annually by a few films, inflation notwithstanding. For instance, Variety ("All-Time Rental Champs," 1980) reports the recent phenomenal success of such movies as Star Wars (1977, $175,685,013), Grease (1978, $96,300,000), and Superman (1978, $82,500,000) in domestic markets. This observation suggests that while movie attendance in general has diminished, there continues to exist what Jarvie (1970: 113) calls "the special occasion audience": normally infrequent filmgoers who attend only selected productions. If this hypothesis is valid, the importance of studying attitudes toward the medium in general has heuristic value for scholars wishing to conduct comparative studies of the population's attitudes toward a variety of leisure-time pursuits.

Unlike utilization of, or participation in, many other of the mass media, moviegoing is an effortful and expensive activity. Unlike television, for instance, cinema requires attendance in addition to substantial commitments of time and money. It will be interesting to study why individuals are or are not willing to make such investments.

Past research

A number of studies have examined a given motion picture's influence on specific attitudes held by individuals (e.g., ethnic and religious groups), but few studies have inquired as to the public's attitudes toward movies. For the most part, movie-audience research has been asymmetric, asking, "What do movies do to patrons?" (Hulett, 1949; Middleton, 1960; Moore, 1971; Peterson and Thurstone, 1933; Raths and Trager, 1948; Rosen, 1948) at the expense of such questions as "How do patrons feel about movies?" In one sense this asymmetric approach to audience research is understandable. Much mass-communications research, especially in the early years, was motivated and designed for commercial reasons (e.g., testing the effectiveness of persuasive messages

(Hovland et al., 1949). But the film industry does not sell advertising. Thus the statement that "it does not need to account to anyone for the size of its audience" (Lazarsfeld, 1947: 162; see also Jarvie, 1970: 5-6, and Riesman and Riesman, 1952: 202) has been invoked as a reason--perhaps "excuse" would be a more accurate term--for the paucity of data on film audiences. Nevertheless, studies that investigate audience attitudes toward the medium offer an important contribution to our understanding of the cinema audience, its behavior, and its motivations.

Finally, though critics of mass entertainment are often wont to rail against what they perceive to be the meretricious nature and debilitating effects of such fare on the public's psyche, as well as on the culture in general,[2] it is of importance that the public itself have an opportunity to express its views. A report by the National Research Center of the Arts (1975: 9) states:

> Few Americans feel that their cultural needs can be satisfied within their own living rooms.... That cultural and artistic activities are important in the daily lives of Americans of all ages is borne out by findings on their interest and wide range of cultural and creative activities.

This chapter discusses research into the public's attitudes toward one such cultural experience.

The earliest report on audience attitude appeared in 1923. Under the sponsorship of the National Board of Review, Charles Arthur Perry wrote The Attitude of High School Students Towards Motion Pictures. However, as reported by Sklar (1975: 325), the results of the study, given its sponsor, are "biased in favor of the movie industry."

In 1930 L. L. Thurstone published his forty-item scale for measuring attitude toward movies. Thurstone developed the movie-attitude scale as a part of the Payne Fund studies, reported in 1933, in which he played a significant role (see Peterson and Thurstone, 1933). The Payne Fund studies, published in twelve volumes, sought to examine the influence of the new medium on society.[3] The focus of Thurstone's report was the development of an attitude-assessment measure rather than its results; as a matter of fact, in this work (1930) Thurstone describes the procedures employed for developing and utilizing this attitude scale but not the results of its implementation.

Thurstone's attitude scale was first used by Williams, who published the results in 1933. Williams offers as the rationale for his attitude study the "value for teacher training": "In the case of teachers, it is reasonable to believe that attitude toward such a problem as that of motion pictures may affect the attitudes and behavior of large numbers of children" (page 222; emphasis added). From his sample of ninety-seven female and seven male teachers-college students he concluded that "this group, on the whole, is more favorably than unfavorably disposed toward moving pictures; and that a large proportion of them exhibit extremely favorable attitudes" (Williams, 1933: 223). Nearly two decades elapsed before another movie attitude study was reported. Patel's (1952) investigation, in India, found that among fifteen- to eighteen-year-olds, males showed a favorable and females an unfavorable attitude toward motion pictures, as measured by a ten-item scale.

Panda and Kanungo (1962), using a scale of thirty items, found that Indian high school and college students held a favorable attitude toward movies. Further, college students were found to have had a significantly more favorable attitude toward films than did high school students. This study also found that males were significantly more favorable than females in their attitude toward films.

In 1977 Bannerman and Lewis reported their study of college students. They made minor modifications to Thurstone's scale and reported that their sample held a slightly to moderately favorable attitude toward motion pictures. However, the method of assessing and presenting their data with regard to their sample's degree of favorability toward movies lacks both clarity and sophistication. Bannerman and Lewis present only frequency data in their report and base their conclusions on only a selection of the attitude statements. They do not present even basic descriptive statistics for each item or the scale as a whole, as Thurstone (1930) suggested. Moreover, subsequent computation of Bannerman and Lewis's data performed by the present writer indicated that their sample held, at best, a neutral-to-slightly-unfavorable attitude toward movies (see Austin, 1981a). The reanalysis of Bannerman and Lewis's data showed that while their respondents tended to disagree moderately with unfavorable-attitude statements, they also showed a distinctly neutral feeling about the favorable items. Further, reanalysis of the Bannerman and Lewis data on all forty attitude statements confirmed that their respondents fell below the neutral point (i.e., toward the unfavorable attitude direction).

The most recent attitude-toward-movies study is my own (Austin, 1981a).[4] My report closely replicates Bannerman and Lewis's (1977). However, whereas Thurstone (1930) and Williams (1933) both offered a three-point, and Bannerman and Lewis (1977) a five-point, response option for their samples, I had the participants in my study respond to each attitude statement on a seven-point rating scale. Increasing the number of response options allowed the respondents to make finer discriminations.

Respondents in my study were college students. For purposes of analysis I placed them in one of two attendance groups: persons who went to one movie a month or fewer were labeled Occasional Moviegoers; those who went to more than one movie a month were Frequent Moviegoers. The respondents were also placed into one of two groups according to the importance they assigned moviegoing as a leisure activity: persons reporting scale values of 1 through 4 on this measure were categorized in the Unimportant Activity group; persons reporting scale values of five through seven were categorized in the Important Activity group.

My findings indicated that although the respondents tended to disagree moderately with the unfavorable-attitude statements, they also showed a tendency to feel somewhat neutral about the favorable statements. In other words, favorable-attitude statements did not elicit a positive endorsement from the respondents. Analysis of the sample's score on all forty attitude statements, a more precise and useful indication of attitudinal inclination, revealed a somewhat unfavorable disposition for the sample as a whole. A three-way analysis of variance test (sex, frequency of attendance, and importance of moviegoing as a leisure activity) found one significant main effect and no significant interaction effects. No sample subgroup achieved a cumulative attitude score above the neutral point, but males had a significantly more positive attitude than females. An examination of the cumulative attitude score for sample subgroups reveals that while the differences between them did not reach statistical significance, Frequent Moviegoers held a more favorable attitude than Occasional Moviegoers and individuals in the Important Activity group held a more favorable attitude than those in the Unimportant Activity group.

My study both confirms and disagrees with previous research findings. As in studies by Williams (1933), Patel (1952), and Panda and Kanungo (1962), males were found to hold a more favorable attitude toward movies than females. Such findings might be expected, given, as numerous researchers have reported (e.g., Gertner, 1980: 32A; Sterling and Haight, 1978: 353; National Association of Theatre Owners, 1976: 32), the positive correlation between frequency of attendance and sex: males are more frequent moviegoers than females. Moreover, research conducted prior to 1950 indicated that males were also more likely than females to go to the movies alone (Handel, 1950: 113). Based upon attitudinal inclination and frequency of attendance, the implication is that males are more ardent movie fans.

Contrary to all previous research on this topic, the participants in Austin's study were found to hold a somewhat unfavorable attitude toward movies. This finding holds despite the fact that within Austin's sample males outnumbered females by a two-to-one margin; males, as noted above, have in the past been found to have more positive attitudes toward motion pictures than females.

My finding of a somewhat negative disposition can be placed in a historical context that shows the public's attitude toward movies as moving from highly favorable (Williams, 1933) to tepid (Panda and Kanungo, 1962), to slightly unfavorable. This shift parallels the declining number of admissions over the years. While acknowledging the dangers of ex post facto explanations, we cannot ignore the intuitive appeal and face validity of such an interpretation. Nevertheless, though movie attendance may indeed have declined because of increasingly negative attitudes toward films (the causes of which can only be speculated on), there are other possible explanations.

I can suggest at least three, not mutually exclusive, reasons for the change in attitude. First, since the earliest movie-attitude study was conducted, both the amount of leisure time available and the number of leisure activities have increased, although not in equal proportions. Frequency of moviegoing has decreased as a consequence, and attitudes may have been adjusted accordingly.

Second, the introduction in recent years of such directly competitive mass media as videodiscs and home videocassette recorders[5] offers consumers a viable (although not necessarily an aesthetically equivalent) alternative to motion pictures. The adoption of such media may have influenced both frequency of movie attendance and attitudes, as did the earlier introduction of television. The decline in favorability

of attitudes toward movies may be a reflection of both the
reduced (perceived) uniqueness of motion pictures and the
growing perception that those functions formerly fulfilled by
the medium are now being fulfilled by other activities or
media.

Third, with the increasing cost of moviegoing, audience expectations may have also risen. One simple (and
incomplete) index of cost is the average admission price,
which has increased from twenty-five cents in 1935 (Sterling
and Haight, 1978: 187) to $2.34 in 1978 (Gertner, 1980: 34A).
The heightened expectations of audiences today are perhaps
not being met, thereby resulting in a less favorable attitude.

Future research

The review of attitude-toward-movies literature presented in
this chapter suggests several avenues for further study.
First, and most obviously and urgently, construction of a
more contemporary movie-attitude scale is needed given the
social changes that have occurred since Thurstone first developed his scale. Perhaps the clearest and most relevant
indicator of social change is audience attendance at films.
Fadiman (1973), among others, has noted that the concept of
moviegoing has shifted substantially from a habitual behavior
to one bearing more special significance. Further, a recent
report (Austin, in press) has found that Thurstone's forty-item scale taps nine attitudinal dimensions. These include
attitudes toward movies regarding their educational value,
potential for social injury, content, and value as a leisure-time pursuit. The most important conclusions to be drawn
from the results of this study are with respect to the attitudinal dimensions that Thurstone omitted. As developed by Thurstone, the scale sought to measure only two aspects of attitude toward movies: overall favorability or unfavorability.
Clearly, there are more attitudinal dimensions held by the
public toward the medium. For instance, virtually absent
from the scale are statements that address the uses and
gratifications perspective of mass-communications research
as applied to the cinema (see, e.g., Blumler and Katz, 1974;
Katz et al., 1973). This functional approach (Wright, 1975)
posits that individuals, in a sense, "manipulate" the media
to satisfy their needs to a larger extent than the media "manipulate" consumers. It can be concluded, therefore, that
the Thurstone scale overlooks an important aspect of attitude
measurement. For if one purpose of attitude measurement

is to help researchers explain and predict behavior, the assessment of audience attitudes as related to their needs, desires, and motivations is essential (Crandall, 1980; Witt and Bishop, 1970).

A major drawback to all of the existing attitude-toward-movies research is the external (especially the population) validity of the samples used. Campbell and Stanley (1963: 5) state that "external validity asks the question of generalizability" (emphasis in original). All of the research studies reviewed in this chapter have used either high school or college students as respondents. The limitations to the results gathered with samples composed of such individuals (in addition to such factors as the demand characteristics of the setting in which the scales were administered) are obvious. While it may be argued that since the majority of filmgoers are of high school or college age,[6] "for film research, the college student may be more representative than students used in other research" (Elliott and Schenck-Hamlin, 1979: 553), this naturally overlooks the larger film audience. Thus attitude measurement performed on samples having a greater range of stratification and demographic attributes is needed.

Still another area in need of investigation is that of discovering the process of formation and change of attitude toward movies. How many exposures to the medium are required before an individual forms a firm attitude? What variables will affect a shift in this attitude? How does the social setting (e.g., theatrical and audience environment) affect attitude formation and change? Furthermore, it has been well documented that interpersonal contact affects individuals' choice of movies (see, e.g., Katz and Lazarsfeld, 1955; Austin, 1981a; Austin, 1981b; O'Guinn, 1981), as well as their evaluation of movies (Burzynski and Bayer, 1977); might not interpersonal influence also affect attitude toward films?

Another question that future research should address is why males tend to have a more favorable attitude toward movies than females. The difference in frequency of attendance and importance of moviegoing as a leisure activity do not appear to offer an answer to this question, since the interaction effect of these variables proved nonsignificant in Austin's study.

Conclusion

Attitudinal research on the audience for motion pictures has been scant. What little we do know suggests the following: 1/ the public's attitude toward movies has undergone a dramatic shift from a very favorable position in the 1930s to a distinctly neutral-to-somewhat-unfavorable position today; and 2/ males appear to have a more favorable attitude toward films than females, a finding that has held over time. The dearth of data on people's attitudes toward motion pictures can be seen as exemplifying the field of film-audience research in general. Systematic study of the film audience properly, but not exclusively, falls within the purview of social scientists trained in such academic disciplines as communications, psychology, and sociology. Although social scientists, enamored of the other major media of mass communications, especially television, have conducted innumerable studies, resulting in encyclopedic volumes, devoted to the audience for the medium of their interest, the research field on film audiences is largely unexplored. Film-audience researchers typically find themselves innundated with verbiage, little of which is theoretically and methodologically systematic, coherent, or valid. It is my hope that this assessment of the state of the art in film-audience research will serve as the impetus to further research endeavors in the future.

Notes

1. It should be noted that the attitude-causes-behavior position is not endorsed by all researchers. Bem (1972), for instance, has discussed the hypothesis that behaviors cause attitudes; Kelman (1974) has examined the reciprocal-causation hypothesis (i.e., attitudes cause behaviors and behaviors cause attitudes).

2. For a concise review of the "origins, functions, and implications" of such attacks see Mendelsohn (1966: Chapter I). Further criticism is presented by various authors in Rosenberg and White (1957). Rejoinders to these remarks are presented by Mendelsohn (1966) and, especially, Gans (1974).

3. For a discussion of this material see Jowett (1976: 220-229) and Young (1935).

4. Two other studies have somewhat tangentially addressed the question of the public's attitude toward movies. In 1973 Louis Harris and Associates, using a national probability sample of 3,005 persons, included three attitude statements, all of which compared movies with theater or television, in their study of <u>Americans and the Arts</u> (National Research Center of the Arts, 1975: 37). The results of this project found favorable attitudes toward both theater and motion pictures among the public. Second, the United States Information Agency commissioned independent research on foreign audiences' reactions to American films, with a special emphasis on their disposition toward the movies' depiction of American life. Results of one such study found that among Japanese citizens "the reaction to American commercial movies ... is decidedly favorable.... American films rank next to their own as the choice of Japanese movie-goers" ("American Films and Foreign Audiences," 1965).

5. For research on the diffusion, adoption, and program preferences among videocassette-recorder owners see Levy (1980a and 1980b), and Agostino et al. (1980).

6. Research presented in the early 1970s showed that eighteen- to twenty-nine-year-olds made up fully forty-eight percent of the moviegoing public (National Association of Theatre Owners, 1976: 40). More recently Gertner (1980: 32A) reports that fifty-eight percent of the total 1977 admissions were accounted for by sixteen- to twenty-nine-year-olds. Individuals with at least some college education comprise both the largest and most frequent moviegoing aggregate.

References

Agostino, Donald E., Herbert A. Terry, and Roland C. Johnson. "Home Video Recorders: Rights and Ratings." <u>Journal of Communication</u> 30 (1980): 28-35.
"All-Time Rental Champs." <u>Variety</u>, May 7, 1980, pp. 182, 232, 244, 248, 252, 256.
"American Films and Foreign Audiences." <u>Film Comment</u> 3 (1965): 50.
Austin, Bruce A. (a) "Attitudes Toward Motion Pictures Among

College Students." Unpublished paper, Rochester Institute of Technology, 1981.

———. (b) "M.P.A.A. Film Rating Influence on Stated Likelihood of High School Student Film Attendance: A Test of Reactance Theory." Ph.D. dissertation, Temple University, 1981.

———. (c) "Film Attendance: Why College Students Chose to See Their Most Recent Film." Journal of Popular Film and Television, 9 (1981): 43-49.

———. "A Factor Analytic Study of Attitudes Toward Motion Pictures." Journal of Social Psychology. In press.

Bannerman, Julia, and Jerry M. Lewis. "College Students' Attitudes Toward Movies." Journal of Popular Film 6, 2 (1977): 126-139.

Bem, Daryl J. "Self-Perception Theory." In Advances in Experimental Social Psychology, edited by Leonard Berkowitz. New York: Academic Press, 1972, Vol. 6.

Blumler, Jay G., and Elihu Katz, eds. The Uses of Mass Communication. Beverly Hills: Sage, 1974.

Bureau of the Census, U.S. Department of Commerce. 1970 Census of Population. Washington, D.C.: U.S. Government Printing Office, 1973, Vol. 1.

Burzynski, Michael H., and Dewey J. Bayer. "The Effect of Positive and Negative Prior Information on Motion Picture Appreciation." Journal of Social Psychology 101 (1977): 215-218.

Campbell, Donald T., and Julian C. Stanley. Experimental and Quasi-Experimental Designs for Research. Chicago: Rand McNally, 1963.

Crandall, Richard. "Motivations for Leisure." Journal of Leisure Research 12 (1980): 45-53.

DeFleur, Melvin L., and Sandra Ball-Rokeach. Theories of Mass Communication. 3rd ed. New York: McKay, 1975.

Elliott, William R., and William J. Schenck-Hamlin. "Film, Politics and the Press: The Influence of 'All the President's Men.'" Journalism Quarterly 56 (1979): 546-553.

Fadiman, William. Hollywood Now. London: Thames and Hudson, 1973.

Gans, Herbert J. Popular Culture and High Culture. New York: Basic Books, 1974.

Gertner, Richard, ed. Motion Picture Almanac 1980. New York: Quigley, 1980.

Handel, Leo A. "Hollywood Market Research." Quarterly of Film, Radio and Television 7 (1953): 304-310.

_____. Hollywood Looks at Its Audience. Urbana: University of Illinois Press, 1950.

_____. "This Thing Called Audience Research." Hollywood Reporter, 1946 Anniversary Issue, unp.

Hovland, Carl I., A. A. Lumsdaine, and Fred D. Sheffield. Experiments in Mass Communication. Princeton: Princeton University Press, 1949.

Hulett, J. E. "Estimating the Net Effect of a Commercial Motion Picture upon the Trend of Local Public Opinion." American Sociological Review 14 (1949): 263-275.

Jarvie, I. C. Movies and Society. New York: Basic Books, 1970.

Jowett, Garth. Film: The Democratic Art. Boston: Little, Brown, 1976.

Katz, Elihu, and Paul F. Lazarsfeld. Personal Influence. Glencoe, Ill.: Free Press, 1955.

_____, Michael Gurevitch, and Hadassah Haas. "On the Use of the Mass Media for Important Things." American Sociological Review 38 (1973): 164-181.

Kelman, Herbert C. "Attitudes Are Alive and Well and Gainfully Employed in the Sphere of Action." American Psychologist 29 (1974): 310-324.

Lazarsfeld, Paul F. "Audience Research in the Movie Field." Annals of the American Academy of Political and Social Sciences 254 (1947): 160-168.

Levy, Mark R. (a) "Home Video Recorders: A User Survey." Journal of Communication 30 (1980): 23-27.

_____. (b) "Program Playback Preferences in VCR Households." Journal of Broadcasting 24 (1980): 327-336.

Mendelsohn, Harold. Mass Entertainment. New Haven: College and University Press, 1966.

Middleton, Russell. "Ethnic Prejudice and Susceptibility to Persuasion." American Sociological Review 25 (1960): 679-686.

Moore, Douglas Cameron. "A Study of the Influence of the Film, The Birth of a Nation, on the Attitudes of Selected High School White Students Toward Negroes." Ph.D. dissertation, University of Illinois at Urbana-Champaign, 1971.

National Association of Theatre Owners. Encyclopedia of Exhibition 1976. New York: National Association of Theatre Owners, 1976.

National Research Center of the Arts. Americans and the Arts: A Survey of Public Opinion. New York: National Committee for Cultural Resources, 1975.

O'Guinn, Thomas. "The Audience's Choice: Movie Selection and Word of Mouth." Paper presented at the Interna-

tional Communication Association conference, Minneapolis, 1981.
Panda, K. C., and R. N. Kanungo. "A Study of Indian Students' Attitude Towards the Motion Pictures," Journal of Social Psychology 57 (1962): 23-31.
Patel, A. S. "Attitudes of Adolescent Pupils Toward Cinema Films." Journal of Education and Psychology 9, 4 (1952): 225-230.
Perry, Charles Arthur. The Attitude of High School Students Towards Motion Pictures. New York: National Board of Review, 1923.
Peterson, Ruth, and L. L. Thurstone. Motion Pictures and the Social Attitudes of Children. New York: Macmillan, 1933.
Raths, Louise, and Frank N. Trager. "Public Opinion and 'Crossfire.'" Journal of Educational Sociology 21 (1948): 345-368.
Riesman, David, and Evelyn T. Riesman. "Movies and Audiences." American Quarterly 4 (1952): 195-202.
Rosen, Irwin C. "The Effect of the Motion Picture 'Gentleman's Agreement' on Attitudes Toward Jews." Journal of Psychology 26 (1948): 525-536.
Rosenberg, Bernard, and David Manning White, eds. Mass Culture. New York: Free Press, 1957.
Selltiz, Claire, Lawrence S. Wrightsman, and Stuart W. Cook. Research Methods in Social Relations. 3rd ed. New York: Holt, Rinehart and Winston, 1976.
Sherif, Carolyn Wood. Orientation in Social Psychology. New York: Harper and Row, 1976.
Simonet, Thomas. "Industry." Film Comment 14 (1978): 72-73.
Sklar, Robert. Movie-Made America. New York: Random House, 1975.
Sterling, Christopher H., and Timothy R. Haight. The Mass Media. New York: Praeger, 1978.
Thurstone, L. L. "A Scale for Measuring Attitude Toward the Movies." Journal of Educational Research 22 (1930): 89-94.
Tittle, Charles R., and Richard J. Hill. "Attitude Measurement and Prediction of Behavior: An Evaluation of the Conditions and Measurement Techniques." Sociometry 30 (1967): 199-213.
Wiese, Mildred J., and Stewart G. Cole. "A Study of Children's Attitudes and the Influence of the Commercial Motion Picture." Journal of Psychology 21 (1946): 151-171.
Williams, J. Harold. "Attitudes of College Students Toward

Motion Pictures." School and Society 38 (1933): 222-224.

Witt, Peter A., and Doyle W. Bishop. "Situational Antecedents to Leisure Behavior." Journal of Leisure Research 2 (1970): 64-77.

Wright, Charles R. Mass Communication. 2nd ed. New York: Random House, 1975.

Young, Kimball. "Review of the Payne Fund Studies." American Journal of Sociology, September 1935, pp. 250-255.

TALKING ABOUT FILM

George F. Custen

Viewer response to film has typically been investigated in the context of film and filmgoing as a part of the economic infrastructure of leisure activities. Film-audience research has been limited in scope. The classic work in the field has simply included: the impact that film content has upon children (the Payne Fund series of the 1930s); as an artifact that is part of the leisure infrastructure of a small community (Warner and Lunt, 1941); as a tool of government mass persuasion (Hovland, Lumsdaine, and Sheffield, 1949); as data in the study of patterns of "culture at a distance" (Mead and Metraux, 1953); or descriptions of audience composition and preferences (Handel, 1950).

"Audience response" to film has rarely meant anything other than head counts or demographic surveys of "who" comprised the audience for certain films and, in a general way, what such viewers like or dislike about movies. The variety of uses that viewers obtain from a given film in everyday life has never been a priority for those who study film and its audiences. This is a grave oversight. For as Sol Worth has noted, if we wish to understand how our responses to a film contrast with our experiences with other modes of communication, we must realize that "the process of interpretation itself as practiced by ordinary as well as elite persons and groups upon ordinary as well as 'great' works could be a goal for the analysis of our symbolic world" (Worth, 1977: 69).

Theorists--notably Eisenstein (1948) and, indirectly, Kris (1952)--have discussed viewer response to film as though knowledge and description of the complex verbal and paraverbal acts that often accompany film viewing were faits accomplis. Whatever changes have been wrought in the technology of image recording and projection since the inception of film, two basic components of film viewing have remained constant: viewers and their object of attention, a film.

This chapter discusses how people talk about movies. It is based largely upon a study in which groups of people talked about a film, Jonathan Demme's Citizen's Band (1977). [1] In particular, this chapter investigates the ways that viewers report "using" a film in their everyday lives; some of the functions that talking about film serves for them; and, to a lesser extent, what "film talk" can encompass for them. For example, one can look at the same film--say, Ingmar Bergman's Wild Strawberries (1957)--as a "work of art," attending to the filmic elements Bergman has selected in a particular sequence, or, in an allusive way, as it pertains to a nonaesthetic concern in one's life ("That story you just told is like Wild Strawberries."). Responses to a film should not be limited to what viewers or critics perceive of as its "message." As Worth has noted (1969; 1974), so little is known about the processes by which we respond to film that there has been a tendency to treat all viewers as though they were either professional filmmakers or else critics "decoding" the "messages" placed in a film by its makers in a process that is a mirror image of how the film was initially constructed.

Films must be studied in the contexts in which they are produced, distributed, viewed, and discussed. They do not exist and are not understandable apart from these social constructions of reality. In learning to respond to a film the viewer is also learning about the shape of his or her own society and the cultural consensuses that prescribe "what" films are or should be good for. From many of our own experiences it should be clear that statements about what the filmmaker "meant" to imply in a film are not the only kind of film talk. If we are to understand film viewing, filmmaking, and talking about film all as socially situated events-- that is, looking at such behavior as extending beyond the immediate duration of contact with a film or audience--the study of how actual viewers respond to a film through talk will illuminate the many potential uses and senses that the verb "to mean" can have for film in our everyday lives.

Talking about Citizen's Band

All acts of categorization, evaluation, and interpretation involve active, shifting processes selected by interpreters. They are not arrived at through conjury, nor are they presented in their entirety as faits accomplis. Interpretations involve the active selection by viewers of a variety of strategies, shifting solutions, and so on. Whether this ongoing activity occurs at the level of "mere" perception (Neisser, 1967) or appears to be more oriented toward the creation of an explicit interpretation, the concept of "frames" (Aiken, 1950; Goffman, 1974), "paradigms" (Kuhn, 1970), or "perspectives" (Mannheim, 1952) all emphasize similar concepts about the nature of interpreters and the events to which they respond. A response is actively constructed by an interpreter and is specifically shaped by the schema selected in interpreting.

In the study noted above, many groups of self-selected peers were separately shown the film Citizen's Band. Following each screening every group of viewers engaged in free, nonchanneled discussion. During these discussions viewers voluntarily interpreted, asked questions, reconstructed the film, and evaluated parts of the narrative, actors' performances, or the attributes of objects within the frame. Viewers also told stories, some of which were suggested by events in the film and others seemingly detached from any direct connection.

Out of the very numerous verbal observations made by viewers less than ten percent of these "responses" were concerned with the "message(s)" that may have been implied by the filmmaker. This finding is most significant when compared with what previous models have presented as the norm for talking about or responding to a film. For without promptings or probes from a researcher talk about film is likely to be talk through film, in which the very situation for after-movie talks serves as a context for many types of discussion. Interpreters are also storytellers, parents, gossips, and so on. To assume that they should play the role of "interpreter" (exclusively) without being asked to do so indicates that unless specifically called for (either by training or situational context) viewers' notions of meaning inhere to the social use of a film and not merely its message. Viewers tend to discuss how the film is meaningful to them in some context present in their lives prior to and apart from the movie. As G. H. Mead (1934: 65) noted of symbolic forms in general, viewers seem to use a particular film in "a selective process by which is picked out what is common." The film viewer and talker, as a social being, "goes out and determines what [he or she] is going to respond to, and organizes that world" (page 25).

The majority of the verbal responses to <u>Citizen's Band</u> were relatively simple acts of evaluation concerning parts of the film a viewer either liked or disliked. In so doing, viewers implicitly raise the issue of what (for them) constitutes an object of value in a film. Rather than attending to "shots," "sequences," or graphic compositions--as ideal interpreter models suggest that one does or should do--viewers talked about "good parts" or specific events or objects (e.g., a song or a car) in the film they enjoyed.

Moreover, these responses--whether interpretations or evaluations--often made use of preexisting personal "real-life" rules and <u>not</u> the rules presented by the "world" in the film as their litmus tests of comparison. For example, there is a sequence in the film in which the two wives of a bigamous truck driver take revenge on their joint husband by breaking into his truck and setting his cargo of cattle free. Several viewers discussed the "improbability" of such a foray by the wives. They noted such real-life constraints as: 1/ the truck would have been well locked; 2/ the police would have been on vigilant patrol; and 3/ the wives would have required special training to operate a forklift truck or deal with a herd of cattle. It is worth quoting extensively from one viewer's discussion to see just how viewers might talk about events that do occur in film but seldom happen in real life.

> There was one thing that struck me as I watched the picture. They took a lot of theatrical liberties. For instance, one that was outstanding to me; you can't convince me that two girls can come out there and open a truck holding a load of cattle without at least using a stick or something to help them. Also, that truck would be very well locked. And, for to open it and watch the cattle come by, that's

stretching it a little bit. But that's the way of the movies, I guess [emphasis added].

This viewer, though still questioning the capability of the two wives in dealing with trucks and cattle, notes that perhaps movies, after all, are a realm of somewhat improbable circumstances where the violation of real-life rules may often occur.

The strength and pervasiveness of a "reality quotient" used at some time by all of the viewers in my study is clearly opposed to the theoretical talk of the ideal-interpreter models. Frequently talk about the film pertained to either personal critiques of events in it ("I know this is not well done because I own a CB radio and the people I talk to don't act like these people") or else attended to events in the film in a manner one might use when dealing with nonmediated material (i.e., without recourse to authors, scripts, or any other hints that belie the fact that the film is a scripted, mediated, event).

It is not that these viewers' responses to the film are "incorrect" or even that they are inappropriate. Rather, viewers' reality orientations indicate that previous notions of how viewers interpret a film should be reframed so to encompass the larger social frames in which all films are made, viewed, and discussed. These findings--that different concepts of "realism" are used as a yardstick for evaluation and interpretation--are in line with Elliot Friedson's study of children's responses to film. As David Riesman has noted of the Friedson study,

> ... in general the children's judgments were cramped by a narrow "realism"--"Why is it that cowboy heroes never get killed?"--although they did move, as they grew older, away from the excitement of "exciting" films (cowboys, gangster, etc.) to the subtler pleasures of supposedly adult films.... Yet perhaps this gradient itself is a sign of "realism": they know what is becoming to their age-grade. They were, perhaps, preparing to make the same sort of judgment later on that many of our friends made about King Solomon's Mines, whose complaint that "Hollywood would have to put in the love interest and keep Deborah Kerr looking too well-groomed for a safari" nearly spoiled the pleasure in an excellent movie. For they, too,

in their purism, were misled by a very rigid idea of "realism" [Riesman, 1954: 198-199].

Although the criteria used in making interpretations and evaluations may change as a person grows older, the basic tenet --in this case, "realism"--can remain unaltered as an evaluative index.[2]

Conclusion

Film, and talk about film, are only two among numerous other kinds of communication systems present in a society. As Malinowski (1956 [1921]: 315) and later LaBarre (1954) and Hockett (1958) observed, one infracommunication system --speech--can serve the purpose of what Malinowski early called "phatic communion," in which "ties of union are created through the mere exchange of words." This notion of phatic communion should be seriously considered as one possible function served by talk about film.

Film talk undoubtedly serves other purposes as well. It is a way for people to integrate socially their communicative needs both as individuals and members of groups. Although Citizen's Band and other films are indeed seen as containing "messages" from which interpretations can be made, viewer responses indicate that one cannot approach their significance in message or meaning terms alone. Viewers entered the marketplace of social discourse through Citizen's Band. They emerged in their discussions with items more "important" to them in their lives outside of a particular film viewing.

There are several limited conclusions we can draw from such film talk. First, response to a film is, for all viewers, an active process. This activity may take a variety of forms. In talking about a film viewers restructure, question, interpret, and engage in other speech acts in a complex process of negotiation with one another. Viewers reach inside and outside the film in attempts to render it understandable and meaningful. Moreover, in the instances from which the illustrations used here were drawn, these acts are performed within limited portions of the film, notably openings, closings, and parts that seemingly violate viewers' cinematic-reality rules. It would be intriguing to see if such a specific location of talk is limited to a single film, film genre, or communication mode, or instead is a pattern pertaining to many symbolic forms and groups of interpreters.

Second, because film talk is but another slice of communication behavior in which viewers, as social beings, constantly participate, interpretations and evaluations are made in terms that are integrative with viewers' daily lives. Film seems to serve a strong "integrative" aspect, both in the "reality" orientations used for evaluations and the practical uses it serves for viewers in their daily lives.

It was not uncommon for a viewer to report general "uses and gratifications" of film--"coin of exchange,"; leisure, aesthetic, or entertainment experience; escapism; and the like. Because film is both a material artifact and a cultural commodity, once it becomes part of the domain of (relatively) "public" culture rather than the bailiwick of a small group of specially trained persons like filmmakers or producers, it is open to specific uses surely unanticipated by its creators. One viewer reported that Heaven Can Wait (1978) helped him "cope" with the death of his parent. Another viewer saw Superman (1978) twice. The first viewing served the use as a "coin of exchange" ("Superman, I saw it the first time because it was new and everybody was seeing it."). The second viewing served a much more idiosyncratic use:

> And I went to see it the second time because I was with somebody I knew would appreciate certain parts of the movie. The girl goes to Vassar, and that's in Poughkeepsie. And there's this one little part where they're announcing the train stops, and one of the stops is Poughkeepsie. So that was the main reason I took her. Because I knew she would get a charge out of it.... She went nuts.

Each film, and each conversation in which film figures, can serve a host of uses or gratify numerous needs of individuals. It is this very polysemic ability of mass communication, as Wright (1975) notes, that makes the empirical investigation of such issues of how we respond to films a high research priority. Along similar lines, one viewer was so enamored of the film Watership Down that she named her car after it. And, most recently, The Rocky Horror Picture Show (1975) has inspired an entire litany of attendant verbal behavior not ordinarily associated with filmgoing or talk about film. Audiences at Rocky dress up as favorite characters in the film and insert dialogue in specific parts of the action. Although one of the uses of talk about film may be the very pleasure gleaned from the cognitive exercise of constructing an interpretation, as Kris (1952: 53) suggests is the case for responses to "art," film is also used in creating meanings other than those initially germane to the filmmakers' intent.

Film should be seen as meaningful not only in regard to the talk we make about its internal orderings but also in the use to which such structures are put by viewers after the film has ended. Interpretations and evaluations are meaningful events that are part of talk about film. However, by limiting the study of meaning in a film to statements made about these intentional structures at the time of any one study's ethnographic present is, I think, to miss the larger frames in which film talk can figure. Just as sociolinguists have realized that speakers and not the organs of speech are the "emitters" of speech, researchers concerned with film and responses to film must understand that the activities surrounding a film (making it, viewing it, or talking about it) provide sources of <u>potential</u> for different kinds of social behavior.

Notes

1. The fuller text of this study is found in Custen (1980).

2. Messaris (1977) has pointed out that one of the weaknesses of "uses and gratifications" research is the failure to take into account precisely such "changes over time" alluded to by Riesman.

References

Aiken, Henry David. "The Aesthetic Relevance of Belief."
    <u>Journal of Aesthetics</u> 9 (1950): 301-315.
Custen, George. "Film Talk: Viewer Responses to Film as a Socially Situated Event." Dissertation, Ph.D. University of Pennsylvania, 1980.
Eisenstein, Sergei. <u>Film Form: Essays in Film Theory</u>,

edited by Jay Leyda. New York: Harcourt, Brace and World, 1949.
Handel, Leo. Hollywood Looks at Its Audience. Urbana: University of Illinois Press, 1950.
Hockett, Charles F. A Course in Modern Linguistics. New York: Macmillan, 1958.
Hovland, Carl I., A. A. Lumsdaine, and Fred D. Sheffield. Experiments in Mass Communication. Princeton: Princeton University Press, 1949.
Kris, Ernst. Psychoanalytic Explorations in Art. New York: Schocken, 1952.
Kuhn, Thomas S. The Structure of Scientific Revolutions. Chicago: University of Chicago Press, 1970.
LaBarre, Weston. The Human Animal. Chicago: University of Chicago Press, 1954.
Malinowski, Bronislaw. "The Problem of Meaning in Primitive Languages." In The Meaning of Meaning, edited by C. K. Ogden and I. A. Richards. New York: Harcourt, Brace, 1921 (1956), Supplement I, 296-336.
Mannheim, Karl. Essays on the Sociology of Knowledge, edited by Paul Kecsekmeti. London: Routledge and Kegan Paul, 1952.
Mead, George Herbert. Mind, Self and Society. 2nd ed. Chicago: University of Chicago Press, 1934.
Mead, Margaret, and Rhoda Metraux, eds. The Study of Culture at a Distance. Chicago: University of Chicago Press, 1953.
Messaris, S. Paul. "Biases of Self-Reported 'Functions' and 'Gratifications' of Mass Media Use." et cetera 34, 3 (1977): 316-329.
Neisser, Ulric. Cognition and Reality: Principles and Implications of Cognitive Psychology. San Francisco: Freeman, 1976.
Payne Fund Studies. 5 vols. New York: Macmillan, 1933.
Pye, Michael, and Linda Myles. The Movie Brats: How the Film Generation Took Over Hollywood. New York: Holt, Rinehart and Winston, 1979.
Riesman, David. Individualism Reconsidered and Other Essays. New York: Free Press, 1954.
Rosenbaum, Jonathan. "The Rocky Horror Picture Cult." Sight and Sound, 49, 2 (1980): 78-79.
Warner, W. Lloyd, and Paul S. Lunt. The Social Life of a Modern Community. Yankee City Series, Vol. I. New Haven: Yale University Press, 1941.
Worth, Sol. "The Development of a Semiotic of Film." Semiotica 1, 3 (1969): 282-321.

———. "The Uses of Film in Education and Communication." In Media and Symbols: The Forms of Expression, Communication, and Education. Chicago: National Society for the Study of Education, 1974, pp. 271-302.

———. "Statement of Plans for Guggenheim Fellowship Application." Studies in the Anthropology of Visual Communication 4, 2 (1977).

Wright, Charles. Mass Communication: A Sociological Perspective. New York: Random House, 1975.

THE SOCIAL EXPERIENCE OF MOVIES

Ian Jarvie

This chapter is about a sociological understanding of film, and, in particular, about understanding changes in the social significance of movies. One of America's foremost sociologists, Edward Shils, writes:

> Society has a center: There is a central zone in the structure of society.... Membership in the society ... is constituted by relationship to this central zone.... The center, or the central zone, is a phenomenon of the realm of values and beliefs. It is the center of the order of symbols, of values and beliefs, which govern the society.... The central zone partakes of the nature of the sacred. In this sense, every society has an "official" religion, even ... a secular, pluralistic, and tolerant society [Shils, 1975: 3].

Movies were once located in the central zone of American society, were part of its "official" religion. This phase lasted about forty years. It was preceded and has been succeeded by phases in which movies are in the peripheral zone. This chapter will describe these phases and the changeover from one to the other.

Introduction

Sociological thinking about

moviegoing differs from commonsense thinking about moviegoing. Common sense tells us that we go to movies for pleasure--as a pastime or because particular movies attract us. Sociology finds such explanations problematic: patterns of taking pleasure, passing time, and considering certain movies attractive themselves need explaining. Sociology explains the social experience of movies by the social functions they serve: some manifest to everyone, others hard to detect, or latent (Merton, 1957).

Even though movies are less than one hundred years old, their functional position in society has already changed twice. From their inception in 1895 until about 1915 they were socially peripheral, comparable to the circus. The movie industry was small, was staffed by raffish personnel, produced vulgar material, and was clearly marginal to the dominant ideas and values of American society (May, 1980; Chapter 2). Sometime during the First World War movies shifted their social position toward the center. They became a prosperous and secure business, run by people who cultivated the image of respectability and propriety, and their stories embodied, projected, and hence sustained the central ideas and values of the society. Mass culture became a part of the center, the "official" religion. Later again, sometime between 1946 and 1956, movies abdicated their central position to television and shifted back toward the periphery, while yet retaining a special aura stemming from their recent centrality and their continuing influence on television.

Over their whole history movies have served several social functions, some more in one phase than another, some manifest, some latent. We can call this the functional "plasticity" of movies. Their plasticity results in a "smearing" of functions over phase boundaries; such smearing reminds us that the phases are not real and distinct entities but rather convenient analytic categories. There are no sharp boundaries between the phases. Also, different sorts of events mark the transition between the first and second phases as compared with the second and third phases. The rapid rise in the social significance of moviegoing that marks the transition from the first phase to the second is explained one way (by reference to the social need to shape the emerging mass society); the slow decline of the importance of moviegoing that marks the transition from the second phase to the third is explained in quite another way (by reference to the appearance of the rival technology of television and to political intervention).

Movies on the periphery of society (1895-1915)

At first the manifest social function of movies was as a novel pastime for city folks, especially the young people and workers who thronged the growing urban centers. Movies offered a haven from the workplace, crowded living conditions, and the weather. A few cents bought admission to a program that might include a chaotic and bewildering array of fictions, newsreels, faked newsreels, documentaries, cautionary tales, pantomime versions of well-known plays and books, and so on. Beginning in storefronts, movie shows graduated to converted theaters and eventually to "picture palaces," while programs and films grew longer.

Movies were an alternative to such established pastimes as the music hall, vaudeville, professional sports, and the saloon. Although some moral concern was expressed about the dark interiors and the proximity of the chairs, the ambience of moviegoing was soon judged to be more suitable for women and children than arenas or bars. This acceptance as family entertainment may help explain why movies later became central to American popular culture; and that centrality, in turn, may help explain the degree of press scrutiny they were subjected to, the intense effort invested to keep risqué and other socially subversive material off the screen (Sklar, 1975: Chapter 8; Jowett, 1976: Chapters IV, VI, IX; Jarvie, 1978: Chapter 1; May, 1980: Chapters 2, 3). During the movies' second phase, another family medium arises, radio. Radio suffered attentions similar to those given to film. In the third and most recent phase, television, the perfect mass medium for a society organized around the nuclear family home, is infantilized by this scrutiny at least as much as movies ever were.

If the nickelodeons and emerging picture palaces were to get repeat customers, they had to have something novel to offer. Movies were (and are) a perishable commodity. Whatever the gratifications people derive from movies (and scholars debate this issue still), ordinary moviegoers rarely want to see the same movie repeatedly, thus there was (and is) a demand for new product. With their emergent popularity, movies differentiated further--between new and interesting movies and new and uninteresting ones, for example. The practice of selling films by the linear foot, as though any piece of film was as valuable as any other, was forced to stop. Firms that resisted or were slow to catch on to audience demands were simply forced out of business.

Besides entertainment, movies in this first phase clearly had the capacity to socialize and educate. Like painting and photography, they brought home distant lands, peoples, and events. They could record scientifically interesting phenomena. Less obviously, fictional movies could embody ideas and values that the audience might be enticed to accept.

Birth of a Nation (1915), which marks the climax of this phase, is a case in point. This full-length, dramatic, and highly profitable film dramatized two of the most aggravated social and political issues in American history: race relations and the Civil War. The script was derived from a passionately pro-South, anti-integration novel; the film was written and directed by D. W. Griffith. In the course of the film it is suggested that patrician white Southerners had cultivated an admirable way of life and that their black slaves had been well treated and happy. The movie implies that miscegenation produces mulattos who are treacherous and lustful. After the war the legislatures of Southern states are shown as packed with grinning "coon"-figure blacks. The Ku Klux Klan is pictured as a noble body of white Southerners gathered in order to prevent pillage and rape (Bogle, 1973; Cripps, 1977; Kirby, 1978).

Birth of a Nation was carefully made and compelling. The audience was not offered the opportunity to reflect on the truth of the ideas and values that it insinuates. This establishes an important link between skill and psychology: movies can propagandize as well as educate. Birth of a Nation provoked violent protests in Boston and New York, demonstrating the potential power of the medium (Carter, 1960; Aitken, 1965; Cripps, 1977). Such publicly expressed fears helped legitimatize attempts to control content, to control access, and to impart a sense of responsibility and accountability to the movie industry. It was in the business interests of the industry to avoid antagonizing the powers that be.

Here we need to clarify the ambiguous notions of "the public" and "the public interest." One public goes to movies often to see films that other individuals declare "against the public interest." The latter are usually elected officials, police officers, licensing bodies, teachers, social workers, journalists, religious spokespeople, and demagogues who speak in the name of a "public opinion" about a "public interest" according to what they sense their constituency to be.

Whether the threat they perceived in movies was genuinely to
the public welfare or rather to their own welfare, is moot.[1]
Moviemakers and theater owners are thus caught between
public opinion expressed in box-office takings and public opinion articulated by self-appointed spokespeople. This conflict
continues down to the present day, where it is most strongly
contested over television.

Turning now from the manifest functions of the mov-
ies--entertainment, socialization, and education--to their
latent functions, we can already discern in this first phase
that they maintained ideas, values, and social bonds of value
to the organization of life under wage labor. It is important
to keep in mind that America at the turn of the century was
changing from a rural into a highly industrialized country
and was also absorbing unprecedented numbers of immigrants,
most of them from rural backgrounds. The music hall, professional sports, and the saloon all predate industrialization;
they neither involve nor gain much from advanced technology.
Movies, however, owe their existence to it. They become
technically possible only after the development of precision
mechanical and chemical engineering in the second half of
the nineteenth century. More subtly, what movies offer society, the manner in which it is offered, and its content are
inextricably bound up with the condition of industrialization.

Movies serve customers who possess certain amenities
of the industrial world. Among these are spare cash and
spare time (neither of which is common among peasants);
homes or workplaces they wish to get away from but to which
they must return; and lives organized around the clock and
the calendar (not around the cycle of the seasons or the
phases of the moon). A movie audience must be tolerant of
secular or religiously neutral activity that is undertaken without significant others and that is not productive. Movies
serve customers who inhabit a demystified natural world,
even when offering mystifying stories.

All this is typical of the organization of life under
wage labor and industrialization, as characterized by the division of labor (Durkheim, 1893). Even time and space are
divided up for specialization: there are work spaces, home
spaces, school spaces, play spaces, common spaces, and
so on. Time is divided up into work time, rest time, meal
time, leisure time, and sleep time. Such division increases
efficiency and the production of wealth, and wealth makes
possible "spare" space, time, and money.[2] The bonds and

divisions that help industrialization work are not the same as the traditional bonds of agricultural society, community, family, and religion.[3] Indeed, in their abstraction (employer, employee) and emphasis on goals (production, wealth) they cut across and weaken those older bonds. An unprecedented individualism emerges, for surplus space, time, and money are allocated to single individuals, not to community, family, or religion. The individual controls the disposition of these rewards but not their size or the structure of their distribution. Industrialization requires of its workers orderly and predictable behavior, governed by the clock and the calendar; disciplined respect for space and property; and orientation to specific goals, such as production, saving, and commodity acquisition. The movie industry converted the diffuse state of enjoyment into a manufacturable and purchasable commodity.

It is not surprising, therefore, that long before these values of industrial society are discernible in story lines they are embodied in the values of moviegoing itself. In the common spaces of the cities, areas that specialize in attracting the leisure dollar emerge. They offer "entertainment" (an abstraction that scarcely exists in traditional society) to consume excess time and money. The unit cost to the customer is modest because of efficient mass production.

Moviegoing thus functioned differently from past performing arts, such as minstrels, strolling players, and traveling theater companies. These sometimes had religious sponsors, or rich patrons, or they in effect begged after performances. Vaudeville and live theater were more commercial but could not be efficiently mass-produced. Traditional myths and stories--the folklore of kinship, religion, and region-- do not present object lessons for effective behavior in industrial society. They do not teach efficiency as a function of specialization and routinization; they do not teach the disciplines of organizing time and space; they seldom embody the kind of individualism essential to both workers and employer; they do not stress the indispensability of literacy and numeracy for full participation in society. Lacking all these lessons, traditional myths were not suitable as foundations of movie stories because they did not foster the kind of bonded cohesion industrial society requires.

Movies are only one part, although the largest, of the growing mass-culture industry of industrial society, along with popular newspapers and magazines, dime novels, popular music, and records. But most of these were tied to the English language, and the newly urban masses from the rural areas of America and Europe rarely commanded standard English.

How fortunate, then, that the movies could mass-produce <u>pantomime:</u> drama not tied to any language. Silent pictures accompanied by music, utilizing titles that could be spelled out or translated in whispers, were culturally rooted yet universally accessible. They offered the possibility of bonding the inhabitants of industrial America in unprecedented ways. They made possible a popular culture that was national rather than regional, modern rather than traditional. This may help explain the worldwide success of American movies. It certainly accounts for the movies' shift from periphery to center.

Movies as socially central (1915-1950)

Both the amount of controversy created by <u>Birth of a Nation</u> and the number of people who saw it are good reasons for using it to mark the point of transition of movies from periphery to center. During the war of 1914-18 (not entered by America until 1917), all the belligerents used movie propaganda to boost recruitment, sell war bonds, denigrate the enemy, keep up morale, instruct troops, and inform the public. No one had used the circus for such purposes.

Movies had a new status. Old functions continued: entertainment, socialization (to be discussed more thoroughly later), education, and reinforcement of the support structures of industrialization. This latter function is complex and spreads its influence from the organization of moviegoing, as a base point, to the very content of movies, which organizes and criticizes experience and contrasts how society is, how it appears, and how it aspires to be. A new development, the star system, also turns out to have functions.

But before coming to those matters I want to discuss the capture of the center. In most European societies the center is associated with the metropolis, the culturally dominant capital city: London, Paris, Rome, Berlin. This coincidence of geography and center has never been true of the United States. Political power is concentrated in Washington and the state capitals; finance has always been concentrated in New York and to a lesser extent Chicago; popular culture has been spread about, with New York long dominant. Movies began in New York, but emigrated to Los Angeles by the beginning of this phase. Radio began in New York also, but drew heavily on stars in Hollywood. Popular music's headquarters, Tin Pan Alley, was in New York, but there were satellite centers like the southern and midwestern homes of jazz and country music. And, finally, television began in New York, but it, too, emigrated West. Shils says the center has nothing to do with geometry, little with geography. My contention is that movies were, in the phase between 1915 and their decline of 1946-1956, the center of the popular culture of the United States. "The movies" meant Hollywood and the local theater.

During this second phase the moviegoing habit spread to an unprecedented degree, penetrating almost every small town and village of America. Theater programming settled into patterns we still recognize today: one or two ninety-minute fictions surrounded by different amounts of short subjects and trailers. Hollywood became a center of attention. Press and radio set up permanent bureaus (Rosten, 1941: Chapter 16). Religious authorities seemed to care greatly what sorts of materials got onto the screens of the nation. [4] Business interests (financial giants like Rockefeller, Morgan, Kennedy, Hearst, and Hughes, as well as the Bank of America all became involved). [5] Public officials time and again took up the issue of censorship at federal, state, county, and city levels. [6] Educationists and social workers expressed anxiety at the effects of movies and hope at their potential. Social scientists mined it constantly (Jowett, 1976). Politicians found the glamour and prominence of the movies useful to enhance their candidacies with support from stars or to give them publicity by crusading against movie people and movie sin (drinking, immorality, irreligion, communism). Diplomats were concerned with movie stereotyping of foreign countries and peoples. Civil servants detected possible violations of federal antitrust laws in the small number of firms that produced, distributed, and exhibited movies.

During this phase Hollywood rarely ground out less than five hundred films a year, even when several of the major studios went into receivership in the mid-thirties. Specialized fan magazines and newspaper columns flooded the public with "information" about Hollywood. Studios maintained publicity organizations and ran fan clubs for their stars. But, most striking of all, moviegoing became a middle-American habit, a weekly or twice-weekly pastime for much of the nation.

To a degree not known before, Americans shared in moviegoing a common institution of entertainment, socialization, and education that helped bind them together around central values and ideas.

A high point of this central phase was the to-do surrounding the immensely profitable film Gone with the Wind (Lambert, 1972: Chapters 2-5; Flamini, 1975). It is said that a movie adaptation of the best-selling novel was contemplated even while it was in galley proofs. Its many readers eagerly anticipated Clark Gable as the male lead. The producer accepted unfavorable contractual terms from MGM, Gable's employers, to secure his services. A nationwide search for a woman to play Scarlett was used to generate publicity and excitement, which did not die down when the choice fell on an unknown British actress, Vivien Leigh. The troubled shooting of the film was widely publicized, and a gala premiere was staged in Atlanta in 1939, with local authorities and celebrities all collaborating. It was the longest and most expensive film made up to that time, and it held the record for box-office returns for more than twenty years.

There is an irony not to be missed about Gone with the Wind. Released twenty-four years after Birth of a Nation, it also concerned the issues at the center of American consciousness: the Civil War and race relations. Although made in more liberal times than Birth of a Nation, it, too, portrayed patrician Southern society in a sympathetic manner. Its black characters, mostly loyal retainers, were more humanized, but still stereotyped. Although less path-breaking than Birth of a Nation, the film has an enduring popularity that makes it a major work of the popular culture of its time.

It is intriguing that two of the most successful films ever made are about the right issues rather than on the right side of the issues: the issues of relations between the states and relations between the races are central to the American experience and much symbolized at the level of "official" values and ideas described by Shils. Though these films project attitudes we (generally or publicly) now find unacceptable, the acceptability of the issues being raised in movies highlights the position of the movies at the center. It is not surprising that movies express popular attitudes--are creatures of their time. More importantly, a central social institution deals with central social and political problems in a manner that is highly acceptable and popular. Movies thus are functioning as means of social integration.

Large-scale and heterogeneous societies are hard to integrate, culturally and socially (Shils, 1975: 48-107). Hollywood may embody and project common preoccupations and values, but some of its customers can be expected to react critically to what is shown, to react against Hollywood itself--just as the federal government's authority may arouse antiauthority sentiments. Institutions of popular culture, even central ones like the movies, have charismatic authority. Charisma is imparted to persons (e.g., stars), institutions (movie companies, Hollywood), symbols (films), "because of their presumed connection with 'ultimate,' 'fundamental,' 'vital,' order-determining powers" (Shils, 1975: 127). Such ultimate "powers" in America are political power, wealth, social status, sexual attractiveness, and fame or "being somebody"--this last we shall call "immortality." During its phase of cultural centrality Hollywood, its personnel, and institutions, seemed to embody and to be able to confer these ultimate powers.

In a new nation, creating itself from scratch (Lipset, 1963) and without consensus on transcendent or religious values, purely secular attributes become the official religion. The actualization of all these powers here on earth (in Hollywood and in movies made in Hollywood)--the ideology that prescribed that anyone can be discovered and participate in these rewards (there are, for example, no social class or ritual/pollution barriers)--gave movies a charismatic authority the function of which was to bind the periphery of the culture (those of us far from Hollywood and those in Hollywood far from the movie industry) to the center. Going to movies, reading, thinking, and talking about movies and about Hollywood doings are functions that bind us to the center. We articulate and internalize the values movies enshrine. Movies treat the central questions of the production and reproduction of American society (Jarvie, 1978: 88-104).

> The center of the authoritative institutional system seeks the legitimating service provided by the creative center of cultural production and reproduction. It has always received a certain amount of that service; a relationship of mutual support between the culture and authoritative centers of society is established [Shils, 1975: 78-79].

Two specific developments in this second phase need to be looked at in detail: the function of stars and the function of content. We shall argue that stars foster and model the individualism appropriate to industrialized society. Stars function as a piece of information. Knowing which star or which picture is "in" is one of several ways the moviegoer can anticipate and hence select the pleasures a movie has in store. Woody Allen's name rouses different expectations from Robert DeNiro's, and Jane Fonda's from Barbra Streisand's. These expectations play a role in movie choice and hence box office. To the companies that dominated this phase the star had a value and became a tradable commodity (as Gable in Gone with the Wind), lending his or her glamour to the company that had the contract and challenging producers and writers to create vehicles that would exploit audience expectations. Unlike the plot, or the creators behind the camera, stars are salable because they are highly visible, on screen and off.

To their fans, stars also function as living proof of the ideas of a self that is its own free creation. A traditional society with fixed roles and statuses, ascribed rather than achieved, allows little leeway for the notion that the individual person can be something else, and hence someone else than he or she now is. Indeed, identity and ascription are fused. Industrial society derives vitality from the conflict between compliance to a given social-status system and an individual with a secure sense of self-identity detached from the ascriptions of tradition, family, and class. Curiously, although industrialization requires docile workers, it also requires that many workers act in the hope that they can be entrepreneurs. The movie star moving from role to role on-screen, likely having risen from humble or unglamorous origins off-screen, enacts the possibility of being able to be a self who is also and constantly someone else.

Finally, in this central phase, we must look at the function of content in socialization. Once the ninety-minute feature film was established as the dominant movie format, it became possible to specify its function. Whereas short films are allowed to be mere fragments and newsreels collages, feature films are called upon to be well-organized and dramatic structures. Even when they are fictional, they present a believable world where there is significance in the kinds of people and events that are portrayed. Feature-film content comes in units we call stories, and stories have shape. Movies are not slices of life, which is notoriously shapeless, confused, chaotic, mysterious, and frustrating. Movies by contrast in this phase show human interaction as coherent and resolvable, goals as reachable, a world in which such values as romantic love, patriotism, family loyalty, compassion, justice, and revenge are acted out. Movies contrast strongly with the myths and legends of other societies present and past, which look to us fragmentary, puzzling, shaggy-dog, cruel, capricious, incoherent, and, in short, shapeless. We might say that one function of the dramatic form that movies take is to present a way of coping with experience in the modern world, life in industrial society. A way of coping that is rational and goal-directed, that organizes and thus controls life by dividing it up into little stories. Each bit of life makes sense, and this leads us to imagine that the overall picture should make sense too.[8] Movies even teach us to view our own lives in this way, as having a beginning, middle, and end, turning points, climaxes, and so on. Such organization is well suited to the rationale of wage labor. The disciplines of the workplace are accepted because of goals we set ourselves, attempts to give our life shape: achievement of goals. The muddle and untidiness of life as it is presented in the stories of earlier times does not give meaning to the disciplined and goal-achieving life. A life that ends only in death is meaningless to industrial society. Hence movies and other forms of popular culture seek to give meaning.

As argued before, the goals striven for, like power, wealth, status, sexual attractiveness, and immortality, are distributed in certain ways in American society. Movies do not always portray those distributions accurately; rather, they portray them as they appear to those who dwell in Beverly Hills--which is perhaps more how some would wish they were than how they actually are. If there are murders and injustices, we want them to be solved or corrected. If Scarlett O'Hara is selfish and hurtful, she deserves her rejection by Rhett. We want the disillusioned hero of Casablanca to join the anti-Nazi cause. We relish the downfall of the egotistical and corrupt Citizen Kane. Life is rarely as satisfying as the movies.

We can take the argument about the function of content one step further now. Power, wealth, status, sexual attractiveness, and immortality are denied those who covet them or who misbehave. This is a far more effective myth than movies simply falsifying the true distribution of these rewards. Better to show these rewards as not worth having, or as corrupting, or as truly belonging only to those worthy of them. To keep going, industrial society needs constantly to extend promise and hope to those without. Stories on the screen, acted out by stars, were paralleled by events in the lives of stars. They, too, sought the power, wealth, status, sexual attractiveness, and immortality that accrued to the most successful. Hollywood's publicity machine kept up hope by giving the public a sense of having a glimpse of the rewarding life, while the gossip-and-exposé industry ameliorated the discontent of the unsuccessful by playing up the dissatisfactions and corruption of success (see Thomas, in press).

The socialization function of movies becomes clearer in this phase. Socialization is the process of transmitting information that assists individuals in becoming socially competent. Children learn about the adult world, rural dwellers about the city, city dwellers about the country, rich and poor about one another, and so on. The capacity of movies to make viewers invisibly present in all kinds of unfamiliar situations also instructs them in what to expect. Movies, however, can mislead as well as educate. Much doubt was expressed throughout this second period as to the movies' reliability as a source of information, especially about crime, foreigners, minorities, and--indeed--"real life" generally (Jarvie, 1970; 1978). One example that recurs throughout the phase of cultural centrality is that of romantic love. Often the problem as cinematically set forth is that the hero or heroine is not complete without romantic love. He or she may be discovered searching for it, rejecting it but secretly yearning for it, or finding it but facing obstacles before it can run its true course. Less innocuously, the Hollywood hero/heroine is sometimes presented as having problems in life (unemployment, turbulent personal relationships, crime threats) that can be resolved solely by the discovery and consummation of true love. One reading of this recurrent theme would be that the individualism encouraged by industrialization is a lonely and isolated condition in tension with bonds of family and kinship, tradition, and community. The incomplete individual, by discovering romantic love for another isolated individual, relieves that tension. Unfortunately, movie myths resolve the structural tensions of society purely notionally.

Movies also perform a problem-solving function (Haley, 1952). The movie story will set up dilemmas or choices and work out the emotional consequences of one course of action. Viewers can treat movies as rehearsals of the consequences they will face as they confront their own dilemmas and choices. Fact will rarely resemble fiction closely, to be sure, as dreams rarely resemble waking, but we readily interpret them as enactments of problems currently on the mind of the dreamer and, often symbolically disguised, as desired or feared solutions to those problems.

To sum up this phase, we can return to Shils's notion that every society--even a secular and pluralistic one like the United States--has an "official" religion. It is clear from our discussion that movies during their phase at the center functioned much like an official religion for American society. They presented myths of the origin of society and thereby offered explanations for why things happened (Birth of a Nation and Gone with the Wind). In both their stories and the life-organization demanded to view them they fostered better integration of newly industrialized American society. They fed back to their audiences values and aspirations. They were less anarchic, challenging, and critical of society during this central phase than before or after (May, 1980: Chapters 2-3; Jarvie, 1978). They defined the sacred and the profane: love, family, motherhood, America, and self-reliance were sacred; crime, violence, lust, greed, and dishonesty were profane. If the movies were the religious texts, the theaters the churches, moviemaking the central mystery of this religion, and Hollywood its shrine, then we must class it as pagan. For the gods and goddesses were, clearly, the movie stars, and Hollywood was their Elysium. Their behavior was sensual and worldly. Hollywood made no secret of this. There is a whole subgenre of films about Hollywood itself that discuss the legitimacy of Hollywood's charisma, its origins, and the more arcane rituals (Thomas and Behlmer, 1975; Parish, 1978). The rituals of moviegoing in the darkened amphitheater are simple compared with the intricate practices of the high priests and scribes resident in Hollywood itself (Rosten, 1941; Dunne, 1968). As always, there is the play between how things are, how they are seen, and how people would like them to be. One story (What Price Hollywood, 1930) remade three times (as A Star Is Born 1937, 1954, 1976), chronicles the decline of a famous star and his love for a rising star who eclipses him.[9] Rise and fall are accepted as inevitable processes, and the means of coping with them are paraded and judged. Alcohol to cope with failure is condemned. Offering sex for advancement is also condemned, as is ruthless devotion to profession and success above all other things. Love is approved, even to the extent of self-sacrificial suicide and devoting oneself to the memory of the loved one. Most films in this subgenre are exposés. The corruption, falsehoods, and depredations lie behind the façade of glamour and success. Hollywood as religion expresses at all levels the conflict between industrialization and the individuals who both benefit from it and resent serving it. The extent to which the devoted audience of the movies also hates and resents them is a subject for further research.

Movies yielding the center (1950 to date)

How could it have come about that movies slipped away from the center, and what difference has this made to their functions in society? The primary factor is technological. A new medium, television, appeared that was even more effective than movies at all the functions we have discussed: entertainment, education, socialization, integration, bonding to the center, and the organization of life and experience under industrialization. It is more effective because it reaches more of the population more quickly and more cheaply than movies do. Available almost twenty-four hours a day, television is flexibly adaptable to the increasingly spread-out working day. Even as religion, the television set's place in the home often makes it a kind of shrine around which people gather.

We saw that moviegoing began in urban America, where living space was limited and mostly crowded. Spacious theaters were for most people a pleasant change. Later, during the central phase, moviegoing was less a refuge and more a means of staying in touch. After World War II America entered a period of great affluence, marked in part by suburbanization--the mass-production of spacious homes for ordinary people. A large percentage of the population now had comfortable home space to spare where the family could watch television. The necessity for the "outing" was lessened, and movie theaters were now inconveniently far away in the old city centers.

The second factor has much to do with the movies' cultural centrality, and the tendency I noted for the charisma of the center to evoke negative reaction. The movies were subject to political scrutiny throughout their period of hegemony, but attempts to institute censorship were turned aside by a system of self-policing (Randall, 1968; Jowett, 1976; May, 1980), and government attempts to utilize them as part of the war effort were also diffused by voluntary cooperation (Jowett, 1976; Koppes and Black, 1977).

After the war, however, two political assaults on this central cultural institution were successful. The first was an antitrust suit accusing the major companies of organizing a monopoly in restraint of trade. Judgment against the major movie companies was given in 1947 and later upheld by the Supreme Court. The major companies had to end their monopoly by divesting themselves of theaters. Second, in 1946 and for several years thereafter, The House Un-American Activities Committee investigated the entertainment industry, especially movies, but also radio, television, and the theater. These investigations led to no significant legislation but succeeded in creating a blacklist and damage to morale. Historians agree that this industry was investigated partly because it was glamorous and much-publicized, part of the central zone of American society; purging it of the sins of monopoly and communism would be a highly visible example to others.

Television and political assault together caused the movies to slip from being the semireligious national pastime of America to being one of several competing pastimes, functioning mainly for people between the ages of fifteen and twenty-five. As the movie business shrank, it receded from the central zone of American society, serving less to make the whole society coherent and cohesive, more to serve the needs of subcultures (Gans, 1966; 1974) within the society. Young people are a very large subculture. There is also the child subculture, to which Disney always catered, and he is now joined by others. There is a blue-collar subculture excited by action and road movies, which made superstars of Clint Eastwood, Charles Bronson, and Burt Reynolds. There is a subculture that enjoys movies that combine old-fashioned values with love of the outdoors. There is an entire subculture of late-night moviegoers who have made cults of various movies. There is a subculture that supports the pornographic movie; another that sustains religious films like <u>In Search of Noah's Ark</u> or <u>The Late Great Planet Earth</u>. All these subcultures have tastes that potentially alienate them from the social and cultural center of American life. Movies made for them tie the subculture together but do nothing to tie the subculture to the center.

Although movies are now less central and more subcultural, the existence of box-office hits among movies of this phase (<u>The Sound of Music</u>, <u>The Godfather</u>, <u>Jaws</u>, <u>Star Wars</u>, and so on) indicates that movies still tap and enrich the stock of myths and formulas laid down when movies were at the center. Their abdication of the center is incomplete.

So the possibly divisive social effect of catering to subcultures is partly ameliorated. Although in profits and "reach" the movie business is smaller than television and popular music, movies still originate myths and formulas of popular culture. Television mines movies for ideas to spin-off as series far more than movies do to television.

A neglected function of movies throughout their history, which some mistakenly think emerges only in this third phase, is that of social criticism (Jarvie, 1978). A society is partly defined by an interpersonal map of how power, wealth, status, sex appeal, and immortality are and should be allocated. Criticism can be directed at both the actual allocation and the proposed allocation. Critique of realities and aspirations has been part of American society since its inception--in the striving to make a society free of the traditional faults of Europe. The American media, and especially the press, have a long history of exposing misallocation and challenging proposed allocation. This has been both manifest and latent in movies in all three phases. Birth of a Nation was explicitly critical of Reconstruction. Over the years many studios made films that exposed social problems, such as corruption in government, the hidden face of organized crime, abuses of the penal system, and juvenile delinquency. Latent criticism at its strongest can be seen in a film like Seconds (1966), whose target is the American dream of eternal youth. A middle-aged man seizes the opportunity of a second chance at life. He leaves his wife and job to be rejuvenated and moves to California. But his dream turns out to be just another commodity provided by business; the dream is a sales pitch. Also, in musicals and comedies there can be found bitter streaks of critical commentary, a recent example being Private Benjamin.

Once movies began to focus on subcultures, they were freed from the restrictions on criticism imposed by their integrative function. No longer did they need to embody and project the central values that keep the society together; now they could embody and project the values of often deviant subcultures. Criticism of American society has become much more general and unsparing in the movies of this latest phase. It is still true that the box-office hits usually embody and project central and cohesive values, which is to be expected, for otherwise they would offend and put off the large numbers of people needed to make their success. Yet highly critical and boat-rocking films can themselves achieve considerable success (Easy Rider, 1969; Joe, 1970).

To sum up the social significance of movies in the present phase, one could say that they function as a massive cult among young people ranging from college-town buffs to drive-in rurals, and they are an occasional outing for the rest of the population. In content they run from the rather safe and old-fashioned values of many outdoor and Disney films to those that press the cutting edge of language, theme, and attitude to the limits of current social tolerance. In all these ways they are unlike television. In religious terms, movies are the Greater or Higher Tradition, television is the Lesser or Lower Tradition (Redfield, 1953) with respect to articulating what affluent America is and thinks it should be. Television is family-centered at a time when the nuclear family has been exposed to unprecedented challenge from anomic individualism. Movies are the Higher Religion of power, wealth, status, sex, and immortality: television is parasitic on movies this way, in the same way that the television industry is parasitic on Hollywood, and television stars copy and aspire to the classic movie-star style. For a long time television was despised and movie stars disdained to appear on it. Being in or on television still plays little role in their general aspiration-fantasies. Yet as an industry the movies are no longer a largish business geared to produce enough material to dominate and permeate the culture. They dominate by more subtle means and deal in specialty products as well as blockbusters.

Conclusion

In this chapter we have developed for the movies the implications of some sociological ideas. Sociology is a neglected area in film studies, and is often confused with economics or psychology. Sociology is a standing challenge to the scholar who thinks that only semiological analysis of movies as texts is fruitful. Sociology situates and explains those texts and their production and reception as understandable parts of overriding social processes, such as socialization and industrialization. With many models available other than the one employed here, sociology is a rich seam for film research.

Notes

1. It is also a moot question what effects there really

are. The locus classicus is Klapper (1960); more recently there is Comstock et al. (1978).

2. The reasons that specialization increases efficiency and hence wealth are to be found in Smith (1776). See also Durkheim (1893), and May (1980: 51).

3. Industrial society is explained in Aron (1967; 1968) and Gellner (1975).

4. Catholic influence was better organized, through the Legion of Decency (Facey, 1974) and the largely Catholic bias of the Production Code and its Administration. Protestant protest was found mainly in the pulpit and the pamphlet. May (1980: Chapters 2-3) shows how in the first phase Protestant protest was better organized.

5. See Klingender and Legg (1937), Huettig (1944), and Mercillon (1953). Some insight into the intricacies of finance is given in Sinclair (1933).

6. See the entries under government documents listed in Huetting (1944), Jowett (1976), and Guback (1979).

7. "Popular culture" is something of a technical term, designating material below or aside from High Culture and Mid-Culture. For discussion of these categories see MacDonald (1954), Brogan (1954), Shils (1957; 1961), and Gans (1966; 1974).

8. Wolfenstein and Leites (1950) regard this as the "moral" of detective and private-eye movies. My reading is much more general. See Jarvie (1970).

9. Some believe the story was based on the marriage of Al Jolson and Ruby Keeler and hence is embodied also in a fifth film, The Jolson Story (1946). If such latitude is granted, then there are countless variants of the story, such as Napoleon of Broadway, All About Eve, Morning Glory, and Stage Struck.

References

Aitken, Roy E. The Birth of a Nation Story. Middleburg, Va.: Demlinger, 1965.

Aron, Raymond. *Eighteen Lectures on Industrialized Society*. Chicago: University of Chicago Press, 1967.

Bogle, Donald. *Toms, Coons, Mulattoes, Mammies and Bucks*. New York: Viking, 1973.

Brogan, D. W. "The Problem of High Culture and Mass Culture." *Diogenes* 5 (1954): 1-13.

Carter, Everett. "Cultural History Written with Lightning: The Significance of The Birth of a Nation." *American Quarterly* 12 (1960): 347-357.

Comstock, George, Steven Chafee, Natan Katzman, Maxell McCombs, and Donald Roberts. *Television and Human Behavior*. New York: Columbia University Press, 1978.

Cripps, Thomas. *Slow Fade to Black*. New York: Oxford University Press, 1977.

Dunne, Philip. *Take Two*. New York: McGraw-Hill, 1980.

Durkheim, Emile. *The Division of Labor in Society*. 1893; Rpt. Glencoe, Ill.: Free Press, 1964.

Facey, Rev. J. *The Legion of Decency: A Sociological Analysis of the Emergence and Development of a Pressure Group*. New York: Arno, 1974.

Flamini, Roland. *Scarlett, Rhett and a Cast of Thousands*. New York: Macmillan, 1975.

Gans, Herbert J. "Popular Culture in America: Social Problem in a Mass Society or Social Asset in a Plural Society?" In *Social Problems: A Modern Approach*, edited by H. S. Becker. New York: Wiley, 1966, pp. 549-620.

_____. *Popular Culture and High Culture*. New York: Basic Books, 1974.

Gellner, Ernest. *Legitimation of Belief*. New York: Cambridge University Press, 1975.

Guback, Thomas. "Theatrical Film." In *Who Owns the Media?* edited by Benjamin M. Compaine. New York: Harmony, 1979, pp. 179-249.

Haley, Jay. "The Appeal of the Moving Picture." *Quarterly of Film, Radio and Television* 6 (1952): 361-374.

Huettig, Mae D. *Economic Control of the Motion Picture Industry*. Philadelphia: University of Pennsylvania Press, 1944.

Jarvie, I. C. *Movies and Society*. New York: Basic Books, 1970.

_____. *Movies as Social Criticism*. Metuchen, N.J.: Scarecrow, 1978.

Jowett, Garth. *Film: The Democratic Art*. Boston: Atlantic/Little, Brown, 1976.

Kirby, Jack Temple. *Media-made Dixie; The South in the American Imagination*. Baton Rouge: Louisiana State University Press, 1978.

Klapper, Joseph. The Effects of Mass Communication. Glencoe, Ill.: Free Press, 1961.
Klingender, F. F., and Stuart Legg. Money Behind the Screen. London: Lawrence and Wishart, 1937.
Koppes, Clayton R., and Gregory D. Black. "What to Show the World: The Office of War Information and Hollywood, 1942-1945. Journal of American History 64(1977): 87-105.
Lambert, Gavin G.W.T.W.: The Story of the Making of Gone with The Wind. Boston: Atlantic/Little, Brown, 1973.
Lipset, Seymour Martin. The First New Nation. New York: Basic Books, 1963.
MacDonald, Dwight. "A Theory of Mass Culture." Diogenes 3 (1954): 1-17.
May, Lary. Screening Out the Past. New York: Oxford University Press, 1980.
Mercillon, Henri. Cinéma et Monopoles. Paris: Armand Colin, 1953.
Merton, Robert K. Social Theory and Social Structure. Glencoe, Ill.: Free Press, 1957.
Parish, James Robert, and Michael R. Pitts. Hollywood on Hollywood. Metuchen, N.J.: Scarecrow, 1978.
Randall, Richard S. Censorship of the Movies. Madison: University of Wisconsin Press, 1968.
Redfield, Robert. The Primitive World and Its Transformations. Ithaca, N.Y.: Cornell University Press, 1953. 1953.
Rosten, Leo. Hollywood: The Movie Colony, the Movie Makers. New York: Harcourt, Brace, 1941.
Shils, Edward. "Daydreams and Nightmares, Reflections on the Criticisms of Mass Culture." Sewanee Review 65 (1957): 587-608.
──────. "Mass Society and Its Culture." Culture for the Millions, edited by N. Jacobs. Princeton: Van Nostrand, 1961, pp. 1-27.
──────. Center and Periphery, Essays in Macrosociology. Chicago: University of Chicago Press, 1975.
Sinclair, Upton. Upton Sinclair Presents William Fox. Los Angeles: Upton Sinclair, 1933.
Sklar, Robert. Movie-made America. New York: Random House, 1975.
Smith, Adam. An Inquiry into the Nature and Causes of the Wealth of Nations. 1776. Many editions.
Thomas, Sari. "Why Television Is Not Art: Toward a Functional Analysis of Art in Western Culture." In press.

Thomas, Tony, and Rudy Behlmer. *Hollywood's Hollywood.*
  Secaucus, N.J.: Citadel, 1975.
Wolfenstein, Martha, and Nathan Leites. *Movies; A Psychological Study.* Glencoe, Ill.: Free Press, 1950.

INDEX

The Adventures of Robin Hood 161
Africa 134
After Many Years 180
Agostino et al. 232
Aiken, R. 250, 262
Air Force 152
Airplane! 81, 94, 122
All About Eve 265
Allen, R. C. 57
Altman, C. 156, 163, 164
American Film Institute 44, 45
The Americanization of Emily 154
Andrew, D. 48, 57
Anthony and Herzlinger 58
anti-Semitism 196, 199
antitrust 21, 23
Apocalypse Now 152
The Apprenticeship of Duddy Kravitz 135
Arkoff, S. Z. 81
Arnheim, R. 2, 9, 113, 124
The Art of Vision 144
Asch and Chagnon 144, 145
Asia 15, 18, 25, 135
Austin, B. 8, 222-36
Avco-Embassy 26
The Ax Fight 144, 145

Balázs, B. 112, 124, 168, 177, 181
Balio, T. 48
Bannerman and Lewis 226, 227, 233
Baposto 133
Baritz, L. 210, 220
Bass, W. 6, 139-46
Bateson, G. 119, 124, 129
Batman 120
Battleground 154
Bazin, A. 9, 112, 124, 174, 182
Becker, F. 136
Bellman and Jules-Rosette 133, 137
Belo, J. 129
Bem, D. 231, 233
Biograph 16
Birth of a Nation 195, 250, 253, 255, 260, 263

Blazing Saddles 158, 202-205
The Blue and the Grey 180
The Blues Brothers 124
Blumer, H. 218, 219, 220
Blumer and Hauser 218, 220
Blumler and Katz 229, 233
Bogle, D. 250, 266
Brakhage, S. 136, 144
Branigan, E. 188, 193
Bringing Up Baby 160
British Film Institute 43
Brogan, D. 265, 266
Browne, N. 193
Buraynski and Bayer 230, 233

Campbell, D. 200, 206
Campbell and Stanley 230, 233
Carey, J. 6, 7, 110-25, 179, 182
Carey, J. W. 136, 137
Carpenter, E. 133, 137
Carter, E. 250, 266
Casablanca 258
Casey, E. S. 105, 109
The Cat People 150
Cawelti, J. 159, 164
Ceram, C. W. 172, 182
Chalfen, R. 6, 101, 109, 126-37
Chapelle, P. 136
Chaplin, C. 17
Charles, W. 9, 195, 199, 207
Charlie Chan and the Curse of the Dragon Queen 192
Chukovsky, K. 109
Cinemascope 24
Cinémathèque Française 43
Cinerama 24
Citizen Kane 142, 143, 258
Citizen's Band 238, 239, 240
Clark, C. 187, 193
A Clockwork Orange 190
Cold War 22, 23
Collins et al. 179, 182
Columbia Pictures 24, 29, 83, 88
Comstock et al. 266
Connant, M. 28, 35, 83, 89-91, 94
Cook, B. 186, 193
Coppola, F. F. 26

Crandall, R. 233
Cripps, T. 207, 250, 262
Cruising 192
Custen, G. F. 8, 237-46
Cutler et al. 92, 94

Dale, E. 214, 220
Dart, P. 187, 193
The Deer Hunter 122
De Fleur and Ball-Rokeach 197, 207, 211, 220, 224, 233
DeMille, C. B. 16
dependency theory 197
The Depression 19
de Sica, V. 23
direct cinema 144
The Dirty Dozen 154
Disney, W. 25, 29, 83, 262
Dixon, W. K. L. 177
documentary 139-46
Dog Star Man 144
Drew, R. 142
Dunne, P. 260, 266
Durkheim, E. 251, 265, 266

Eastman-Kodak 15
Easy Rider 263
Edison, T. A. 15, 16, 172, 177
Eisenstein, S. 238, 244
Elias, D. 58
Elliott and Schenck-Hamlin 230, 233
The Empire Strikes Back 81, 122
Emshwiller, E. 136
Eskimo 134
Europe 17, 18, 23, 210, 253

Faccinto, V. 136
Facey, R. 265, 266
Fadiman, C. 229, 233
Fairbanks, D. 16
Family Focus 136
Family Portrait Sitting 136
Feilitzen and Linné 187, 193
Felman, J. 231
Film Portrait 136
Flamini, R. 255, 266

Index 271

Flight of the Phoenix 154, 161
Fox, W. 16, 20, 28, 32
France 15
Freedom Force 120
The French Connection 124
Freud, S. 187
Friedson, E. 241
Fuzz 190

Galbraith, J. K. 54, 55, 56, 57
Gans, H. 137, 192, 193, 197, 207, 231, 233, 262, 265
Geertz, C. 136
Geiger, P. 32, 35
Gellner E. 265, 266
genre 147-64
Gentleman's Agreement 195, 199, 204
Géricault 99
Gertner, R. 223, 228, 229, 233
Gibson, J. J. 170, 182
Gino's Pizza 144
The Godfather 262
Goffman, E. 239
Gombrich, E. 98, 109
Gomery, D. 5, 48, 53, 54, 55, 57, 81-94
Gone with the Wind 20, 255, 257, 260
Gorer, G. 129
Gottesman, R. 58
Grainger, R. 151, 155-56, 157, 159, 163-64
Grand Illusion 143
La Grande Casse 190
Grease 224
The Great Train Robbery 14, 177
Green, J. R. 5, 37-59
Gregory, R. L. 102, 109, 170, 182
Griffith, D. W. 113, 176, 177, 180, 182, 250
Gross, L. 108
Growing Up in Paradise 136
Guback, T. 30, 35, 92-94, 266
Guback and Dombkowski 28, 35

Gulf + Western Corporation 25, 29
Gusfield, J. 210, 220
Gustafson, R. 5, 60-80
Guston, P. 100
Guzetti, A. 136

HUAC 34, 262
Halloran, J. 192, 193
Hampton, B. 48, 57
Handel, L. 223, 228, 233, 237, 245
Hanet, K. 192, 193
A Hatful of Rain 117
Hayes and Hayes 170, 182
Hayley, J. 266
Healy, W. 212-13, 220
Heaven Can Wait 242
Heroes 136
Herrnstein and Loveland 170, 182
Herskovits, M. 169, 182
Hill, J. 136
Hill and Crittenden 133, 137
Hoban and Van Orner 195, 198, 207
Hochberg, J. 170
Hochberg and Brooks 170, 171, 182
Hockett, C. 245
Hodgdon, D. 136
Hollywood 19, 21, 24, 32, 150, 195, 222, 254
Hovland et al. 9, 10, 225, 234, 237, 245
Huettig, M. 28, 35, 265, 266
Hulett, J. 224, 234
hypodermic model 196

identification 188, 190, 191, 217
imitation 188, 190, 191, 217
"impossible figures" 102, 107
In Search of Noah's Ark 262
"independents" 16, 28, 34, 83
It Happened One Night 160, 191
Italy 15

Jacobs, L. 48, 58, 176, 177, 182

Jarvie, I. C. 4, 8, 48, 56, 58, 197, 207, 224, 225, 234, 247-67
Jaws 122, 262
Joe 263
The Jolson Story 265
Jowett, G. 8, 209-21, 231, 234, 249, 254, 261, 265, 266
Jowett and Linton 186, 194
Jowett et al. 184, 191, 194

Katz, J. S. 136, 137
Katz and Brialy 200-01, 202, 207
Katz and Lazarsfeld 197, 207, 230, 234
Kauffmann and Henstell 171, 180, 182
Kennedy, J. 170, 183
Kindem and Teddlie 7, 195-208
King, A. 144
Kirby, J. 250, 266
The Kiss 177
Kitses, J. 159, 164
Klapper, J. 192, 265, 266
Klingender and Legg 28, 35, 265, 267
Koppes and Black 261, 267
Kpelle 133
Kracauer, S. 2, 9, 10
Kris, E. 238, 244, 245
Kuhn, T. 239, 245

La Barre, N. 245
Laemmles, C. 26
Lambert, C. 255, 267
Langness, L. L. 132, 137
La Piere, R. 200, 207
Lasky, J. 16
The Late, Great Planet Earth 262
Latin America 19, 21-22, 25
Lazarsfeld, P. 223, 225, 234
Leach, E. 164
Leacock, R. 142
Levine, B. 136
Levine, J. E. 26
Lévi-Strauss, C. 148, 150, 152, 154, 164

Levy, M. 232, 234
Life of an American Fireman 176
Linset, S. 266
Linton, J. 9, 184-94
Linton and Jowett 192
Little Caesar 162
Lloyd's of London 117
Loews 28
The Long Goodbye 158
Love of Gold 177
Lumières 146
Lund, D. M. 4, 13-26
Lynd, H. and R. 215-16, 221

MGM 23, 83, 88
McArthur, C. 159, 164
McCabe and Mrs. Miller 158
Maccoby, E. 187, 194
MacDonald, D. 265, 266
MacDougall, D. 136, 137
McGilligan, 33, 34, 35
McGuire, W. 198, 202, 207
McQuail, D. 185, 190, 194
Makavejer, D. 103
Malinowski, B. 147, 149, 153, 164, 242
The Maltese Falcon 161
A Man for all Seasons 116
Mann, J. 201, 207
Mannheim, K. 239, 245
A Married Couple 144
May, H. 209-10, 221
May, L. 249, 260, 261, 265, 266
Mayer, J. 221
Mayer, M. 33, 35, 83, 94
Mead, G. H. 240, 245
Mead, M. 128, 129
Mead and Metraux 128, 137, 237, 245
Medium Cool 103
Mekas, A. 136
Mekas, J. 136
Méliès, G. 16
Melton, H. 58
Mendelsohn, H. 231, 234
Merton, R. 248, 267
Messaris, P. 7, 168-83, 244, 245
Messaris and Gross 179, 183
Metz, C. 106, 109

Mialaret and Méliès 174-75, 176, 178-79, 183
Middleton, R. 195, 199, 202, 206, 208, 224, 234
Mitchell, A. 216, 221
Monogram 24
Moore, D. 224, 234
Morning Glory 265
Morse Code 105
Motion Pictures Patent Co. 16
movie palaces 15, 249
Mowry, G. 220, 221
Mulvey, L. 192, 194
Musello, C. 137
Museum of Modern Art 42, 43, 48, 53

Nana, Mom and Me 136
Napoleon of Broadway 265
Neisser, U. 169, 183, 239, 245
Netzer, D. 58
The Nitake Film 136
No Lies 144
Noble, G. 176, 177, 179, 183, 187, 189, 194
Nothing but a Man 202, 203, 204, 205

Oberholtzer, E. P. 209, 221
O'Grady, G. 56, 58
Ohrn, K. B. 137
oligopoly 16, 34, 88

painting 1
Pallenik, M. 179, 183
Panda and Kanungo 226, 227, 228, 235
Paramount Pictures 18, 21, 23, 25, 28, 29, 81, 83, 87, 88, 89
Parish and Pitts 260, 267
Patel, A. 226, 227, 235
Pathé Frères 16
Payne Fund Studies 9, 195, 217, 219, 237, 245
Pennebaker, D. A. 142
perception 169-70
Perry, C. 225, 235
Perry, D. 31, 35

Perry, T. 58
Peter, C. 217-18, 221
The Philadelphia Story 160
Phillips, A. 58
photographs 169
Pickford, M. 17
Planet of the Apes 118
Polaroid 23
Pollock, J. 100
Porter, E. S. 14, 176
The Poseidon Adventure 154
The Practical Joke on the Gardener 146
Price, K. B. 105, 109
Prieve and Allen 58
Private Benjamin 263
Procession 136
Psycho 152
Pudovkin, V. 174, 183
Pye and Myles 245

RKO 21, 24, 28
The Raft of the Medusa 99
Ramsaye, T. 171, 172, 177, 183
Randall, R. 261, 267
Raths and Irager 224, 235
Redfield, R. 264, 267
ReFlex Film/FamilyFilm 136
"reflexivity" 144-45
Reid, L. 105, 109
Reisz and Millar 112, 125
Renoir, J. 143
Republic Pictures 24
Riefenstahl, L. 141
Riesman, D. 241-42, 245
Riesman and Riesman 225, 235
The Ring of Rings 117
Rocky 243
The Rocky Horror Picture Show 243
Rose, E. 59
Rosenbaum, J. 245
Rosenberg and White 235
Rosten, L. 254, 260, 267
Rothschild, A. 136
Rouch, J. 144
Rubbo, M. 144
Rundstrom, D. and S. 136
Rydall, T. 159, 164

Sapir, E. 97, 109
Scaramouche 161
Schatz, T. 148, 156, 165
Scheurer, T. 148, 156, 165
Schlesinger, A. 220, 221
Screen Gems 25
Scruffy 120
selective perception 196
Shadoian, J. 159, 165
Shils, E. 8, 247, 256, 265, 267
silent film 18, 171-72, 249
Simonet, T. 223, 235
Sinclair, U. 265, 267
Six Filmmakers in Search of a Wedding 136
Sklar, R. 48, 235, 249, 267
Small, E. S. 136, 137
Smell-o-vision 24
Smith, A. 265, 267
The Sneeze 177
Snow White 28
Sobchack, T. 149, 165
Sobchack, V. 6, 147-164
Sobchack and Sobchack 148, 151, 156, 157, 158, 163, 165
social class 15, 161, 257
The Sound of Music 262
Soviet Union 18
The Squaw Man 16
Stage Struck 265
Staiger, J. 48, 58
Stanley and Riena 194
A Star Is Born 260
Star Wars 81, 122, 158, 262
Stella Dallas 162
Sterling and Haight 223, 228, 229, 235
The Sting 119
Sudnow, D. 133
Summers, G. 199, 208
Sutton and Harris 50, 52, 58
Sweet and Sour 136
syntax 104, 106, 112, 168

Taylor, J. R. 186, 194
Teddlie, C. 7
television 2, 6, 29, 40, 48, 186, 224, 248, 261, 262
Thomas, S. 1-10, 259, 261, 267

Thomas and Behlmer 267
3-D 24, 172
The Three Musketeers 161
Thurstone, L. 9-10, 195, 196, 198, 199, 206, 208, 223, 225, 255
time/space transitions 114-19, 179-80
Tittle and Hill 225, 235
Todd-AO 24
Tovland, G. 143
The Towering Inferno 154
TransAmerica Corp. 25, 29
Triumph of the Will 142
Tudor, A. 186, 187, 188, 194, 196, 198, 208
Twentieth Century-Fox 23, 29, 83

United Artists 25, 26, 29, 83, 88
Universal Studios 21, 29, 83, 88
Urban, W. 105, 109
Urban Cowboy 81

vertical integration 16
Vertov, D. 144
video recording 228

W. R.: Mysteries of the Organism 103
Waiting for Fidel 144
Warner and Lunt 237, 245
Warner Bros. 19, 23, 25, 28, 29, 83, 88
The Warriors 190
Warshow, R. 159, 165
Wasko, J. 5, 27-36
Watership Down 243
Weakland, J. 129, 137
Weise and Cole 235
Weiss, E. 136, 138
Welles, O. 143
The Wild One 191
Wild Strawberries 238
Williams, J. H. 227, 235
Wilson, J. 168, 183
Wilson, S. 136
Winick and Winick 176, 183

Witt, P. 236
The Wolf Man 150
Wolfenstein and Leites 9, 10, 129, 137, 267
World War I 17
World War II 22
Worth, S. 5, 6, 7, 97-109, 128, 134-5, 137, 168, 183, 237, 245-6
Worth and Adair 107, 109, 137
Wright, C. R. 9, 10, 229, 236, 246
Wright, W. 150, 165

Yanomamo 133
Young, C. 58
Young, D. 213-14, 221
Young, K. 231, 236
Young Frankenstein 158

Zazzo, B. 173, 174, 175, 178, 179, 183
Zeitlin, M. 36
Zeitline and Star 136
Zigler and Child 211, 221
Zimmerman and Hochberg 170, 183
Zolberg, V. L. 58
Zukor, A. 16, 18